The Peace Formula

Economic forces play a major role in the outbreak and perpetuation of violence, but they also hold the key for positive change. Using a nontechnical and accessible style, *The Peace Formula* attacks a series of misconceptions about how economics has been used to foster peace. In place of these misconceptions, this book draws on rich historical anecdotes and cutting-edge academic evidence to outline the "peace formula" – a set of key policies that are crucial ingredients for curbing armed conflict and achieving a transition to lasting peace and prosperity. These policies include providing jobs (work), ensuring democratic participation (voice), and guaranteeing the security and basic functions of the state (warranties). Investigating specific political institutions and economic policies, this book provides the first easily accessible synthesis of this work and explains how "smart idealism" can help us get the incentives of our leaders right. The stakes could hardly be higher.

DOMINIC ROHNER is a professor at the Geneva Graduate Institute and the University of Lausanne (on leave) and holds a PhD in economics from the University of Cambridge. He is also affiliated to the Centre for Economic Policy Research and the OxCarre Center at the University of Oxford. His research on the economics of conflict has won various prizes and been covered by major news outlets worldwide. He leads an international expert group on policies for peace.

The Peace Formula

Voice, Work and Warranties, Not Violence

DOMINIC ROHNER

University of Lausanne

CAMBRIDGE
UNIVERSITY PRESS

CAMBRIDGE
UNIVERSITY PRESS

Shaftesbury Road, Cambridge CB2 8EA, United Kingdom

One Liberty Plaza, 20th Floor, New York, NY 10006, USA

477 Williamstown Road, Port Melbourne, VIC 3207, Australia

314–321, 3rd Floor, Plot 3, Splendor Forum, Jasola District Centre,
New Delhi – 110025, India

103 Penang Road, #05–06/07, Visioncrest Commercial, Singapore 238467

Cambridge University Press is part of Cambridge University Press &
Assessment, a department of the University of Cambridge.

We share the University's mission to contribute to society through the
pursuit of education, learning and research at the highest international
levels of excellence.

www.cambridge.org
Information on this title: www.cambridge.org/9781009438315

DOI: 10.1017/9781009438322

First published 2024

Printed in the United Kingdom by CPI Group Ltd, Croydon CR0 4YY

A catalogue record for this publication is available from the British Library

Library of Congress Cataloging-in-Publication Data
Names: Rohner, Dominic, author.
Title: The peace formula : voice, work and warranties,
not violence / Dominic Rohner.
Description: Cambridge, United Kingdom ; New York, NY: Cambridge
University Press, 2024. | Includes bibliographical references and index.
Identifiers: LCCN 2024003006 | ISBN 9781009438315 (hardback) |
ISBN 9781009438322 (ebook)
Subjects: LCSH: Peace-building. | Conflict management. |
War – Prevention. | Idealism.
Classification: LCC JZ5538 .R636 2024 | DDC 327.1/72–dc23/eng/20240326
LC record available at https://lccn.loc.gov/2024003006

ISBN 978-1-009-43831-5 Hardback

This book is dedicated to my parents, Brigitte and Fridolin, as well as to my wife Géraldine, and my children Camille, Nicolas and Sophie.

Contents

Acknowledgments

For a tree to grow, it requires basically three ingredients, a seed, sunshine and rain. For academic research and books, it may not be very different. You need ideas (the seeds), fruitful discussions and encouragement from colleagues, coauthors and friends (the sunshine) and constructive critique from referees and unconvinced peers (the rain), nudging you to improve the argument and step up the empirical evidence. In what follows, let me focus on the sunshine: the numerous peers who have supported and encouraged me over the last twenty years, during which much of my research has focused on explaining the drivers and consequences of armed conflicts.

As a starting point of this journey, I would like to highlight the inspiring teaching of Geneva-based political scientist Urs Luterbacher, in whose course I first encountered academic research that strives to make sense of the dark side of politics. Then, as next stops on my roller-coaster ride through academia, I encountered in Cambridge my PhD supervisor, Sir Partha Dasgupta, and in Oxford Sir Paul Collier, whose willingness to tackle really grand and deep questions has been an inspiration ever since. Back in Switzerland after my doctoral dissertation, I had the privilege of working with Fabrizio Zilibotti (then in Zurich, now at Yale). He has been a formidable boss and mentor, teaching me so much about research methods, academic writing … and Italian wine and cuisine.

Since these first years, I have become a faculty member myself at the University of Lausanne (and since September 2024 at the Geneva Graduate Institute), and a wonderful group of colleagues, coauthors, PhD supervisees and students have shared their knowledge and insights with me about science in general and conflict in particular. They are too numerous to enumerate, and some such as Mathias Thoenig and Massimo Morelli have become serial coauthors.

As I won't be able to do justice to everybody, let me in what follows just stick to those scholars with whom I have coauthored the works to which I refer in the current book (see the Bibliography for details): In particular, I am very much indebted to Siwan Anderson, Andrea Berlanda, Nicolas Berman, Francesco Caselli, Matteo Cervellati, Sir Paul Collier, Mathieu Couttenier, Bénédicte De la Brière, Anastasiya Denisova, Ulrich Eberle, Elena Esposito, Joan Esteban, Deon Filmer, Patrick Francois, Quentin Gallea, Luis Garicano, Christian Gollier, Michael König, Michael Lehning, Jérémy Laurent-Lucchetti, Andrea Marcucci, Massimo Morelli, Hannes Mueller, Frederik Noack, Veronica Petrencu, Patrick Premand, Dena Ringold, Alessandro Saia, Rogerio Santarrosa, David Schönholzer, Tommaso Sonno, Julia Steinberger, Uwe Sunde, Nicolas Tetreault, Mathias Thoenig, Evelina Trutnevyte, Beatrice Weder di Mauro, Ekaterina Zhuravskaya and Fabrizio Zilibotti.

I am also grateful for all the support and thoughtful suggestions to the editor Philip Good, the rest of the team working for Cambridge University Press, including Simon Fletcher, Chris Hudson and Veena Ramakrishnan, as well as to the anonymous referees reviewing the book proposal. The excellent help with language editing provided by Ethan Catanzariti and Benoit Hayman is also gratefully acknowledged.

Last but not least, I would like to very much thank my wonderful family for all the love, support and understanding.

PART I   **Apocalypse No!**

Why We Should Care

I Smart Idealism and the Peace Formula

Introduction

If we don't end war, war will end us.

H. G. Wells

The fight had already been going on for what seemed an eternity when a series of blows caused his opponent to stumble and ultimately fall to the floor. Blood, sweat and tears flowed and the surrounding crowd of 60,000 spectators started to cheer. The scene also captivated over a billion spectators in front of their TVs at home, making it one of the biggest TV events to date. Shortly thereafter, Muhammad Ali was declared winner by knock-out over George Foreman in the "Rumble in the Jungle" – one of the most famous matches in boxing history, which took place in 1974 in Kinshasa, Zaire (now the Democratic Republic of Congo, DRC). While the nominal winner and loser of this epic fight were, respectively, Muhammad Ali and George Foreman, it may well be argued that its greatest beneficiary was Zaire's ruthless dictator, Mobutu Sese Seko, and the biggest loss was at the expense of the Congolese population, whose plundered wealth was used to pay part of the bill for this mega-event.

Less than a decade after gaining power in a coup in 1965, Mobutu was relishing his international reputation and prestige. He essentially prided himself on being a darling of various major powers, each competing for his attention. From its very beginning, Mobutu's presidency was characterized by public executions of rival politicians (drawing live audiences greater than that for the Rumble in the Jungle), bloody suppression of demonstrators (with the aid of foreign mercenaries), gruesome torture of dissidents, kleptocracy on a breathtaking scale (he amassed a personal fortune worth several billion US dollars), and an appalling lack of democracy and

3

development. This, however, did not prevent Western leaders from generously supporting their ally against the Soviets. Mobutu was a regular guest at the White House, having had warm relations with Presidents Richard Nixon, Ronald Reagan and George Bush Senior. Even under the somewhat more distant Jimmy Carter, Zaire received nearly half of the US foreign aid allocated to sub-Saharan Africa. This financial help was not put to good use – to put it mildly – as the country still suffers from alarming levels of political violence today, is democratic in name only, and is ranked 226th (out of 229 countries) in terms of real gross domestic product per capita.[1] No matter what ranking of governance, human development, human rights protection, or socioeconomic development is used, the country is consistently close to the bottom.

How could such a tragedy occur in a country blessed with abundant natural resources and great potential? It is almost a textbook example of what can go wrong in the presence of several (sadly common) misperceptions. In short, similar to many other cases, Western governments favored short-term stability and the strategic upside of supporting an anticommunist dictator over the promotion of actual democracy. Beyond this cynical Cold War realpolitik, many well-intentioned policymakers endorsed the shady peace deals mastered by Mobutu (who had the habit of offering *"plata o plomo"* (silver or lead), that is, either buying off or killing detractors). Their underlying assumption was that bargaining and cutting deals between the dictator and the current opposition could promote peace. Since the independence of the DRC from Belgium in 1960, time and again Western powers supported (and sometimes saved) Mobutu and other cronies financially and militarily and brokered peace talks and ceasefires, which invariably proved short-lived and failed to deliver lasting peace. As shown in this book, the logical fallacy of such an almost exclusive focus on short-term bargaining is that whenever one given rebel leader has been bought off at the negotiation table, other aspiring warlords are already in the starting blocks. As in the ancient Greek Hydra myth, for each rebel removed, two new challengers arise. When the breeding ground for political unrest persists (poverty, bad institutions, natural resource rents to grab, low productivity and public insecurity), there will always be armed movements ready to capitalize.

Another misconception of Mobutu's Western allies was that they hoped to "buy" peace through cash transfers that were largely embezzled by a kleptocratic regime. In contrast, productive "investments" in human capital did not receive much consideration (e.g., the DRC's schools are infamously underfunded, and security risks and violence have been major obstacles to schooling in the past decades). Finally, the need to, first and foremost, establish public security as a basis for any policy hoping to bring positive change has been widely underestimated – and lack of public safety has indeed been a major factor jeopardizing any promising reforms or policy measures, an example being the fight against the 2018–2019 Ebola epidemic. In a nutshell, poverty and lack of democracy, as well as insecurity, have been the root causes for renewed political violence in the DRC over the last six decades. As shown in this book, key elements of a formula for peace – both for the DRC and around the world – include policies that provide a *voice, work* and *warranties*.

BEYOND THE DRC: A DIRE STATE OF AFFAIRS

Sadly, the tragedy in the DRC is not a unique case. We live in dangerous times. When switching on the TV and watching the news, on an average day one may hear about several dozen civil conflicts worldwide. The more mediatized of them include the civil wars in Syria, Yemen and Libya, or the fighting in Afghanistan, Iraq, South Sudan, the DRC and Somalia. The subjective perception of an escalation in such political violence is confirmed by cold-hearted statistics: The fifty-six distinct instances of ongoing wars and conflicts in 2022 correspond to a record number since 1946.[2]

At the forefront of the news are also drug-related massacres and organized crime, for example, in Mexico, Colombia or Honduras, in addition to mounting international tensions, most prominently between the current superpower, the United States, and its rising rival, China, as well as the conflict between Russia and Ukraine, and tension between Russia and neighboring countries, such as Georgia. Even Western democracies are not spared. Populism is on the rise across rich countries and democracy is on the decline. Again, this subjective perception is consistent with statistics from Freedom House, suggesting a decline in worldwide average democracy/freedom scores for the seventeenth consecutive year.[3] There are also mounting social tensions in several countries, most notably in the United States, with waves of protest by the Black Lives Matter movement after recent incidences of police violence against black citizens.

The recent COVID-19 pandemic has further aggravated various forms of social and political violence.[4] As discussed in this book, poverty and lack of human capital are crucial root causes fueling the threat of conflict and violence. The pandemic has led to spiking levels of unemployment and poverty (especially among the most unfortunate, who work in the informal sector and do not have access to formal insurance mechanisms). Access to schooling is also under severe stress – among others for sanitary reasons. This may well constitute a fertile breeding ground for further violence to come. Furthermore, the imperative of fighting the virus has provided a formidable pretext for populists and autocrats to limit freedom of assembly and expression, and to step up surveillance. Last but not least, a pandemic tends to reduce international trade and business relations. Declining interdependence between countries thereby reduces the economic cost of international wars (and hence makes them potentially more likely, as discussed in more detail in Chapter 3).

Does this affect us directly or is it just some depressing intermezzo we watch on the TV news before turning on the next Netflix series or feel-good movie? Well, it turns out that we are in this together. Nobody is an island and violence – like a virus – does not stop at country borders. Mischief travels not only across space but also through time, as wars today sow the seeds of future poverty and discord, through a series of vicious cycles. Throw in global warming, pandemics, grand economic transformations and demographic transitions, and you have an explosive concoction threatening global stability and well-being. Just as the murder of Archduke Franz Ferdinand in 1914 in Sarajevo triggered World War I and fighting around the globe, the rise to power of Adolf Hitler in Germany in 1933 led to a chain of events resulting in millions of people dying not just in Germany but thousands of miles away up to a dozen years later. Hence, even if some of our lives appear on the surface like a long, winding river flowing down the same valley since eternity, in reality, conflict and war can exert a global grip on society, with each one affecting us directly – like a worldwide pandemic.

Thus, the time has come to take the bull by the horns and act at once to ensure a prosperous and peaceful future for generations to come. Just as for the *torero* at the *corrida*, inaction is fatal and will be punished by history. To tackle threats to peace, we first need to understand why people fight and how to prevent it. As it turns out, economic forces play a major role in the outbreak and perpetuation of violence, but they may also hold the key for positive change. In particular, having *work* and a *voice* provide the nutrients and sunlight required for the seeds of future prosperity and peace to blossom.

Sadly, too often the economic root causes for turmoil are ignored in favor of peace plans focusing on cutting deals with the powerful, leaving the real underlying reasons for conflict unaddressed. There has been an alphabet soup of naive or cynical top-down policies, cooked up by powerful international leaders and policymakers. The ingredients in this indigestible brew include ill-prepared mediation, biased military assistance and untargeted food aid. As detailed in this book, such measures can fail spectacularly and ignite the social tensions and civil unrest which ravage our time.

This book will argue that, instead, bottom-up policies are required to align economic incentives for peace, achieved through a well-designed blend of peace-promoting institutions, state capacity building and health, education and labor market policies. There is also a crucial role for the international community (and ordinary citizens) in regulating and monitoring international firms, migration policies and funding the right initiatives. In a nutshell, while this book explains how well-intended yet naive policies backfire, often with disastrous consequences, it also sketches a path forward. Drawing on decades of careful academic research on conflict, it makes the case for "smart idealism," that is, a set of policies shown to foster incentives for sustained peace.

INFLUENTIAL – YET FATAL – MISCONCEPTIONS

In what follows, we shall first revisit some common misconceptions – already encountered in the example of the DRC – that have given birth to failed peace policies for decades, before outlining promising ingredients for successful peacebuilding and revisiting some successful transitions to democracy, peace and prosperity.

Misconception 1: "He Is an A-Hole, But He Is Our A-Hole" (Alias "Better the Devil You Know")

This logic has been invoked to prop up autocrats around the world for decades, even centuries. During the Cold War, for example, being anticommunist may have been enough to warrant support from Western powers – independent of how dismal a nation's democratic and human rights track-record was – whereas swearing alliance to Marxism, similarly, was enough to get the USSR on board. A good illustration is provided by Nicaragua's fight in the 1980s between the Sandinista (supported by the Kremlin) and the Contras (supported by the Ronald Reagan administration). While neither the United States nor the USSR were convinced by the moral, political or economic appeal of their protégé group, they actively supported their ally in the goal of preventing their own zone of influence from shrinking. Similar cynical calculations are made today in the Yemen war and when it comes to backing particular fighting groups in Libya (linked to particular gas pipeline projects). As argued in this book, backing bad regimes and despots in exchange for short-run influence and (seemingly) lucrative deals is not just morally wrong but may also backfire politically and economically.

Take the case of Muammar Gaddafi's regime. Coming to power in a coup in 1969, Gaddafi consolidated a tight grip on power and became *persona non grata* in many Western democracies in the 1990s owing to his financing of various terrorist and extremist groups globally, and following Libya's role in the Lockerbie bombing of Pan AM flight 103, which killed 270 innocent people in 1988. Some years later, after Gaddafi turned in the alleged perpetrators of the Lockerbie bombing and paid financial compensation and stopped his unconventional weapons program, all was forgiven and forgotten. Once more, Western diplomats were busy rolling out the red carpet for an autocratic ruler. The race to please Tripoli's despot was so frantic that any human rights abuses by the Libyan regime were duly ignored by Gaddafi's new-found Western friends, who acclaimed him with the highest honors during state visits. In 2008, Gaddafi's son Hannibal was accused of beating up his servants and arrested by Swiss police in Geneva. During the subsequent diplomatic turmoil between Switzerland and Libya, one of Switzerland's oldest allies, France, refused to take sides between the Swiss insistence on equality of the law versus Gaddafi's thirst for vendetta (which culminated in the arrest of two high-level Swiss businessmen in Tripoli for alleged visa irregularities, and Gaddafi calling for jihad against Switzerland). In 2010, the then French foreign minister Bernard Kouchner famously talked about a "dispute between their Swiss friends and their Libyan friends" in which France did not want to take sides and "distribute responsibilities and errors."[5] Little did it matter that one of the French "friends" was one of the continent's oldest democracies, which in this affair could be accused of nothing else than applying the rule of law and respecting the judiciary's independence, while the other (new-found) French "friend" was a dictator with a decade-long track record of human rights abuses, supporting terrorism and violently repressing opposition at home.

Sadly, realpolitik and ignorance of human rights abuses of "useful" dictators is often the rule rather than the exception. The problem is that – besides being morally wrong – it does not work. As discussed in this book, there is ample recent academic research showing that the price to pay for short-run stability and attractive deals is mounting anti-Western sentiment in the long-run. The population in destitute countries finds it hard to understand why champions of democracy at home help to prop up corrupt regimes abroad. This hypocrisy results in rejection and hate of the West and its values – which are perceived as phony. For example, a systematic study of international terrorism shows that US military aid to doubtful regimes in the last few decades has resulted in *more, not fewer*, terror attacks from beneficiary countries against the United States, prompting the authors to wonder in the title why the United States were willing to be "Paying them to hate US?"[6] Another study, examining US military aid to Colombia, found that – if anything – it strengthened illicit armed groups to the detriment of weakened domestic political institutions.[7]

As argued in this book, rather than cutting shady deals with despots and distributing, without scrutiny, vast sums of military aid, rich and stable Western countries should endeavor to foster peace by helping to lay the groundwork for a peaceful society. Having work, a voice and security warranties ensures citizens do not have incentives to engage in political violence – an investment more beneficial and durable than supporting autocrats.

Misconception 2: Sending Enough Cash Can Curb Conflict

Another widespread misconception is that fostering peace is directly linked to the amount of money spent for this purpose. As argued in this book, "buying" peace by simply disbursing cash does not work – yet "investing in" peace by strengthening human capital and productive capacities does. The core pervasive misconception is that any amount of financial means put at the disposal of a given country will lead to similar effects, no matter the modalities, as typically money will be put to best use. Unfortunately, this logic is as watertight as a teabag. The problem is that the presence of large, accessible resources naturally triggers the incentive to appropriate them – a phenomenon occurring in rich and poor countries and in democracies and autocracies alike. When something is "up for grabs" there will typically always be people trying to get their hands on it. While the thirst for rent-seeking may not differ between rich democracies and countries torn by civil war, what prevents the worst excesses in democratic states is that strong state capacity and a powerful legal apparatus keep people's behavior in check. However, in unstable countries with a weak state, having a sudden inflow of rents to grab can be disastrous – as can be easily illustrated by oil holdings. As discussed in Chapter 4, recent studies have found that while oil reserves can have positive effects in strong, stable states such as Norway, for less stable countries such as Venezuela, Sudan, Chad, Nigeria, Angola and so on oil money is often a critical source of instability and turmoil. The "resource curse" of in-fighting for rents has been a key reason why, despite impressive oil and mineral revenues, many oil- and mineral-producing states have not achieved the level of prosperity one may have expected. Incidentally, as argued in this book, a "smart" green transition yields the double dividend of tackling climate change and at the same time reduces the scope for toxic petropolitics, which, in turn, fosters the prospectives for peace.

The trouble is that sending cash or goods can have – in some cases – remarkably similar effects to having oil in the ground. For example, a recent study has found that US food aid on average – if anything – *increases rather than reduces* the risk of fighting in the beneficiary regions.[8] In the presence of political instability and a weak state, it is not surprising that various armed groups would typically try to appropriate food aid and sell it – which can fuel further fighting.

Does this mean that Western democracies should resign and renounce any aid to unstable regions? No: Thankfully there exist ways to provide aid that do not suffer from the "resource curse" logic. As discussed in this book, there is a place for *smart idealism*, and, in particular, *investments* in human capital which drive a series of virtuous effects. First of all, better education and better health will improve the chances of attaining attractive employment, causing both the motives and time available for engaging in violence to decrease. Second, and even more crucially, *physical* capital can be stolen, while *human* capital cannot. Turning cash into education and better health not only boosts productive capacities and the opportunity cost of fighting but also reduces the financial resources that are up for grabs. As discussed later, it has been found, unsurprisingly, that resource-rich countries fare better when investing money from natural resources in schools rather than elsewhere. Vast schooling programs (such as the INPRES program in Indonesia) have experienced spectacular success in curbing violence.[9]

Misconception 3: Winning Over Hearts and Minds First; Security Second

A third dangerous misconception is that a "charm offensive" is a great first step to winning over local support, which will then (almost automatically) lead to reduced grievances and tensions, thereby curbing conflict. According to this logic, communication efforts are stepped up and amenities are provided to win over the hearts and minds of the local population. While theoretically this may be appealing, the trouble with such a strategy is that in practice it has rarely worked. The reason is simple: When security is so scarce that your family faces severe risks every day, you naturally won't care much about amenities and politics. As shown in a series of studies discussed in this book, there is a pyramid of needs, and the most basic one is security and basic state capacity and infrastructure (water, electricity). Hence, for any other policy to be successful, at the very beginning it needs to be ensured that the most basic functions of the state (security, infrastructure) are put in place (either by the country in question or by an international peacekeeping force). Once these basic needs are satisfied, people are more receptive in a "war of ideas" to think about the virtues of having a democratic society and equal civil rights for all societal groups. As discussed in more detail later, in Iraq, for example, the provision of services did, in a first phase, nothing to curb violence, and only helped later when some minimum level of basic safety had been established.[10]

To get armed rebel groups to the negotiating table, security warranties are fundamental. Picture yourself as a rebel leader: You may not be willing to hand over the AK-47 if you have a justified fear of being massacred afterwards. Therefore, providing security guarantees for all groups is a key role that the international community can play: The willingness to invest considerable resources during postconflict reconstruction renders a revival of the conflict all but impossible, with postwar reconstruction even succeeding in very hostile environments. Think of the Bosnia-Herzegovina power-sharing agreement brokered in Dayton, Ohio in 1995. While it has yet to lead to an integrated melting pot society, it ended a brutal three-year war and has prevented the renewal of large-scale violence ever since. International peacekeepers have been instrumental in this success. By the same token, the occupation of Nazi Germany and the maintenance of a large contingent of US troops has, in the long run, favored the transformation of Germany from a fascist murder state to a stable democracy today.

SUCCESS STORIES: THE ROLE OF WORK, VOICE AND WARRANTIES

In fact, the *denazification of Germany* is almost a textbook example of how to transform a fascist rogue state into a peaceful and prosperous democracy. It contains many ingredients of the *peace formula* advocated in the current book. First of all, the Allies wisely did not engage in deal-making with the Nazi's worst offenders. Instead, they investigated abuses in the Nuremberg trials and built the modern Bundesrepublik (BRD) on the solid foundation of a new generation of politicians, of which the highest representatives had not been entangled with the most ruthless *Sonderkommandos* of the Third Reich.

Admittedly, various Nazi supporters did go under the radar of the denazification process and "recycle" themselves in the new BRD administration – but at least at the highest level, the denazification achieved a *tabula rasa* and the Allies insisted on Germany becoming a real democracy, where each and every citizen has a *voice*.

At the same time, the Marshall Plan was put in place and resulted in an unprecedented boom in economic investments, supporting the rebuilding of infrastructure and boost of human capital. The German *Wirtschaftswunder* provided *work* and economic prospects to the citizens of the newly created BRD. This was a vital puzzle piece for lasting peace and prosperity. Crucially, from the beginning, the Marshall Plan had the intention of not simply disbursing poverty relief funds, but also investing in an economically productive Europe, with a clear goal of cutting red tape, reducing barriers to trade and rebuilding industry. This boost in productivity made it more attractive to seek a career in business rather than going back to the old ways of bad politics.

Last but not least, one needs to remember that the United States wisely helped to restore the basic state administration and infrastructure in record time and kept postreconstruction Germany on a short leash militarily. A large number of US troops were charged with guaranteeing security and a smooth transition to democracy. Even if some old Nazi nostalgic had the bad idea of staging a coup against the nascent BRD, he would not have gotten far. The restored state capacity and security guarantee proved determinant in preventing backlashes and resurgences of antidemocratic politics.

Japan's post-World War II recovery shares many characteristics with Germany's. The United States also played a fundamental role between 1945 and 1952, under the leadership of General Douglas MacArthur. As with the denazification in Germany, the Allies removed the old elite who engaged in massacres and organized trials to punish war crimes committed by Japanese individuals. The US occupiers also imposed a new democratic constitution in 1947, limiting the political role of the emperor and giving a *voice* to all Japanese citizens. At the same time, a large US army contingent occupied Japan, *warranting* security and preventing relapses during the transition to democracy. Concurrently, the Marshall plan logic was applied to Japan's recovery with massive infrastructure and human capital investments, which provided *work* and fueled the Japanese economic miracle. As for Germany, the result was spectacular: In a few years Japan was transformed from a terrifying war machine spreading fear throughout Asia into a stable and prosperous democracy with a pacifist constitution that has been a force for good ever since.

One may counter these examples as, in most other cases, democracy imposed from abroad backfired. This point is well taken: As shown in this book, the conditions under which radical democratization driven from the outside can succeed are restrictive, and hence I will not naively advocate for wild interventionism. What made Allied post-conflict reconstruction work in Germany and Japan was, first of all, that these countries were, after losing World War II, in a desolate position and morally, financially, politically and militarily bankrupt. This was indeed a fertile terrain for making a *tabula rasa* and planting the seeds of democracy, despite once being a hostile territory of widespread fascist and militarist ideology. Besides these preconditions, what crucially contributed to success was the consequent and massive application of key ingredients of what I call "the peace formula": unprecedented investments in creating *work*, insisting without compromise on a democratic *voice* for everybody and providing massive and long-lasting security *warranties*. So, no, it is not by chance that such interventions worked for Germany and Japan but often backfired elsewhere, where either the preconditions for intervention were less favorable or – more often – the principles of the peace formula were discarded for the benefit of shady deals.

In what follows, we shall turn to examples where much of the heavy lifting of democratization was domestic, with the international community in the role of a supporting actor. *South*

Africa is an example of such a "home-grown" democratic transition crowned with success. After turning a blind eye to the inhuman apartheid state of South Africa for decades, at the end of the 1980s international pressure on the rogue regime of Pretoria finally mounted and international economic sanctions and boycotts took their toll. Olaf Palme nailed it in 1986 at an anti-apartheid rally one week before his murder: "Apartheid cannot be reformed; it needs to be eliminated."[11]

Once international support and shady deals with the South African *Unrechtsstaat* were history and when the leader of the African National Congress (ANC), Nelson Mandela, insisted on "one person, one vote" rather than the semidemocracy proposed by the old elite, South Africa set sail for a better future. Insisting on full democracy and fully removing past despots from power has proven crucial for a successful transition to the rule of law. While the "Rainbow Nation" achieved the difficult task of transitioning to democracy and giving every citizen a *voice*, its track record is more dismal when it comes to investing in productive *work*, building up state capacity and *warranting* security. While South Africa boasts one of Africa's strongest economies, the education sector still faces important challenges and homicide rates are still high.

In these three tales of success, the international community played a substantial role in helping the transition toward democracy – as a leading actor in Germany and Japan, and as a supporting actor in South Africa. However, there also exists a multitude of cases where a country's move toward democracy was largely home-grown and achieved through domestic pressure from the street. The involvement of the international community was limited to maintaining international pressure and "nudging" the domestic political cast toward democratic reforms.

After having discussed these examples from Europe, Asia and Africa, let us now turn to Latin America. Stories of transformation are abundant: Uruguay finally escaped the grip of the military *junta* led by Gregorio Alvarez in 1985, Chile got rid of the authoritarian dictatorship of General Augusto Pinochet in 1990 and Peru's dictator Alberto Fujimori finally resigned in 2000. In each case pressure from civil society played a key role. What surely helped was that the Cold War had already started to fade away amid Mikhail Gorbachev's perestroika and glasnost in the mid-1980s and concluded after 1989. This robbed right-wing dictators of the Western support they may have enjoyed decades earlier and that may have helped them to cling to power. Removing the former bad regimes of strongmen did not lead to chaos – as some cold warriors may have feared earlier – but led all three countries away from being conflicted and repressive autocracies with blood on their hands toward stable democracy, peace and prosperity. In all three cases, a mix of rule of law and civil rights (*voice*), reasonable economic performance (*work*) and considerable state capacity and security enforcement (*warranties*) were instrumental in fostering peace.

When we refer to the *peace formula*, we often highlight these three key ingredients, *voice*, *work* and *warranties*. Still, it is important to keep in mind that beyond these fundamental pillars (or cornerstones) of the edifice of peace, various specific policies play important roles as well, holding the basic structures together as if with mortar and reinforcing them. It is a bit like with homemade pizza dough. While there are three key ingredients (flour, water and yeast), the taste also depends on plenty of further components that you add in small quantities (salt, olive oil, maybe sugar), as well as contextual factors that matter (how long you let the dough rest, the type of oven, etc.). You get the point. Well, as highlighted in the book, in addition to *voice*, *work* and *warranties*, a series of policies that foster trust and reconciliation are of paramount importance. Further, we will stress that a battery of programs and policies requiring international coordination make a big difference, ranging from a well-designed green transition, transparency initiatives in resource extraction, commercial practices and monitoring of multinational firms to a generous and well-coordinated refugee admission policy.

WHY IS THE PEACE FORMULA NOT APPLIED MORE OFTEN?

The aforementioned examples of success should be complemented by many more, but unfortunately the list of failed states and aborted democratization processes is equally long. Why is our peace formula not universally applied? It is not rocket science after all. Well, the problem with *smart idealism* is twofold: Concerning the *smart*, several of the scientific results underlying the arguments of this book are recent. Only cutting-edge empirical studies have clearly shown that supporting bad regimes is not only morally wrong but also unsuccessful. Similarly, it is also novel evidence that shows that human capital investments are key, that handing out cash can backfire and that winning hearts and minds does not work when safety is absent.

Now, beyond the fact that these are new insights, the second problem with *smart idealism* is the *idealism*. Fostering peace is a long-run endeavor and requires massive investments. After World War II, the Allies managed to turn Germany, Japan and Italy from fascist mass murder states to functioning democracies, but this came with a steep price tag. Preventing World War III was a powerful enough imperative to rally political support for pumping billions into former adversaries and committing to a massive army presence for years. A US president asking Congress to spend similar sums and efforts on fostering peace and prosperity in, say, Somalia, would face an uphill battle with tainted reelection perspectives. Moreover, and maybe even more importantly, a politician's term is limited to around four years in most countries; hence the incentives are geared toward short- and medium-run projects rather than massive, long-run investments that yield fruit to be collected by the successor government. And, sadly, in the very short run there may be political benefits for Western leaders to engage in shady deals with despots that prove counterproductive in the long run.

This brings us to a key point of the current book: We cannot comfort ourselves with simply trusting our elected politicians to do the "right thing." Instead, popular pressure from civic society to uphold democratic ideals and foster education around the world is key for championing democratic change. It was ordinary citizens who fueled the economic boycotts and sanctions of the South African apartheid state and thereby supported the ANC-led resistance movement. Similarly, domestic prodemocracy activists persisted in fighting the rogue regimes of Alvarez, Pinochet, Fujimori and their cronies – despite often paying a very steep personal price (think of the hundreds of *desaparecidos* throughout Latin America). Global solidarity helped their cause by applying and maintaining international pressure. One cannot overstate the role of ordinary citizens in championing positive political change. In the words of Jim Valvano, "In every single day, in every walk of life, ordinary people do extraordinary things."[12]

Are sound policies that promote peace and prosperity worth fighting for? After all, during the last decade – if anything – haven't more countries receded in terms of democracy, coupled with a record level of ongoing civil wars around the world? Yes: Despite these setbacks it is crucial to fight for democracy and for evidence-based policies for the greater good, as they have persistent effects. Democracies that slide down the slippery slope toward authoritarianism may remain nondemocratic for a while, but are likely to eventually bounce back, drawing resources from the remnants of a "democratic capital" of a bygone era (as illustrated by Argentina's democratic comebacks). Or in the words of Abraham Lincoln, in 1863 in a letter to Stephen Hurlburt, "Those who shall have tasted actual freedom I believe can never be slaves, or quasi slaves again."[13]

2 Loss of Lives, Livelihoods and Love

Wars Are *Not* Good Business

In war, whichever side may call itself the victor, there are no winners, but all are losers.

Neville Chamberlain

In peace sons bury their fathers. In war, fathers bury their sons.

Herodotus

Conflicts come in all shapes and sizes. To meet expectations, it is important to state upfront what the various terms mean, what types of conflicts will be covered in this book, and what is beyond its scope. Figure 2.1 illustrates a possible categorization. To start with, the subject of the current book, *(armed) conflict*, is the umbrella term that designates various forms of organized, politically motivated violence. This is different from other phenomena such as crime (which is not politically motivated) and unarmed interpersonal conflict (which is typically not organized). Obviously, the distinctions can be blurred, but generally speaking, we only focus on armed conflicts and do not treat crime or nonviolent interpersonal conflicts in this book.

There are several subgroups of armed conflict events which are all part of the scope of this book: A first distinction drawn by scholars in the field is between *one-sided* and *two-sided* political violence. The former often refers to situations where the state engages in violent repression and attacks its own people, and where massacres target helpless civilians unable to protect themselves. Examples include the Stalinist purges in Russia or the murderous regime of the Red Khmer in Cambodia. Civilian massacres perpetuated by terrorist groups or rebel forces are also part of the definition of one-sided political violence.

In contrast, the latter, two-sided conflict, designates battle-related violence where both sides have some military capacity and at

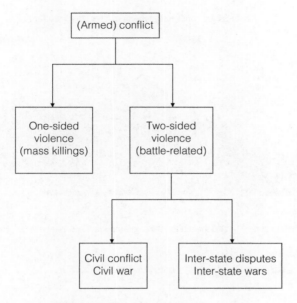

FIGURE 2.1 Categories of armed conflict

least some share of the fatalities are suffered by both sides. Examples include the American Civil War or the current (2024) civil war in Yemen. In many datasets civil conflicts are defined rather broadly, and various forms of noninternational political violence are also included in the civil conflict basket. This is, for example, the case for rebellion (where rebels fight against the national army), coups (where parts of the army strive to overturn a regime) or riots (where often fighting takes place between different ethnic groups).

There are of course also many conflicts that feature both one- and two-sided political violence. The (one-sided) Rwandan genocide of 1994 perpetrated by Hutu Interahamwe fanatics against helpless civilians was only stopped by the military victory of the Tutsi-led Rwandan Patriotic Front in the (two-sided) civil war taking place during the same period.

While our book will also treat (one-sided) mass killings, most of the studies referred to focus on (two-sided) armed conflict, which can, in turn, be split into two subcategories. First, there is *domestic/*

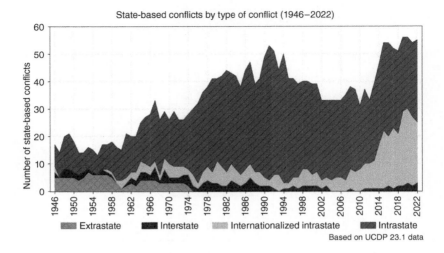

FIGURE 2.2 Evolution of conflict types over time

internal fighting within a given country, which is also referred to as *civil conflict* (for incidents with more than twenty-five battle-related fatalities) and *civil war* (when the threshold of over 1,000 battle-related deaths is reached). The second category of two-sided armed conflict consists of international fighting, where small-scale events are called *interstate disputes*, while large events with more than 1,000 battle-related deaths are labelled *interstate wars*.

In recent years most scholars have focused on explaining civil conflicts, which can be accounted for by the fact that this category has become increasingly important over time. Figure 2.2 displays the evolution of conflict types, highlighting how radically our world has changed.[1] When in 1946 humanity finally woke up from the nightmare of World War II, one of the most frequent grounds for fighting was the willingness to free oneself from the chains of colonization and create an independent nation state. Examples include the Indonesian National Revolution from 1945 to 1949, opposing Indonesian independentist forces under the leadership of Sukarno and Mohammad Hatta against the Dutch colonial troops, as well as the Algerian War from 1954 to 1962 where the National Liberation

Front combated the French colonizers. In the jargon of conflict, scholars call these decolonization wars "extrastate" conflicts (marked in
grey in Figure 2.2). As becomes clear from the chart, these types of
war had all but stopped by the mid-1970s.

Similarly, interstate conflict became a relatively less frequent
category over time. There were a fair number of interstate wars up
to the 1980s, such as for instance the 1967 Six-Day War opposing
Israel to its neighbor states, or the Indo-Pakistan War of 1971. After
the fall of the Berlin Wall in 1989 and the implosion of the communist bloc, in the following years somewhat fewer interstate conflicts
broke out, yet there was an important surge in civil (intrastate) wars.
In the 1990s, the number of conflicts worldwide totaled more than
fifty in some years, and several lethal civil conflicts broke out, for
example, in the Balkans and in Rwanda.

In the new millennium a previously mostly ignored type of
hybrid conflict became more and more prominent, the so-called
internationalized intrastate war. These wars often start as civil wars,
but rapidly escalate and attract the intervention of various foreign
powers, leading to an internationalization of the warfare. A particularly tragic example of this phenomenon is the Second Congo
War, also known as the Great War of Africa, that started in 1998
and officially ended in 2003 (although fighting has continued on a
shockingly large scale thereafter). This war has, by some estimates,
led to more than 5 million casualties, and has involved many other
African nations as war parties, such as, most prominently, Uganda
and Rwanda.[2] Another more recent example of a very lethal internationalized intrastate conflict is the current war in Syria, which
has involved military interventions by various international powers. Worryingly, in recent years both civil wars and internationalized
intrastate wars have surged, resulting in record-high conflict counts.
To make matters worse, a previously dormant (and considered ana-
chronic) type of war has also made its comeback, the interstate war,
with the Russian large-scale attack on Ukraine starting on February
24, 2022. Given that many recent scientific advancements are about

civil and internationalized intrastate conflicts, a substantial share of the book will be devoted to these findings. This being said, some key results on interstate wars will also be discussed.

SO MANY LIVES LOST

The whole point of going to war is to use force and violence to achieve political goals. Hence, unsurprisingly, fighting results in large-scale human suffering. Establishing a death count for armed conflict is complex, as there are casualties that occur directly from the violence (e.g., if somebody is killed by a bomb or firearm), but there are other, indirect ways in which wars kill. For example, the misery and precarious sanitary conditions caused by warfare can favor the spread of infectious diseases and epidemics. This is well illustrated by the terrible "Spanish flu" epidemic in 1918, finding an easy prey in the undernourished and weakened population after four years of unprecedented fighting in World War I. The Spanish flu is estimated to have killed over 50 million people, costing more than twice as many human lives than World War I itself (for which battlefield deaths are estimated as 8.5 million, and civilian fatalities as 13 million).[3] Beyond World War I this pattern is more general, and it has been found in a wide array of settings that the number of indirect fatalities from these wars (e.g., through diseases) is roughly of the same order of magnitude as the direct ones. Which means that to know the "real" death count of a war, one has, on average, to multiply the official fatality numbers by two.[4]

Braving these tricky challenges of computing death counts, Charles Anderton and Jurgen Brauer have strived to put a number on the total fatalities from (one-sided) massacres of helpless civilians over the last two centuries.[5] Their conservative estimates of direct mass-atrocity-related deaths since 1900 amount to 100 million lives lost. When it comes to estimates of (two-sided) direct battle deaths, we can consider the estimates of James Fearon and David Laitin.[6] Focusing on the shorter time period of the second half of the twentieth century (1946–1999), they put the numbers of battle-related casualties from interstate wars over that period to 3.33 million and civil war battle deaths to 16.2 million. Consistent with the story told by Figure 2.2, civil conflicts have become the dominant form of armed warfare in the second half of the twentieth century.

WARS ARE *NOT* GOOD BUSINESS

If it is quite easy to intuitively understand that wars lead to much human suffering, their economic impact is harder to grasp. A dangerous misconception is that wars may be good business. The argument goes that reconstruction may boost investment and create jobs in the construction industry. This could lead to an investment multiplier similar to that in the case of an ambitious road construction program or Franklin D. Roosevelt's New Deal to get America out of the Great Depression. This reasoning couldn't be more wrong, as first of all, investment programs not only create potential multiplier effects, but also create value to start with (better infrastructure, more schools and hospitals, etc.). In contrast, reconstruction after war only gets the infrastructure back to prewar levels. Hence, unsurprisingly, in terms of macroeconomic impact at country level, a war leaves a country substantially poorer than before its outbreak, as has been shown by a multitude of studies. A recent measurement effort has been performed by Hannes Mueller and Julia Tobias, who investigated the evolution of gross domestic product (GDP) in the years following a conflict outbreak.[7] The news is not good: There is a rapid drop in economic output, hitting the floor four years after the onset of fighting and leaving the country almost a fifth (18 percent) poorer than in the prewar period. Just as worrying is the pattern of recovery over time. Even ten years after the start of hostilities no notable recovery can be detected in the data. And the world is sadly not short of examples to illustrate this: Countries as different as Burundi, Mozambique, Afghanistan, Sudan, Yemen, Tajikistan, and Libya have in common that the postconflict recovery has been a rocky road paved with setbacks and ambushes rather than a smooth sail to sustained prosperity.

Measuring the economic consequences of war is by no means as easy as it may seem. Some studies just follow a pure accounting approach, summing up dollars and dimes spent directly or indirectly to obtain an overall number. In this vein, Nobel Prize winner Joseph Stiglitz and Linda Bilmes estimated the cost for US taxpayers of the Iraq conflict to be 3 trillion USD.[8] While such estimates allow at least a partial regard of the public finance implications of international powers fighting abroad, it would be hopeless to apply similar estimates for countries where fighting takes place. The reason is that beyond military expenses, wars destroy physical infrastructure (and human and social capital, as discussed later) in both the short and long run. This makes it hard to estimate the impact of a given conflict, as it is difficult to pin down the counterfactual, that is, how the country would have evolved in the absence of conflict.

An ingenious solution to this tricky problem has been provided by Alberto Abadie and Javier Gardeazabal, drawing on an approach popularized as the "Synthetic Control Method."[9] The principle is a bit similar to the creation of synthetic tissues aiming to recreate clothing with similar features to one made of, say, cotton or silk. In order to have a good idea of how a given place might evolve in the absence of a given policy, they create an artificial unit that shares the key characteristics with the place that is being analyzed. Put differently, if there has been a huge earthquake confined to Iowa and you want to know how it would have fared without one, you take a bit of Missouri, a bit of Nebraska and a bit of Ohio and mix them together in the right proportions in order to create an "artificial twin" of Iowa that has escaped the natural disaster. The fascinating thing is that a statistical algorithm spits out the right proportions of similar states or regions to create the synthetic unit. Abadie and Gardeazabal applied exactly this method to estimate the cost of the conflict in the northern Spanish Basque Country region. This armed struggle has roots that go back over half a century. In 1959, the separatist organization Basque Homeland and Liberty (Euskadi Ta Askatasuna, ETA), grew out of the Basque Nationalist party and chose to use terrorism with the goal of achieving an independent Basque state. Until ETA's official disbanding in May 2018 this decades-long political violence claimed more than 800 lives.[10] To estimate the economic impact of ETA violence, Alberto Abadie and Javier Gardeazabal's algorithm constructed a synthetic, artificial "clone" of the Basque Country, drawing on characteristics of all other Spanish regions. This clone turns out to be a mix of 85 percent Catalunya and 15 percent Madrid region and matches the economic evolution of the Basque Country before the onset of violence really well: To spot any meaningful difference between the trend line of Basque Country and its fake counterpart requires much concentration and eagle-sharp eyesight. Then, magically, when violence starts there is a striking drop in the real Basque Country curve vis-à-vis the synthetic counterfactual, with the missing GDP gap growing to 10 percent. Put differently, even in a conflict that has a death count far lower than the millions of the Second Congo War, the impact on the economy is very substantial.

SHOCK WAVES OF WAR ARE GLOBAL

Strikingly, political turmoil and instability also impose costs beyond the domestic economy, especially when a country plays a central strategic role. This can, for example, be illustrated by the oil price shock that followed the invasion of Kuwait by Saddam Hussein's Iraq in 1990. The most symbolic images of this are Kuwait's burning oil wells, deliberately set on fire by Iraqi combat troops, which still haunt our memories. The doubling of the oil price contributed to the fueling of an economic recession in the United States and beyond. Analogously, the 2022 Russian invasion of Ukraine has not only led to terrible suffering by the Ukrainian population and to a huge contraction of the Ukrainian economy, but has also led to a global spike in gas and food prices, triggering record levels of inflation and dragging down global business cycles.[11] While the full extent of the worldwide economic costs of this current crisis will not be known for some years, a team of scholars from the London School of Economics and Barcelona has been able to compute the negative externalities of political instability and violence in another, more specific, context. In particular, they exploited a sudden deterioration of the security situation in Somalia in spring 2008.[12] The vessels that were attacked in that year in the Gulf of Aden were as diverse as the French luxury yacht MS *Le Ponant*, the Spanish tuna fishing boat FV *Playa de Bakio*, and cargo ships from the United Arab Emirates, Jordan, the Netherlands and Germany, among others. The hijacking and ransom-taking in this crucial, narrow passage led to a spike in shipping cost mark ups, filtering in risk premia. Comparing the evolution of shipping costs with respect to other, less risky routes allowed an estimation of the "welfare cost of lawlessness." These excess expenditures owing to political risks led to an overall shipping cost increase of around 10 percent. This is a huge waste: While generating around 120 million USD of criminal revenues, the Somali pirates imposed a welfare loss of roughly 630 million USD, making piracy an extremely expensive way of "obtaining transfers."

DEADLY BUSINESS

Is the case of the Somali pirates the exception or the rule? Is it a general pattern that political violence leads to heavy losses of lives and livelihood, while making the fortunes of an unscrupulous few whose wealth builds on the bones of the defunct? Remember Leonardo Di Caprio in the Hollywood blockbuster *Blood Diamond*. The movie depicts rebel forces fueling their fighting efforts with the cash from diamond sales. While Hollywood has a history of choosing drama over facts, in this particular case key stakes in Sierra Leone's civil war were captured rather well. While war is poison for most ordinary businesses, its impact on the diamond industry is more ambiguous, as the "lawlessness" brought along by bloody fighting can be exploited by diamond producers who may be able to dodge regulations and evade royalty payments. Hence, a natural winner from devastating conflict may well be (parts of) the diamond industry. To investigate this, scholars need to draw on the tool kit of forensic science to prove their case. This is exactly what Italian economists Massimo

Guidolin and Eliana La Ferrara have done.[13] They have focused on
the diamond industry during the Angolan civil war – in which natural resources have famously played a prime role – and have found
an ingenious way of detecting the winners of war. The unexpected
and sudden death of rebel leader Jonas Savimbi on February 22, 2022
was associated with a rapid end to the long-standing conflict that had
ravaged this beautiful country since 1975. Unexpected news should
be reflected in the stock market, they thought, and they conducted
a study on the evolution of stock returns around Savimbi's dying
day. What they found was striking: Stocks of diamond firms heavily
entrenched in Angola *plunged* compared with other diamond firms
not operating in Angola! The end of a decade-long brutal war was not
good but bad news for Angola's diamond firms, which suggests that
the war was not such bad business for them after all, while of course
it ripped the rest of the country to pieces (the twenty-seven years of
civil war have resulted in the deaths of an estimated 800'000 people
and a displacement of nearly 4 million).[14]

But the econ-detectives have not finished their investigation
yet and have embarked on another case. Della Vigna and La Ferrara
have developed "forensic economics" methods further to detect the
illegal arms trade, covering eight countries under a United Nations
arms embargo for 1990–2005: Angola, Ethiopia, Liberia, Rwanda,
Sierra Leone, Somalia, Sudan and Yugoslavia.[15] As a next step, they
have identified eighteen unexpected events that represented critical junctures when the prospects for peace improved or deteriorated
suddenly. Analyzing abnormal returns for 153 weapon-producing
companies within a three-day window around the unexpected
events, they are able to show whether "bad news for peace" (a pro-
longing of hostilities) is good or bad news for the expected sales of
a given company. "Clean" firms respecting the embargo should be
expected to suffer from a longer war (and hence a longer embargo)
while firms engaging in illegal arms trade should benefit from a
longer war. The verdict is again very stark: The stocks of weapon
producers from corrupt countries thrive when peace prospects

deteriorate, suggesting that they indeed engage in illegal arms trading. Conversely, stocks from firms from low-corruption countries slump when war is prolonged, consistent with the notion that they respect arms embargoes.

In a nutshell, we have seen in this chapter that wars lead to huge levels of human suffering and are poison for the general economy, which on average contracts by nearly a fifth. Still, for a slim yet scrupulous minority in the country and abroad, war is a great financial opportunity. The more people die, the richer they become. The trouble is that this small group of people does not want the war to end and often has the means to prolong it, for example by illegal sales of diamonds and minerals, which finance the fighting, or by illegal arms trade. As argued in later chapters, to dry out war financing and weapon inflows requires coordinated international action, and particular institutions and policies, such as traceability and transparency protocols for natural resource trade.

Yet beyond these stereotypical villains and spoilers for peace, there are sadly also a series of vicious cycles that can lead countries into war traps with recurrent fighting, which is what we discuss in Chapter 3.

3　Vicious Cycles of Conflict

Why Wars Today Threaten Our Future

> I object to violence because when it appears to do good, the good is only
> temporary; the evil it does is permanent.

Mahatma Gandhi

A sunny June day in Geneva, some years ago. A group of friends
are sunbathing at the Bains des Pâquis, on the shores of Lake
Geneva, right across the street from the Palais Wilson, where the
headquarters of the League of Nations were historically located.
This precursor organization of today's United Nations (UN) was
championed by then American president, Woodrow Wilson, which
explains the current name of this famous landmark, which today
hosts the headquarters of the UN High Commissioner for human
rights. The air is mild, the waves gently caress the peddle beach
and we are chatting lazily about childhood, growing up and getting
older. At some point during the discussion, I realize that three of
the friends with whom we celebrated the previous night, originally
from Peru, Angola and Sri Lanka, have something crucial in common, despite having grown up on different continents in very different contexts: Their countries of origin have been on and off at
war for much of the past decades, which has left a persistent mark
on their lives. Where they live now, how they have spent their
childhood and early adult lives and their plans for the future have
all been affected by political violence in their origin countries. One
can think of these common destinies being a mirror image of the
universalism of the UN, located at the Place des Nations barely
a few hundred meters away. Put differently, persistent and recurrent warfare is not an "African" or "Asian" or "Latin American"
phenomenon, attributed sometimes wrongly to rotten local social
norms. Instead, there are forces plunging countries more and more

into violent mayhem that stretch across continents, local specific-
ities and particular events.

Consider first Peru over the past decades, starting with the
guerrilla warfare in the 1960s perpetrated by the National Liberation
Army (Ejercito de Liberacion Nacional) and the Revolutionary Left
Movement (Movimiento de la Izquierda Revolucionaria). Then, some
years later, violence related to the Shining Path (Sendero Luminoso)
communist guerrilla group peaked in the 1980s and 1990s during the
dictatorship of Alberto Fujimori.[1] After a period of calmer politics,
recently there has again been an uptake of political confrontation of
militants against the government. Poverty and inequality and historical political marginalization of indigenous population groups are
some of the ingredients in an uneasy blend that leads to low trust
between groups and regular surges in social tensions.

There are many parallels with Angola's recent history.[2]
During the 1960s and 1970s the independentist movement became
ever stronger, championed by various armed groups that combated
the Portuguese colonizing force. When in 1975 independence from
Portugal was finally won, the desperately hoped-for peace was sadly
still decades away, as former guerrilla groups now turned their rifles
against each other in a fight over political control. A typical Cold
War proxy conflict erupted between the communist-backed Popular
Movement for the Liberation of Angola on the one hand and the
capitalist-backed National Union for the Total Independence of
Angola (UNITA) and the National Front for the Liberation of Angola
on the other hand. This brutal war waged on until 2002 when peace
was finally achieved after UNITA swore off armed combat. Since then,
the country has strengthened institutions and engaged in reconstruction, yet fighting is still ongoing in the enclave of Cabinda province,
where the rebel movement Front for the Liberation of the Enclave
of Cabinda continues to fight for secession. First and foremost, the
persistent decades-long violence in Angola highlights the violent legacy of colonialism and how proxy wars fueled by superpower rivalries can tear apart a country. Yet, as in Peru, poverty, inequality,

discrimination and mutual distrust between groups are also among the root causes that helped the fire of hatred to burn for such long periods and light up afresh after periods of reduced violence.

Finally, the sorry tale of long-lasting political violence of recent decades in Sri Lanka bears many parallels with Angola.[3] In this multiethnic state the largest population group are the Sinhalese, accounting for roughly three-quarters of the population, with the Tamils the largest minority group, predominantly based in northern Sri Lanka. Historical tensions increased over time and in 1976 the Tamil Tigers (a byname of the Liberation Tigers of Tamil Eelam) were founded with the goal of achieving by force an independent Tamil state in northern and eastern Sri Lanka. From 1983 onwards violence escalated on a shocking scale, and raged for over a quarter of century until the Tamil Tigers were militarily defeated in 2009, bringing an end to a brutal civil war that cost over 80,000 lives.[4] Poverty and grievances over discrimination and political exclusion, together with deep distrust between rival population groups were among the factors that led the fighting to carry on over such a long period.

In a nutshell, while all of these three conflicts in Peru, Angola and Sri Lanka have individual causes and specific drivers (such as natural resource abundance, superpower rivalries, remittances), they have much in common in terms of poverty and inequality, grievances over political disenfranchisement and discrimination, and deepening mistrust between different ethnic and societal groups. Sadly, at least some of these factors have also contributed to prolonged fighting in dozens of other countries around the world, such as Afghanistan, DRC, Guatemala, Iran, Iraq, Myanmar, Nigeria, Pakistan, Somalia, Sudan, Syria and Uganda, to name just a few.

But the aforementioned countries are by no means the only states in the world with high poverty rates, multiple ethnic and religious groups and imperfect political inclusion. Why have they experienced lengthy and/or recurrent wars shattering the lives of whole generations of young people, while others have been spared? Economists would call this "path dependency," which is jargon translating in this case into something like "persistent tough luck," owing to vicious cycles that imply that violence today sows the seeds of future fighting.

POOR PERSPECTIVES: A FIRST VICIOUS CYCLE PERPETRATING WAR

Sadly, misfortunes never come singly and when it rains it pours, which in our case means that there is not just one type of vicious cycle but there are several! Maybe the most straightforward to relate to is poverty. As discussed in Chapter 2, wars impoverish the population. And as we shall discuss in much depth in Chapter 4, poverty is maybe the number one risk factor for hostilities breaking out. Hence, persisting poverty creates vicious cycles of deprivation and disputes. Namely, poverty provides the breeding ground for violence, as the lack of income and perspectives make it relatively more appealing to join an armed rebellion. This, in turn, further impoverishes the country, which risks fighting further down the road, and so on. Importantly, it is not unusual that good or bad income shocks lie outside the power of any given economy. First of all, there can be adverse weather shocks. Famously, bad harvests contributed to price spikes for bread in France of the 1780s, paving the way for escalating unrest that played a role in the French Revolution. But in an interconnected world even events taking place thousands of kilometers away can strongly affect a given country. Take, for example, global recessions caused by unexpected disease outbreaks (such as COVID-19) or international banking crises that start in the financial hub of a rich country. The shock waves hit all countries around the world, but not all are equally fragile. Switzerland, for example, has had the means to mitigate the economic effects of COVID-19 relatively well, as a low debt-to-gross domestic product ratio did not constrain too much the rolling out of financial help for companies. In contrast, according to estimates of the Kaiser Family Foundation (KFF), Angola was the country that was economically hit hardest worldwide in the first

COVID-19 year (2020), and experienced in that year much political contestation, repression and violence, according to Human Rights Watch, a nongovernmental organization.[5]

Similarly, a developing country's economic exposure to the effects of the Russian invasion of Ukraine in 2022 has varied considerably, depending on whether it is a net exporter or importer of food and energy. According to recent estimates from World Bank researchers, countries such as Armenia and Georgia were particularly hard hit by the surging world food prices, leading to an over 5 percent drop in household incomes.[6] Sadly, this exogenous shock may further aggravate the severe political turbulences experienced by both Armenia and Georgia, related, among other factors for Armenia to the heated public debate about how to best protect the civilian population of Nagorno-Karabakh (that very recently experienced an attack from Azerbaijan), and for Georgia to pro-Western versus pro-Russian groups clashing in March 2023 over the so-called foreign agent law. Above all, this illustrates that good versus bad luck can matter, with comparable countries experiencing different types of shock at different times – some being hit harder when they are already fragile while others are "lucky." The trouble is that bad luck today may not be a single random event in the great scheme of things (or the law of large numbers, as statisticians would call it), but may perpetuate itself, leading to tough luck tomorrow, owing to the vicious cycle of poverty breeding conflict, which in turn triggers more destruction and poverty, and so on.

BOWLING ALONE FOREVER: A SECOND VICIOUS CYCLE

When Robert Putnam published his bestseller *Bowling Alone* two decades ago, he focused on the declining social capital in the United States.[7] This is, however – if anything – just the tip of the iceberg when it comes to the global issue of building cohesive and harmonious societies with intergroup trust and social capital. Many countries around the world actually fare much worse than the United States when it comes to intergroup trust – despite America's mounting political polarization. Hostilities between ethnic or religious groups can go as far as triggering "ethnic cleansings," in which people are slaughtered by neighbors for the sole reason that they belong to a different group. Human history is full of examples, from Rome's brutal siege and sacking of Carthage, to the Massacre on Saint Bartholemew's Day in medieval France, the Herero and Nama Genocide by German colonial troops in Namibia at the beginning of the twentieth century, the Holocaust during World War II and more recently the Rwandan genocide and the massacres in the Balkans during the 1990s. Dozens of further instances of these mass killings could be added to this shameful list.

If intergroup hatred has triggered atrocities, the violence – if anything – further fuels mutual distrust and grievances.[8] To illustrate this, we shall zoom in on Uganda, an East-Central African country that has had a rich history of centralized kingdoms from at least 1200 AD onwards. After becoming a British protectorate in 1894, it gained independence in 1962. This landlocked country is full of contrasts between tropical climate in the south and semi-arid regions in the north and ranging from flatlands to mighty peaks over 5,000 meters. The 48 million strong population is equally diverse, with over fifty ethnic groups and sizable communities of Protestants, Catholics and Muslims. Sadly, its recent political history has been tormented. The reign of terror of Idi Amin between 1970 and 1979 has entered history as one of the most despotic regimes in recent history. During Amin's one decade reign, which has been thematized in movies such as *The Last King of Scotland*, an estimated 300,000 to 500,000 people were killed.[9] Furthermore, after Amin's demise, under the following ruler, political violence continued. The current president, Yoweri Museveni, came to power by insurgency in 1986 and has now been in power for almost four decades. His National Resistance Movement has, as its main constituency, the Bantu-dominated south and has historically faced armed opposition in several parts of the country, especially in the northern Acholiland region, which is the ethnic homeland of the

Acholi group, and where the Lord's Resistance Army (LRA) has been active, as well as near the border area with the DRC, which has been a hotspot of insurgency by another rebel group, the Allied Democratic Forces (ADF).

In a study called "Seeds of Distrust," which I carried out together with my Lausanne-based colleague Mathias Thoenig and Yale-economist Fabrizio Zilibotti, we investigated the impact on social capital of the Museveni government's military campaign Operation Iron Fist.[10] As for some of the examples here, a global shock taking place thousands of kilometers away has played an important role: In the aftermath of 9/11, the 2001 US Patriot Act outlawed Uganda's two main rebel groups, the LRA and ADF, including them on the list of terrorist organizations. This led to a withdrawal of support from the Sudanese National Islamic Front, which had previously offered sanctuary to the LRA, and Museveni seized this formidable window of opportunity for a military crackdown on these two groups, with a major operation launched in March 2002 against LRA, dubbed Operation Iron Fist.

In order to capture the impact of this surge in military fighting that peaked in the mid-2000s, we drew on individual survey data from two waves of the Afrobarometer opinion poll survey – in 2000, just before Operation Iron Fist, and in 2008, immediately after. A major methodological difficulty was of course that a surge in fighting may be nonrandom – say, if in a place most people despise the government, fighting may arise much more in that region than elsewhere, unrelated to the military operation. Thankfully, we could identify a major determinant of the intensity of fighting: The distance to the Sudanese border (where the LRA previously had its sanctuaries) explains much of the variation in violence during Museveni's military campaign, and we exploited this information to obtain a measure of how a given respondent was exposed to fighting, independently of her/his characteristics.

Statistical analysis of this data reveals that exposure to more intense fighting in a given area very substantially undermined trust in other people from Uganda. To quantify this, we found that an intermediate surge in violence can account for a gap in trust between, say, the Netherlands, one of the most trusting countries in the world, and Brazil, where trust levels are much lower. These seeds of future distrust are even more striking when a respondent's ethnic group is directly involved in fighting events and when a person is better informed about politics. At the same time, we also observe a large-scale surge in ethnic identity as opposed to identification with the country as a whole.

In order to make sense of these findings we stress in related work how vicious cycles of distrust can emerge.[11] Picture two groups in a given region whose members work together, trade together and interact frequently. To fix ideas, think of the French-speaking Swiss and their German speaking conationals. Trust between people from these groups is high, business abounds and interactions are generally peaceful. In this good state of the world, a civil war between these groups would be prohibitively costly, as all these families, businesses and friendships build the cement holding the two groups together. Imagine now a conflict arising out of the blue between the groups, maybe due to miscommunication. Despite both groups having a cooperative attitude and being civically minded, this unexpected war leaves profound traces and depletes mutual trust. Suddenly ties become looser, more business and interaction shift towards within-group links, there is less intermarriage, fewer friendship links and less travelling to the other part of the country. Relations become as cold as ice and next time a much smaller quibble arises, the risk of escalation and wars is now much larger, given that the missing inter-linkages between groups do not perform their function as ramparts against extremism anymore. And with additional spells of hostilities trust may further go down and trigger further violence. While such a scenario is thankfully very far-fetched for current Switzerland, such spirals of hatred, grievances and fighting characterized much of Swiss history in medieval times, with frequent clashes between Catholics and Protestants. And also, around the world, many examples of vicious cycles of distrust and war persist, as illustrated, for example, by the conflict about Kashmir.

If buildings can be reconstructed swiftly, restoring trust between groups after atrocities is much harder and takes longer. Unsurprisingly, an army of economists has in recent years focused on unveiling deep-rooted historical origins of current discord. The historical persistence of social norms, attitudes and intergroup relationships have in many cases been traced over periods spanning several decades. A systematic big-picture analysis has been performed by the Italian economist trio Luigi Guiso, Paola Sapienza and Luigi Zingales.[12] Exploiting a great number of individual survey responses across Europe, they document that centuries-old bilateral war histories still shape trust today. In line with the mechanism sketched earlier, lower trust also results in less bilateral trade. For example, France and the United Kingdom trust each other less and have weaker economic links than one would expect, owing to their tormented history of frequent wars centuries back. Put differently, the Uganda story also applies to a whole group of countries located on another continent, with a different history and varying economic structures. This can also be showcased for one particular case study, Greece–Germany, investigated by Vasiliki Fouka and Hans-Joachim Voth.[13] Drawing on very fine-grained data on where exactly German massacres took place during World War II, they studied how these painful memories persisted over time. While deep trauma may have been buried inside for many decades, it resurfaced in 2009 during the Greek debt crises, when Germany's fiscally conservative stance was met by a massive political backlash in Greece. Strikingly, areas that suffered more from German atrocities during World War II experienced a greater drop in German car sales and surges in votes for anti-German parties. In a nutshell, the strong and long-lasting depletion of intergroup trust can lead to a powerful vicious cycle of lower trust, low trade and frequent hostilities, which amplifies initial discord and can account for the striking patterns of path dependency in conflict highlighted here.

SCHOOLING AND HEALTH UNDER FIRE:
A THIRD VICIOUS CYCLE

Sadly, this is not the end of the story, as a third powerful vicious cycle is also to blame for countries ending up in "war traps" and struggling to get out. While the first vicious cycle of wars creating devastation and poverty may deplete in the short run by destroying jobs and livelihoods, it may also be addressed rapidly, through reconstruction aid and investments (think of the Marshall Plan after World War II!). In contrast, wars can also undermine reconstruction in the longer term, as emphasized by the third vicious cycle, by causing a lasting destruction of productivity (or what economists may call "human capital"). Hence, the third vicious cycle studied concerns education and health, with low education and poor health fueling fighting (higher unemployment easing rebel recruiting), and subsequent wars destroying schools and damaging physical and mental health.

Many studies have highlighted how exposure to conflict constitutes a painful break in the school curriculum of a child or young adult and leads to a loss of education that typically cannot be fully recovered later in life. Going back to Peru, with which we started this chapter, Barcelona-based Peruvian economist Gianmarco Leon studied the detrimental impact of political violence on schooling.[14] Drawing on fine-grained data on where exactly in Peru conflict events took place and which birth cohorts were exposed, he found that, conditional on being exposed to violence, an average person accumulates roughly a third of a year less education as an adult.

Similar results have been found for a variety of countries. Another influential study, for example, was penned by Olga Shemyakina on the impact of the war in Tajikistan that took place between 1992 and 1997, killing tens of thousands of people.[15] Exploiting information on the location of the fighting and the birth cohorts affected, she showed a strong negative impact of war exposure on the likelihood of completing mandatory schooling and the enrollment of girls, while no effect was found for boys. While the size of estimated effects varies and some studies uncover gender effects while others do not, the overall picture is bleak: Wars destroy precious education months and years that never come back and haunt people for the rest of their lives.

Similarly, exposure to political violence may lead to lasting injuries that may entail lifelong pain and suffering and can also result in poverty, especially in countries with a lacunary social safety net. While some physical injuries are the direct result of fighting (such as becoming tetraplegic or losing a leg), wars also favor the spread of infectious diseases (think of the Spanish Flu at the end of World War I), and lead to lasting mental health damage. For example, long-lasting negative consequences on mental health have been documented for bombing in Vietnam.[16] A 1 percent increase in early-life exposure to bombing during the Vietnam war has been associated with an increase in severe mental distress in adulthood by sixteen percentage points. Such large effects of trauma and lasting mental suffering have been documented for war exposure in various countries across the globe. Strikingly, not only civilians suffer, but combatants as well, as testified in many interviews with army veterans, for example in the recent documentary series *American Veteran*. In terms of numbers, the US National Center for Post-Traumatic Stress Disorder (PTSD) estimates that between a tenth and a fifth of veterans who served in Iraq or Afghanistan currently suffer from PTSD.[17]

But what are the underlying mechanisms of this third vicious cycle that deploys effects over the medium and long run? The sad, thoughtful eyes of Che Guevara that greet us from many T-shirts and posters every week are misleading – there obviously exist some Che Guevara-types among rebels, who fight for a cause they believe in (say, universal communism or jihadism), but a very sizable share of fighters in wars around the world are "hired guns" who may more or less identify with the political goals of an armed group, but still fight for a living. Hence, any armed group –whether regular army or armed rebels – needs to recruit fighters and pay them a salary. Part of the equation is the funding for this, as discussed in Chapter 5. Yet even if some funds have been raised, a "rebel entrepreneur" needs to be able to recruit sufficient fighters within the budget. And this of course depends on the outside options of target recruits. Someone who is well fed with a stable, well-paid job and financially comfortable will be much less keen to risk life and health to fight for some obscure cause than somebody who is out of luck and struggling to find the means to buy food every day. And that is where the third vicious cycle kicks in: If their physical and mental health are ruined and their schooling is jeopardized, war victims will be less fit for the labor markets decades later when the initial war is maybe long over. Unemployed and out of luck former war victims or combatants are hence easier prey for rebel recruiters, who try to build the largest army possible for a given budget. If their job is easier, then larger-scale fighting may resume rapidly, shattering countless lives today and for decades to come.

This being said, economists are maybe focusing too much on cold-hearted cost–benefit calculus and neglect another channel of transmission through which war victimization fuels future aggression: Beyond easier recruiting, the mental trauma caused by war exposure may directly increase willingness to use force later in life, independently of economic incentives, owing to, for example, more difficulties in controlling impulses. Studying whether there is a long-run effect of war victimization causing violent future behavior is tricky. The reason is simple: People often remain in the toxic context in which they have experienced violence. If somebody has been victimized in, say, the First Libyan Civil War of 2011, and has stayed in Libya thereafter, it would be hazardous to attribute trauma later in life to this episode, as insecurity, corruption, lack of rule of law, violent crime, armed fighting and discrimination have remained widespread even after the end of the war. Hence, whether any PTSD years later was actually due to war victimization or more generally due to exposure to living in a "failed state" would be hard to disentangle.

Why should we care? Is this debate not purely academic and devoid of any useful policy implications? Well, not really. Knowing how much mental distress is due to ancient violence exposure and which part is due to current triggers is key, as it allows us to get a handle on how mental distress is about to evolve in countries that experience a successful postconflict reconstruction. Take for example, the people of Croatia, who were exposed to armed violence in the early 1990s, when Croatia declared independence. Since the end of hostilities, Croatia has managed a successful postconflict reconstruction, with a strengthening of institutions, economic growth and EU membership. If solely current triggers matter, its government won't have to focus on mental-healing policies, while if past trauma continues to haunt war victims, a well-designed strategy to combat mental distress is needed.

Several studies suggest that war involvement has long-lasting detrimental effects on mental health, even once the people exposed have left the risk zone and are in the safe harbor of a democratic country with a functioning rule of law. Some of the evidence focuses on former combatants who are now back home. For example, an article in the *British Journal of Psychiatry* examined a sample of over 1,000 US veterans who were deployed in Iraq and Afghanistan, and are now back home.[18] It found that almost a tenth of them had engaged in severe violence and about a quarter in other physical aggression, where a combination of PTSD and alcohol misuse constituted a key risk factor.

Is this effect of trauma favoring future violent behavior confined to militarily trained soldiers or can war victimization also make civilian refugees more violent later in life? Some years ago, together with my current and former Lausanne colleagues Mathieu Couttenier, Veronica Preotu and Mathias Thoenig, we set sail to study this question.[19] It was neither a smooth sail nor an easy journey, as we first faced the difficulty of separating past war experience from current bad conditions. As mentioned earlier, there are countries such as Croatia where after the war postconflict transition has been relatively swift and successful, but in many contexts the decades after the most acute fighting have been still tough, and characterized by weak institutions, high insecurity and poverty. Isolating the impact of war trauma from this toxic mix is like finding a needle in a haystack. Then a solution arose: Study people who have left their homes and are living now in democratic, peaceful and quiet surroundings. What better context for this than Switzerland, which has since the publication of Johanna Spyri's bestseller *Heidi* in the late nineteenth century been associated with peaceful Alpine landscapes with grazing cows and snow-covered peaks. And so we started out on our journey of investigation, with as first task the need to access data. This was not the most straightforward stage of the endeavor, as the individual data needed on asylum seekers in Switzerland and on crimes committed could hardly be more sensitive. If such data got into the hands of far-right extremists, they might cook up some misleading statistics for political purposes. If the data get into the hand of journalists, they may selectively highlight "catchy" crimes but neglect the big picture patterns, and if some criminals obtain data access, they may use it for extorting ex-cons who in the meantime had made a fortune. So we took a train to picturesque Neuchâtel, a medieval town on the shores of a lake with the same name, where the headquarter of Statistics Switzerland is located, and convinced them with our academic credentials that we are scholars and not part of the three aforementioned categories. Once the data were obtained (and securely stored) the actual work began. After many months of data crunching and a never-ending stream of statistical robustness checks we finally held the results in our hands.

We found that cohorts exposed to civil conflict or massacres during childhood (and now living as asylum seekers in Switzerland) are about a third more prone to violent crime later in life than the average cohort. This effect is particularly strong when somebody was victimized during very early childhood, and much of the violent crime behavior is directed towards conationals. Put differently, if two groups have been at war at home and members of these groups have fled to Switzerland to ask for refuge, their intergroup grievances move with them; even in a completely different context, of a new country of residence, intergroup hatred persists. This has been illustrated recently by severe tensions within the Eritrean diaspora in Switzerland, resulting in clashes between factions either in favor or against the current Eritrean regime. Thankfully, this ever-perpetuating hatred and these grievances are not immutable: In the second part of our article, we showed that inclusive integration policies and access to the labor market can eliminate two-thirds of this trauma-crime effect.

THE PEACE MULTIPLIER

As discussed in this chapter, wars today sow the seeds of wars tomorrow. This highlights that stopping violence early is key, before the economy, the social fabric and individual education and health have fallen victim to the madness of war. Scholars studying conflict like to talk about a "peace dividend," but in light of these vicious cycles this term may be misleading, as a dividend evokes a one-off payment made to a stockholder.[20] In reality, the impact of war is *dynamic*, and does not only destroy lives today but also the futures of many coming generations. Hence, it is more accurate to talk about a peace *multiplier*, given that stopping hostilities has payoffs not just today but for many decades to come. Yet this is easier said than done: We still have not yet answered the question of how we can stop fighting. This is what the remaining chapters will examine. In particular, we shall first investigate in more depth the actual key root causes of political violence, and will then explore a series of concrete policy suggestions.

PART II The Logic of Evil

Why Wars Occur

4 Poverty, Populations and Petrol

Why Do People Fight?

That war is an evil is something that we all know, and it would be
pointless to go on cataloguing all the disadvantages involved in it. (...)
The fact is that one side thinks that the profits to be won outweigh the
risks to be incurred, and the other side is ready to face danger rather
than accept an immediate loss.

Thucydides

Poverty is the parent of revolution and crime.

Aristotle

Before finding the cure, a doctor must first understand the disease. It is
the same for economists. This chapter will provide a "crash course"
of key explanations in economics and political science on why wars
break out and drag on in the first place, focusing on explaining the
powerful logic of perilous promises and hidden information, and the
dangers of low opportunity costs and lucrative rents.

The starting point of many explanations of war is the question of
why peaceful bargaining cannot prevent it, despite the fact that war is
so costly (remember from Chapter 2 –war may destroy as much as a fifth
of economic output). This is sometimes called the "war inefficiency
puzzle," and the classic reasons for its occurrence were described some
decades ago in a seminal work by Stanford's James Fearon.[1] While most
of our book is about civil conflicts, the following theories of why bargaining may fail apply both to civil as well as interstate wars. The deep
and fundamental question on the scope of peaceful bargaining to prevent destruction is as old as humanity itself, and already in the Bible
negotiation under the threat of death received prominent attention
through the tale of King Solomon's judgement. It goes as follows:

> One day two women came to King Solomon, and one of them said:
> "Your Majesty, this woman and I live in the same house. Not long
> ago my baby was born at home, and three days later her baby was
> born. Nobody else was there with us. One night while we were all
> asleep, she rolled over on her baby, and he died. Then while I was
> still asleep, she got up and took my son out of my bed. She put him
> in her bed, then she put her dead baby next to me. In the morning
> when I got up to feed my son, I saw that he was dead. But when I
> looked at him in the light, I knew he wasn't my son." "No!" the
> other woman shouted. "He was your son. My baby is alive!" "The
> dead baby is yours," the first woman yelled. "Mine is alive!" They
> argued back and forth in front of Solomon, until finally he said,
> "Both of you say this live baby is yours. Someone bring me a
> sword." A sword was brought, and Solomon ordered, "Cut the
> baby in half! That way each of you can have part of him." "Please
> don't kill my son," the baby's mother screamed. "Your Majesty,
> I love him very much, but give him to her. Just don't kill him."
> The other woman shouted, "Go ahead and cut him in half. Then
> neither of us will have the baby." Solomon said, "Don't kill the
> baby." Then he pointed to the first woman, "She is his real mother.
> Give the baby to her." Everyone in Israel was amazed when they
> heard how Solomon had made his decision. They realized that God
> had given him wisdom to judge fairly. (The Bible, Kings: 3:16–28)

As illustrated by this famous Bible quote, failed bargaining may end
up completely destroying what is as at stake. Hence, one would expect
that in most situations solutions for peaceful sharing can be found.
For example, in a nonnegligible share of divorces parents manage to
maintain functional relationships for the children's sake and find a
modus operandi that splits family time and financial contributions in
ways that are acceptable for both. Obviously, such peaceful outcomes
do not always work, as illustrated in the 1989 blockbuster movie *The
War of the Roses*. When it comes to politics, statistics suggest that
most disputes actually get solved peacefully, and wars are rather the
exception than the rule. While in recent years most scholars have

focused on civil wars, the category with the lion's share of events in recent decades, in the distant past most scientific attention concentrated on explaining wars between states. So, unsurprisingly, when it comes to long time series recording different types of disputes, of varying magnitude, scholars of international relations between states still have an edge. The so-called "Correlates of War" project has assembled a detailed database of disputes between states ranging as far back as 1816. This covers everything from border disputes to the Gulf Wars, classifying incidents into different categories. When crunching the data, it is striking that, of the several thousand incidents since the Congress of Vienna, only roughly 5 percent escalated into full-blown wars. Put differently, when France and the United Kingdom quibble about fishing rights or Switzerland and Germany about noise from airports in the border area, these disputes typically end with compromises (in these cases, fishing quotas and different landing routes), rather than the English torpedoing French fishing boats or Germany shooting down Swiss passenger planes. It is important to keep in mind that bargaining often works, which means that in many disputes a natural initial question emerges: Can we negotiate a compromise?

THE FOG OF WAR

But then, if bargaining often works fairly well, why does it sometimes backfire? Let us answer this question with another one. Why was the 2023 alleged balloon spying by China such a big deal, leading to new lows in the relationships between the rising Middle Country and Uncle Sam? Well, spying is a big deal, because military secrecy is. As illustrated by famous military ruses throughout millennia of military history – from the Trojan Horse to George Washington's unexpected attack by crossing the Delaware river during a treacherous storm – surprise is a key component of battlefield success. Hence, it is unimaginable that a given military power would send precise information on the details of troop location, strength, equipment, training, morale and preparation to its foes. Yet information asymmetry is exactly one of the reasons why estimates of winning chances may vary substantially between warring parties. And if all foes overestimate their chances of a swift victory they may reject negotiated settlements and entrench themselves in prolonged fighting. The difficulty to accurately predict winning chances is illustrated by the beginning of the Russian invasion of Ukraine on February 24, 2022. Many well-established (and some self-declared) military experts around the world declared on live camera that the fall of Kyiv was imminent and that the Russian victory, with full control over all Ukrainian territory, was only days away. If experts could hardly have been more off, this is not because of a lack of competency, but simply the inherent imperative of military secrecy that makes it difficult to credibly communicate exact military strength to the outside. In a nutshell, *asymmetric information* has been invoked in countless scholarly articles as a first key driver of bargaining breakdown.

PERILOUS PROMISES

The second classic roadblock on the path to peace settlements is distrust – or as it is called in the jargon, commitment problems. Some telling metaphors have entered popular culture, ranging from "negotiating with a gun to one's head" to "plata o plomo" – an expression popularized by Colombian drug lord Pablo Escobar on the choice between a bribe or a bullet. The movie version of this is the famous scene in *The Godfather*, where the "padrino" makes "an offer you can't refuse." Less colorfully, scholars distinguish three types of commitment problems. The first subcategory is referred to as "preemptive war" or "first-striker advantage." Military history is spiked with examples where the first attacker in a battle has capitalized on this element of surprise to gain an edge. Beyond George Washington's audacious attack in the Battle of Trenton, one can think, for example, of the Six-Day War, where Israel –in response to apparent mobilization of neighboring states – in the early morning of June 5, 1967, launched a massive surprise air assault, wiping out more that 90 percent of the mighty Egyptian air force still glued down to the tarmac. If, in a given hostility between enemy fractions first-striker advantages are large, then any peace deal may prove brittle, as the foe's intentions are difficult to trust.

Another subcategory of commitment problems poisoning negotiations are so-called preventive wars. This refers to situations in which a rising power is getting stronger by the day and an enemy force judges it wise to attack while the foe is still containable, rather than later when the chance of winning is lower. Or in the words of Bob Marley in his tune "I Shot the Sheriff," "Kill them before they grow." Again, examples abound in history, with one well-known episode of warfare attributed to preemptive motives being the devastating Japanese attack on Pearl Harbor during World War II. Allegedly, some Japanese commanders thought war against the United States was inevitable and were worried about the long-run effect of embargoes and of the American military industry stepping up its game. Importantly, attacks that "succeed" in the short run can backfire in the long-run. If Japan won the battle, it lost the war. To sum up, when relative military strength is shifting over time, preconditions for peaceful bargaining are under strain.

The third and final subcategory of commitment problems is often referred to as strategic territory. When the object of bargaining confers future power, it is difficult to conclude an agreement. Take the logic of being the "king of the hill." Once having captured control of strategically valuable territory, future battlefield success becomes more likely. To illustrate this, we shall shift our attention back to the Swiss city of Geneva, today a worldwide hub of international organizations and often referred to as "city of peace," but in medieval times it was a hotspot of sectarian violence between Catholics and Protestants. Charles-Emmanuel Ier, the Catholic Duke of Savoy, who was desperate to force the Protestant city of Geneva to its knees, learnt the logic of "strategic territory" the hard way. In 1602, when, after a series of failed attempts, the Savoy troops prepared a large-scale –and as they hoped – final assault, they did many things right. They wanted to capitalize on the aforementioned element of surprise by staging an attack overnight and brought cutting-edge equipment with them, in particular long ladders destined to scale the city walls and surprise Geneva's inhabitants in their sleep. Protected by the still of the night, the Savoy squads advanced silently, with professional calm. However, they underestimated the inherent advantage of their Protestant foes who were controlling a strategic territory – as old town Geneva lay dominantly on a steep hill. According to the local legend, the valiant city of Geneva was saved by an elderly lady (Mère Royaume) who was cooking a boiling hot vegetable soup. When she spotted the intruders, in desperation she threw the large soup cauldron at nearby Savoy soldiers mounting a ladder. Their cries of terror when hit by the boiling brew broke the night's dead silence and mobilized the Geneva defense that repelled the invaders. Beyond this legend –the accuracy and salience of which remains unclear – the key factors for Geneva's triumph were the great defensive advantage of occupying this easy-to-defend strategic site as well as unexpected misfortunes for the assailants (such as the very rapid loss of their key lieutenant Brunaulieu). Further, historians' accounts have stressed the different morale of the troops: While Savoy troops were mostly composed of financially motivated mercenaries, the Geneva population was, at the end of the day, fighting for liberty and survival. What is clear is that this failed assault was decisive, as the Savoy troops have not attempted a large-scale attack since. It goes without saying that Geneva celebrates this occasion every year with one of Europe's largest folklore festivities and parade, called the Fêtes de l'Escalade. Beyond this specific example, strategic territory has also been disputed in recent years, such as, for example, the fighting at the Golan Heights (Israel and Syria). The way in which strategic territory jeopardizes bargaining, is that when strategic territory is attributed to one warring party as part of a peace deal, it is difficult to credibly promise not to exploit this battlefield advantage later on (perhaps by starting a new war some years further down the road).

The literature stresses the existence of a series of further hindrances to negotiation, one of which is indivisibilities. If, say, a disputed city contains sites that are considered holy for several world religions, dividing parts of the city between warring factions is inherently difficult and may render infeasible some of the possible bargaining outcomes.

SELFISH DESPOTS VERSUS DEMOCRATIC PEACE

The last reason for bargaining failure that we shall emphasize may be called political bias.[2] This captures situations where the overall costs of war are not properly accounted for by the ruling elite of a belligerent country, as it may benefit disproportionally from the spoils of war (say, lucrative oil or gas deals or cementing domestically its grip of power) while facing fewer costs from fighting than the average citizen (e.g., if disproportionally the poor or ethnic minorities give their blood for their motherland, while the children of the rich and powerful escape the draft or risky assignments). Overall, the more autocratic the regime, the greater the political bias. In the worst regimes a narrow junta, or sometimes even a single person, can decide to sacrifice generations of young lives for a war that nobody wants. This higher political bias in autocracy may also be the underlying reason for the famous "Democratic Peace" result uncovered by scholars of international relations.[3] This striking empirical finding stresses that interstate wars between two democracies are excessively rare, almost impossible, while other combinations (an autocracy against a democracy or two autocracies against each other) are much more frequent. This prominent regularity is sometimes even called one of the rare (physical) "laws" in social sciences. An implication of this is, of course, that if more major powers around the world were democracies, the earth would be a much more peaceful place.

Interestingly, while political bias is typically substantially larger in autocracies, democracies are not fully devoid of it. A recent study examines the voting pattern of US legislators with draft-age sons versus those with daughters of the same age, related to the four conscription wars of the twentieth century.[4] Strikingly, American politicians with "kin in the game" were much more reluctant to vote in favor of proconscription bills relative to comparable politicians with draft-age daughters. This is maybe the most direct evidence to date that even in democracies politicians have "political bias," and are less warprone if they pay the same personal costs as their cocitizens.

If asymmetric information, commitment problems, indivisibilities and political bias make bargaining failure more likely, what are the factors that help bargaining succeed? Basically, it is the so-called peace dividend that spans the bargaining range, making peaceful solutions cheaper than fighting.[5] Put differently, the more costly and destructive conflict is relative to the potential spoils of victory, the greater the scope for preventing conflict by negotiation. If war has a considerable potential to destroy much wealth in a rich country with a complex, trust-based economy such as Switzerland (think of banking and pharma), it is relatively cheaper when the opportunity costs of fighting are low relative to the high stakes of controlling the government (think of a country with high poverty rates but abundant natural riches, such as the DRC). Similarly, the stakes of controlling the state are also greater in an ethnically polarized country in which different factions have radically divergent conceptions of the public goods and laws they would like to put in place. In a nutshell, the peace dividend is lower (and the rampart against bargaining failure frailer) in the presence of poverty, abundant natural resources and high ethnic polarization. We shall now discuss them in turn.

POOR PERSPECTIVES

As discussed earlier, poverty is such a powerful root cause for war, as despair and desolation make easy recruits for would-be warlords. Being out of work and out of options makes somebody easy prey for rebel headhunters as they have less to lose and employment as a rebel soldier may constitute in periods of deep crises one of very few options for feeding a family. While scholars have suspected for a long time that poverty is not only a consequence but also a cause of conflict, for decades they have found it difficult to show this statistically. Showing a pure association is obviously not enough, as such a correlation could spuriously pick up some other confounders or the reversed causality from war to poverty. Confusing correlation and causality can yield seriously wrong conclusions. When you build a nice graph with the number of storks on one axis and the number of babies on the other, you may find a striking positive association – places with many storks have also high birth rates (say, a small town in a rural area) while in areas with fewer birds babies are also scarce (say, in the center of a cosmopolitan city). Is this proof that storks deliver babies, in line with the popular legend? Of course not. Any such correlation could, for example, be due to the fact that storks need a rural environment to thrive and at the same time in rural areas the demographic composition and social norms may be different than in very dense urban environments. Anyway, the point of this example is that by documenting that poverty and violence move together we don't learn much. Thankfully, a team of scholars had a brilliant idea in the early 2000s: By exploiting income shocks caused by the weather caprices of Mother Nature, they could find some change in economic fortunes that is plausibly unaffected by conflict or its covariates.[6] While humanity has already invented plenty of daring (and sometimes dangerous or harmful) innovations, the manipulation of rainfall patterns has, to date, not been added to this list. The result they have found is spectacular: Adverse meteorological shocks (such as droughts or heat waves) that harm agricultural productivity are key drivers of a surge in civil conflict. While this pioneering contribution has the merit of being among the first, it has hardly been the last: In the last years, literally dozens of articles have been written that exploit a similar statistical strategy and have similarly found that bad weather makes political violence more likely.

Beyond this general statistical relationship that exists throughout various regions of the world, a very telling recent example is the Tunisian Revolution of 2011, sometimes dubbed the Jasmine Revolution. In late 2010 and early 2011 popular anger was boiling throughout this Mediterranean country, fueled by high unemployment, food price inflation and widespread corruption. The then longtime president Zine El Abidine Ben Ali became the target of these grievances, and the slogan "Ben Ali dégage" ("Ben Ali get out") rallied vast parts of the Tunisian population. The event that triggered this upheaval was the self-immolation of Mohamed Bouazizi, who set himself on fire in despair after the confiscation of his wares by public officials. The ensuing widespread unrest led to the resignation of the autocratic ruler Ben Ali on January 14, 2011, and the revolutionary fire turned towards igniting the flames of discontent throughout the Arabic world, leading to the so-called Arab Spring.

POLARIZATION AND POLITICAL VIOLENCE

Another key factor that may shrink the bargaining range is when strong ethnic rivalries raise the stakes of controlling the state. The role of ethnicity in politics has been documented for many countries around the world for a long time. But scholars have found it difficult to arrive at precise predictions of what specific constellation bears the greatest risks. There were just too many parameters to get one's head around – the number of groups, their size, their location and how much their social norms and preferences differ, to name a few. Two old friends – Joan Esteban and Debraj Ray – studied the problem from the opposite direction, leaving the beaten tracks of existing approaches.[7] Rather than starting from anecdotal evidence or regularities in the data, they started from a mathematical model. Following in the footsteps of John Nash – popularized in the movie *A Beautiful Mind* – they followed a game-theoretic approach (put simply, this amounts to assuming rational choice and emphasizing strategic interaction between various groups in society). After pages and pages of algebra, their model spit out a prediction: Peace was at greatest danger in a setting with just two big groups of similar size. It turned out that having many small groups – maybe surprisingly – did not put a country at greater risk of war than a completely homogeneous society. Yet having a few sizable groups led to a substantial surge in risk. The intuition of their framework is quite simple, but powerful: Groups need to mobilize their "troops," and while a single small group has difficulties capturing power and coalitions of several small groups may be hard to enact, being a larger group leads to a powerful combination of greater winning chances and relatively easier collective action.

In some follow-up work, a series of articles confronted this pre-diction with the data.[8] To test this conjecture, one first needs to build an ethnic polarization measure for each country or subnational unit. This is actually quite easy (at least for the simplified formula) as it requires only two ingredients: census data on population sizes of dif-ferent ethnic groups, and their ethnic polarization index. Note that the formula can be applied to any scale of observation – if underworked and bored, one could even compute the ethnic polarization of one's hometown or religious polarization of one's own extended family. But nerdy pastimes aside, polarization scores have been computed in literally hundreds of academic studies.[9] Sadly, the existing empirical research articles have found overall that ethnic polarization is indeed a powerful predictor of conflict and atrocities against civilians. This sug-gests that infamous historical examples of ethnic violence may only be the tip of the iceberg. The political manipulation of ethnic hatred was at the heart of not only the murderous attacks in Rwanda in 1992 by extremists from the majoritarian Hutu ethnic group against the sizable Tutsi minority, but also of the ethnic cleansing perpetrated in Bosnia by pro-Serbian troops during the Bosnian War of 1992–1995 – where the population was composed of roughly half Bosniaks, a third Serbs and most others Croats, which corresponds to very high ethnic polariza-tion levels. Furthermore, the demography of troubled Northern Ireland (with similar sizes of the Protestant and Catholic population groups) illustrates well the perils of high ethnic or religious polarization levels.

So does this mean that high ethnic or religious polariza-tion leads inevitably to conflict, which is an unavoidable fatality? Thankfully not! As illustrated in the Irish case, the Good Friday Agreement contributed to peace in Northern Ireland, despite very high polarization. Or take the case of Switzerland, which also has very large religious polarization (similar numbers of Protestants and Catholics) and on top of that a sizable linguistic polarization (with about 62 percent German speakers, 23 percent French speakers and 8 percent Italophones).[10] After a string of religious wars tormenting Swiss society during late medieval times, a well-crafted constitution with checks and balances and power-sharing institutions brought relief. As will be discussed in more detail in Chapter 6, skillful institutional design can address the perils of polarization.

A last remark on demographics before moving on. While the Esteban-Ray polarization measure captures well the number of groups and their size (and in its original version even preference distances between groups), it remains silent on group *locations*. Yet geography is key. For example, when one examines an ethnic map of Bosnia before the massacres, it is striking that both Srebrenica and Sarajevo (where terrible atrocities were committed) are located close to ethnic borders. The worst ethnic violence tends to erupt in areas where rival factions are in close contact with one another and find themselves within shooting range. Similarly, victimization in the Rwandan genocide depended not least on the proximity of a given village to major roads (as well as on weather conditions affecting the mobility of the Interahamwe murder squads), as shown by Vancouver economist Torsten Rogall.[11] Last but not least, Belfast offers a stunning example of how urban geography affects the risk of escalation. When I last arrived in Belfast after travelling through the British and Irish isles, my final stop before the capital was the Giant's Causeway, where hexagonal basalt columns have been formed over thousands of years by underwater volcanic actions. A similar logic of tectonic plates hit me when I reached Belfast, where the most explosive religious neighborhood borders have been secured using so-called peace lines (also called peace walls), keeping potential support of the Irish Republican Army (IRA), the Ulster Freedom Fighters and other paramilitary groups apart. Peace lines range from simple barbed wire fences to actual walls, and when reading up on the background of the violence, it becomes clear what purpose they serve. Often, the modus operandi of, say, an IRA raid was to hit a target in a nearby opponent stronghold and then within a minute slip back into the relative security of their own neighborhood before British troops or police arrived. Such rapid, targeted attacks on (perceived) foes at striking distance were combated through the establishment of the peace line, which de facto created an additional effective distance between rival factions at hotspots of sectarian violence. This may of course have two countervailing effects: On the one hand, separating combat parties who are in the midst of fighting may be a good idea for preventing clashes in the short run, while on the other hand, in the medium and long run, positive and peaceful contact between previous foes may help foster trust and peace, as discussed in Chapter 9.

The Northern Irish example of how distance affects intergroup violence has also struck other scholars trying to understand the drivers of combat. Hence, I teamed up with Hannes Mueller and David Schoenholzer to study the role of distance for ethno-religious violence.[12] While the "bright side" of being close (such as more trade and innovation) had for decades received ample attention in academia, we rapidly noticed that the "dark side" of proximity had been all but ignored. Drawing on fine-grained location data of various fighting groups in two dozen countries around the world, we documented that –once fighting has started – there is a curse of being close, and that violence steeply declines as distance increases. In fact, more than half of the ability to project military power is gone when a target is more than 350 kilometers away. Finally, we found some support for erecting peace walls, as in Northern Ireland. Yet while this may be a potent second-best policy to contain violence in the short run, in the long run the only way forward is building trust and fostering peaceful interactions between hostile factions.

OIL AND BLOOD

> And then Prime Minister Margaret Thatcher slapped her handbag on the table, a gesture made famous in thorny EU negotiations, and said with a firm voice: Gentlemen, let's cut the crap, we all know what we are talking about. Clearly, it is not about bloody human rights, or democracy or some other abstract principle. The reason I tell you we need to go to war with Argentina over the (admittedly tiny) Falkland Islands is...

The scene obviously never happened quite like this, but it may have unfolded somewhat similarly. This is at least how some historians may imagine debates within the British War Cabinet formed after the invasion of the Falkland Islands by Argentinian troops in 1982. And they all have their own interpretations on what the three dots could mean. Many have argued that they refer to reelection as indeed the swift victory led to a renewal of popularity of the Thatcher government by voters and a landslide Conservative electoral victory in the following year. This being said, another popular explanation for the UK engagement to keep the Falkland Islands is oil. This archipelago of hundreds of islands located next to the Argentinian shore is mostly uninhabited and holds a total population of about 3,000 people, but the surrounding area is indeed rich in offshore oil. And this second explanation has received renewed interest after recent revelations in the *Guardian* and other newspapers that declassified documents showed the UK government had already shown interest in oil exploitation before the 1980s.[13]

In the light of the bargaining framework sketched here, oil reduces the peaceful bargaining range by lowering the relative weight of the opportunity cost of war relative to the grabbable resources. There will always be a bargaining range giving birth to a peace dividend, but if natural resources are very abundant (and hence the stakes of war high), then the lost wages or destruction cost in conflict will become relatively less salient (compared with the high stakes of appropriating resource windfalls). If the relative importance of oil in the Falklands War is still hotly debated, for other interstate wars such as Iraq's invasion of Kuwait, there is not the slightest doubt that it played a role. In fact, prominent disagreements between Iraq and Kuwait included the alleged overproduction of oil and slant-drilling at the giant Rumaila oil field by Kuwait. Together with unsuccessful bullying by Iraq for debt relief, these economic motives substantially contributed to Saddam Hussein's attack decision. Consistent with this willingness of keeping oil prices high and holding back a major competitor is the disastrous decision of the Iraqi regime to follow a scorched earth policy and set on fire over 600 oil wells when retreating from advancing US troops.[14]

But are these examples simply anecdotes or are they the rules rather than the exceptions? In order to study systematically the role of oil and gas in international hostilities, I teamed up some years ago with Francesco Caselli and Massimo Morelli.[15] Our starting point was that oil is likely to matter, but that the devil lies in the details. If for Saddam Hussein it may have looked attractive to assault oil-rich Kuwait, it may never cross a leader's mind to invade Russia to grab their oil in Siberia. Beyond the military clout of Russia, what plays a role is that many of the largest oil fields are geographically very far from international borders. What is more, if, say, the United States had the bad idea to try to snatch an Eastern Siberian offshore oil field, in case of defeat they may well lose Alaskan oil fields, several of which are located in West Alaska, close to the Russian border. This illustrates that what matters strategically is not just the presence of oil, but also the distance to bilateral borders, and relative asymmetry between countries. Put differently, a given country may be most tempted to invade a neighbor that is richer in oil and which is located closer to the bilateral border than one's own oil. Once the logic of oil conquest was clarified, we then engaged in data collection and computation of oil distances from the border for bilateral country pairs across the world. The results of the statistical analysis proved surprisingly striking. The aforementioned critical constellation of oil asymmetry – one country has oil close to the bilateral border while the other has none or fields far away from the border – results indeed in a much greater conflict likelihood than when oil is absent or equally distributed geographically.

Yet despite the existence of various further examples and this systematic analysis of oil-fueled interstate conflicts, one should not forget that oil plays a similarly detrimental role in the outbreak of civil wars. Remember, for example, the brutal Biafran War (also called the Nigerian Civil War) from 1967 to 1970 and the ensuing terrible famine. The war had been looming for several years but broke out after the oil-rich secessionist Southern Nigerian Biafran region declared independence in 1967. A major reason for the war was ethnic polarization and hostility between the large ethnic groups, such as the Yoruba people in the west, the Igbo people in the east and the Hausa-Fulani people in the north. Yet the lucrative oil fields located in the Biafran region without a doubt played a significant role, as illustrated by the dispute arising when the Biafran government wanted to obtain oil royalties, which was harshly contested by the federal authorities. Beyond Nigeria, dozens of examples of oil fueling armed fighting can be found across the world, from Angola over Chad, Sudan, Yemen, Libya and Iraq to Venezuela and Colombia.

My serial coauthor Massimo Morelli and I again wanted to understand whether this relationship holds generally across a large set of nations and how the specifics of oil location matter.[16] We found that it is not just oil's presence in general that is key, but that, again, the geographical distribution of oil matters crucially. In small countries with huge reserves (say, Qatar) there is so much "black gold" that distributional conflicts are quite limited, while the most dangerous constellation arises when the oil distribution in a country is unequal – when some regions have lots of it and others have little. In this case the oil-rich areas may have powerful incentives to split. This general pattern is confirmed when we compute an index of unequal oil distribution, which we call "Oil Gini." It turns out that this measure is strongly associated with civil conflict. To further refine the risk profile, we were keen to also consider whether the ethnic groups located in oil-abundant regions were politically included or discriminated. The most explosive brew consists of extremely unequal oil holdings, with the groups populating the oil-rich areas being politically discriminated against. They are treated badly and know that by seceding they may potentially be better off – which almost guarantees the establishment of separatist movements that are likely met with violence.

Importantly, this curse of resource abundance is not confined to oil and gas, but extends to minerals. Think, for example, of the gold-rich Eastern Congo region of Kivu, that has suffered from armed violence and combats for the control of mining resources for several decades. Or consider the role of diamonds in Sierra Leone's brutal civil war from 1991 to 2002, popularized by the Hollywood block-buster *Blood Diamond*. While major movie productions are typically good at being "catchy," their reputation for accuracy is more dismal. So are these rare cases getting disproportionate attention – or are they what statisticians would call "outliers"? To answer this million-dollar question, my French colleagues Nicolas Berman, Mathieu Couttenier and Mathias Thoenig and I teamed up for an article dubbed "This mine is mine!"[17] We started by assembling a data-set from a variety of sources that lays a geographical raster all over Africa. A bit like in a puzzle, the continent is cut in little squares of roughly 50 times 50 kilometers; in each of them we know which minerals are depleted. Now simply comparing places with, say, gold versus areas with, say, silver and other resource-free regions would be misleading, as particular mineral deposits may correlate with territorial features that can impact fighting. Imagine, for instance, that gold mines are located predominantly in rough territory with dense vegetation that provides formidable hiding grounds for rebels. In that case, maybe any gold war effect could be wrongly attributed to the metal, while the actual culprit would be jungle guerrilla tactics. In order to get around this methodological roadblock we followed a simple yet powerful approach pioneered earlier on, among others, by our brilliant colleagues Oeindrila Dube and Juan Vargas for oil and coffee in Colombia: We take deposits as given, but exploit the annual evolution of world price shocks for different minerals between 1997 and 2010, driven mostly by the rich world's thirst for electronic gadgets and other consumer goods.[18] This period was characterized by a historical surge in prices of at least some minerals, often referred to as the "commodity super-cycle." If, for example, a new smartphone comes on the market, the prices of key ingredients such as copper or lithium may go up, and in, say, a solar panel boom, silver and zinc may be subject to price rallies. To cut a long story short, we found that that there is a large-scale effect of price spikes for particular minerals, and that the general mineral price boom during the commodity super-cycle of the early 2000s can explain up to a quarter of the violence in Africa during that period. Put differently, the movie *Blood Diamond* is not an exception, but rather the tip of the iceberg.

Beyond civil wars, government massacres of ethnic minority groups have also been found to be fueled by natural resource abundance. A telling example is Iraq's oil-rich Kurdistan region, which suffered from several waves of massacres by Saddam Hussein's government. Between 1987 and 1989 alone, a campaign of organized atrocities including the widespread use of chemical weapons led to over 50,000 Kurdish fatalities.[19] Joan Esteban, Massimo Morelli and I investigated whether, beyond battlefield fighting, governments engage in resource-rich regions more often in atrocities directed against helpless unarmed civilians.[20] Crunching the numbers from all the most horrific episodes of mass killings of civilians since the end of World War II we find that there is indeed a very strong pattern of resource abundance making ethnic minorities more vulnerable to the ethnic cleansing of murderous regimes. One possible explanation, which we develop in a mathematical model, is the unwillingness of the ruling junta to share future resource rents with other groups, fueling their cynical strategy of killing potential future challengers or driving them out of the country. What makes natural resources tilt the balance in favor of this most despisable despotic behavior is the fact that extracting resources doesn't often require much local labor (in extremis, all gets outsourced to multinationals paying royalties), allowing murderous regimes to grab a bigger part of rents without endangering future resource depletion.

To sum up, in this chapter we have highlighted major reasons and factors favoring conflict. Thankfully, though, the surge in politically motivated violence is not a fatality but can be addressed by well-designed policies. Much of the remainder of this book is about exactly that.

5 The Killer in the Boardroom

How Fighting Is Funded

Endless money forms the sinews of war.

Marcus Tullius Cicero

Alberto Graves Chakussanga was born in Angola in 1978, when times were tough. A civil war had broken out three years earlier in 1975, opposing the communist People's Movement for the Liberation of Angola (MPLA) and the anti-communist National Union for the Total Independence of Angola (UNITA). The population was already exhausted by the violence and suffering from the conflict and was hoping for a swift settlement, allowing them to overcome fear and trauma and get back to a peaceful life. Sadly, this did not happen. Chakussanga's first day of school, his entire teenage years, his first love and first kiss, and his coming of age were all overshadowed by the horrors of war, until the shooting finally stopped in 2002, after over twenty-six years of civil war. Tragically, Chakussanga – a well-known radio host for Radio Despetar and critic of the government – was not able to enjoy a long life in peace: He was murdered in 2010, at the age of only thirty-two and on the day his fourth child was born. His murder has never been solved. This illustrates first and foremost how wars fundamentally affect the lives of those exposed to it. Yet beyond this, the sheer length of the Angolan civil war is also striking. How can it be that fighting can carry on for so long and how can warring factions finance this decades-long war economy?

There are two features of the Angolan civil war that are emblematic of long-lasting conflicts where the cash for killing seems to never run out. First of all, Angola is very natural resource-abundant, with its soils' riches ranging from oil and gas, to various metals and diamonds. According to specialist estimates, between 1992 and 1999 alone, the UNITA fighters earned about 2.5 to 3 billion USD from black market diamond sales.[1] This spectacular figure allowed an armed faction to buy large quantities of new arms and pay the salaries of sizable combat units. Beyond these global estimates, black market diamond sales can also be detected through abnormal stock market returns of diamond firms. As discussed at greater length in Chapter 2, the unexpected death of Angolan rebel leader Jonas Savimbi on February 22, 2022, was associated with swift peace negotiations. Yet, maybe surprisingly, good news for peace did not constitute good news for diamond firms: Around Savimbi's dying day, stocks of diamond firms doing business in Angola dropped drastically relative to other diamond firms, suggesting that illicit diamond sales during warfare represented a flourishing business for the cynical few (while destroying uncountable civilian lives).[2]

This link between generous windfalls from Mother Nature and long-lasting civil wars also holds outside Angola, with the smuggling of natural resources having been claimed to profoundly influence the decades-long wars in Colombia (where a key role was played by cocaine sales), Myanmar (with widespread opium contraband) or Sierra Leone (where again diamond black market sales mattered strongly – as thematized by the movie *Blood Diamond*). Beyond these particular cases, there exists a general pattern when war duration is studied for a great number of conflicts across the world over several decades, as shown by the American political scientist James Fearon.[3] In particular, he found that for the seventeen conflicts that can be coded as contraband-fueled, the estimated mean civil war duration was over forty-eight years compared with about nine years for other civil wars.

The second typical ingredient for long civil conflicts is international involvement and support for warring parties. In Angola's case the usual Cold War logic of proxy warfare applied, with the

Soviet Union's backing up of the communist faction (MPLA), providing arms and training, while the United States supported the anticommunist counterpart (UNITA). Importantly, proxy wars and international involvement in domestic fighting are not confined to the Cold War period and the rivalry between a capitalist US-led block and the communist Warsaw pact countries. Local conflict can also be affected by rivalries between, say, the major Shia power, Iran, versus major Sunni nations such as Saudi Arabia. In the ongoing war in Yemen that started in 2014, for example, the Houthi insurgents are a Shia group with ties to Iran, while the Sunni-led government benefits from the backing of a coalition of Gulf states under the leadership of Saudi Arabia.

CONGO'S TRAGEDY

Yet it would be misleading to see these two key forces for escalation – resource abundance and international meddling – as separate. On the contrary, it is often the perspective of grabbing windfalls for rich soils that (at least in part) motivates foreign intervention. This is illustrated well by the fighting in the DRC, where international interventions were overproportionally frequent around the particularly resource-rich Kivu area. Crucially, not only major regional powers intervene, but also smaller armed groups may be attracted by resource rents. It follows that understanding warfare can become even more complicated when local ethnic affiliation and regional power dynamics both play a role, as Michael König, Mathias Thoenig, Fabrizio Zilibotti and I discovered when studying the Second Congo War (also known as the Great War of Africa).[4] While any colonial regime in the past centuries did indefensible wrongs and has caused unimaginable human pain and suffering, with long-lasting consequences, Belgian king Leopold II's Congo Free State, founded in 1885, provides a telling illustration of such regimes of horror. Infamous for its brutality, according to some estimates, half of the Congolese population died from repression and malnutrition. Sadly, in 1960 when the DRC finally gained independence from Belgium, it was not easy to turn the page and build a stable and peaceful nation. The ghosts from the past were haunting the young state, which suffered from the heritage of extractive colonial-era institutions and distrust between different ethnic groups that has been deliberately fueled by colonial divide-and-rule strategies. Hence, unsurprisingly, the following decades have been characterized by unstable politics and recurrent armed violence. Tensions subsequently intensified and the Congolese state became a powder keg in the 1990s when the fragile equilibrium between ethnic groups was shaken up. The whole region's destiny faltered when, in 1994, the Rwandan genocide took place: In one of humanity's darkest hours, over 800,000 Tutsis and moderate Hutus died at the hands of the Interahamwe Hutu extremists, fired up by propaganda from the Radio Télévision Libre des Mille Collines.[5] The Rwandan killing only stopped when the Tutsi-led Rwandan Patriotic Front, under the leadership of current president Paul Kagame gained power on the battlefield and ousted the previous government.

This change of power led to a mass exodus of over a million Hutus fleeing from Rwanda to the DRC, ruled at that time by the dictator Mobutu Sese Seko – infamous for kleptocracy, cruelty and his leopard skin hat. The Rwandan Hutu refugees hosted by Mobutu were a heterogeneous group containing both civilians and former genocidaires, clashing regularly with local Tutsi population in the Kivu region where the DRC borders both Rwanda and Uganda. Ethnic tensions mounted and a Uganda- and Rwanda-led coalition supported the rebellion of Laurent-Désiré Kabila's forces against Mobutu. Kabila eventually proved victorious in the First Congo War from 1996 to 1997, becoming the DRC's new ruler. Yet relations with Rwanda and Uganda rapidly turned sour, and Kabila ordered all their troops to leave the country. New ethnic clashes in Eastern Congo then rapidly escalated into a full-blown war, the Second Congo War, which started in 1998 and officially ended in 2003, yet even after that date fighting continued at a very high intensity. This led to a notoriously high death toll, making it one of the worst wars –if not *the* worst – since World War II. Fatality counts vary widely, but a recent computation by the International Rescue Committee puts the total deaths caused directly or indirectly (e.g., through diseases or malnutrition) to 5.4 million.[6] One obstacle to pacification was the great complexity of the war, featuring multiple fighting groups. In particular, during the Second Congo War Uganda and Rwanda supported a Tutsi-led rebel group, the Rallye for Congolese Democracy. On the opposing side, the main Hutu-led military organization, the Democratic Forces for the Liberation of Rwanda, backed Kabila, as did Angola, Chad, Namibia, Sudan and Zimbabwe. When crunching the data from almost 5,000 geolocalized violent events, we count as many as eighty armed groups fighting in this war, including four Congolese state army groups, forty-seven domestic nonstate militias, eleven foreign government armies and eighteen foreign nonstate militias.

After gaining this overview of the armed actors involved in the Second Congo War, we wanted to investigate if and how the complex web of alliances and enemy links affects the fighting behavior of a given group. The hope was that understanding regularities in the supposed chaos of unpredictable violence would help us to lift the fog of war and propose policies for pacification. Yet at that point we hit the first methodological roadblock. The problem we faced has become famous in network analysis under the name of "Manski's reflection problem." If you and your friend Susan mutually influence each other, it is hard to know what exactly your influence is on your friend, as she influences you as well. So if both of you start taking tennis lessons, say, it will be hard for the statistician to tell who came up with the idea by looking at the data alone. Put differently, given that links run both ways, it is hard to establish causality one way or the other, or even to isolate network effects from common shocks. In this example, maybe you both ended up playing tennis because a new tennis club opened up in your neighborhood, and the friendship link did not play any actual role. In order to get a handle on this, one needs to isolate some external influence that is outside the connection between two people or groups. To cut

a long story short, we made use of the "old trick" in this literature, exploiting rainfall shocks. Imagine that a given armed fighting
group, say the Rallye for Congolese Democracy in Goma (RCD-G),
operates in an area that is hit by a historic drought. The local population is desperately trying to make ends meet and find enough food
for their families, hence becoming an easy prey for rebel recruiters.
The bad weather plays into the hands of the RCD-G, and they are
able to step up their military action. This will influence their allies
as well as their enemies. Drawing on this statistical strategy, we
have finally been able to isolate the impact of one group on another
throughout the network.

So what did we find? First of all, and maybe expectedly, rivalry
relationships between particular groups mutually wind up the
opponents and trigger an escalation of fighting. Second, and maybe
more surprisingly, allies tend to freeride on the fighting efforts of
their brothers in arms. If your ally is doing well, you end up sav-
ing your troops and bullets and let the allied troops take the risks.
This mechanism is well illustrated by the mutual accusation of the
American and British troops on the one hand and the Soviet forces
on the other hand at the end of World War II. They both claimed
that the other did not fight hard enough against Hitler, in order to
have their allies – and soon-to-be enemies in the Cold War – pay the
higher price on the battlefield. At a more metalevel, the analysis
also demonstrates that having a complex network with dozens of
fighting groups makes a bad situation worse and that many groups
actually have a much worse indirect effect than is caused directly
by their own military actions. If my group engages in a battle where
a number of people die, the overall effect may be multiplied by the
fact that my enemies are provoked to step up their fighting efforts
as well. Overall, we found that removing all foreign groups from
the Second Congo War would have reduced the total fighting by
almost half, highlighting the detrimental effect of mingling by outside powers and proxy warfare. One of the pacification policies
that proves highly effective in simulations is bilateral pacification

between particularly aggressive foes. Thus, maybe unexpectedly, even in complex wars with dozens of groups, holding bilateral peace talks with a couple of factions may make a big difference.

MINING CASH AND MILITARY

So far, the perils of war funding have been shown for Angola and the DRC. Yet are these outliers or just the tip of the iceberg? Sadly, the tragic tale of these large countries generalizes to many other nations. As discussed in Chapter 4, booming mining prices can account for a substantial part of armed fighting in Africa. But, while much has been said about mining cash fostering the *motivation* for appropriation, it also fuels the *ability* for engaging in armed conflict. To disentangle these harmful effects of mining wealth, we can go back to our mining data for the whole of Africa, described in Chapter 4.[7] Our data not only contain the location of mines, but also show where given armed groups have their traditional homelands and who wins a particular battle. Why are these elements of information important? Well, they allow us to learn much about the financing of fighting, drawing on evidence for a whole continent, Africa. When crunching the data, one striking result that appears is that capturing a mine is a game changer for the ambitious warlord! The impact is huge, as it triples the fighting effort of a given group in the future, allowing a drastic expansion in the range of their activities. Sadly, this of course results in an escalation of war and dimming perspectives for peace. The data also allow for an alternative way of pinpointing the salience of cash for conflict. It turns out that another funding source for the pushy rebel "entrepreneur" is to drain resources from the original homelands of a given fighting group. Indeed, many armed groups are dominated by one or a few ethnic groups. For example, the infamous Lord's Resistance Army is originally from the Northern Ugandan region Acholiland, home of the Acholi ethnic group. Strikingly, when mines located in the ethnic homelands of a given armed group experience a price boom, this translates into greater resources available for its armed struggle and leads to a diffusion of fighting operations across space, as found in the data. Hence, put differently, whether it is from capturing a given mine or from drawing on one's homeland's mining cash, the resource windfalls constitute powerful fuel for armed combat.

A COMMON MISCONCEPTION OR THE RISE OF STATIONARY BANDITS

A common misconception stems from the thousands of Che Guevara posters and T-shirts we have encountered in our lives, alongside those of Bob Marley, James Dean and The Doors' Jim Morrison. These icons of pop culture have in common the notion of rebellion – to overthrow norms, traditions or … the state. Ernesto Che Guevara's journey throughout vast areas of the world is striking, with most visits being carried out as a diplomat and some as a fighter. This globetrotter politics illustrates his global ambitions: Overthrowing the brutal and kleptocratic Batista regime in Cuba was not nearly enough, as Che Guevara's aspirations were global. Never would he rest before the whole world had embraced communism. Well, using the language of statisticians, Che Guevara was an "outlier," and very much the exception rather than the rule (which may also explain why he made it onto all these T-shirts, contrary to basically all other rebel leaders in recent history). The common misconception that rebel leaders are like Che Guevara could hardly be more wrong. While there are of course parallels in, say, the willingness to use force, the overall non-monetary goals of a Che Guevara type are –if anything – not so frequent. In contrast, many rebel leaders do not have global ambitions and a substantial share of them run their organizations not unlike organized crime syndicates. This of course does not prevent them invoking grand idealistic goals – which in some cases have some real bearing but in others are just clever yet phony marketing, not very different from the greenwashing of some firms. So even if one of the main goals is to steal stuff, marketing 101 in the warlord's playbook implies adding attributes such as "Freedom," "Democracy" and "Lord" to the organization's name.

For warlords aiming at gaining military control of a financially attractive area, Eastern Congo is the place to go, as documented meticulously by Chicago's Raul Sanchez de la Sierra.[8] His team has travelled extensively in the North and South Kivu regions of the DRC where the state has lost much of its original monopoly on violence. In many areas the evident power vacuum has been gladly filled by various local armed groups. With the help of a team of ten surveyors, several hundred villages and corresponding mining sites have been mapped out and data on political control have been collected. These support the conclusion that the various armed groups often aim to mimic traditional state functions and operations, ranging from public goods provisions to taxation. Acting as so-called stationary bandits, they tend to build infrastructure that allows them to better extract windfalls from natural resource production. Like many recognized states, they even have to think about how to avoid tax evasion! The Sanchez de la Sierra team found that for bulky minerals such as coltan – that are virtually impossible to conceal – taxation is easy, while for easily concealable metals, such as gold, the armed groups extort funds in the locations where the money is spent – analogously to the value-added tax that is a key instrument of many tax administrations around the world. It goes without saying that what keeps the pseudostate administrations of armed groups going are the rents from valuable natural resources, illustrating yet again how resource abundance can entrench armed rebellion for a prolonged period by financing fighting operations.

BETTING ON BAD TIMES

If vultures prepare an assault when the target is down and out, rebel leaders also bet on bad times. Farmers' tough luck constitutes hiring opportunities for the "entrepreneurs of death." Put differently, while funding sources for fighting matter in general, they are even more crucial when times are tough – as each dollar stretches further. To illustrate this, we shall now move to India's so-called Red Corridor where the Naxalite-Maoist rebellion has cost thousands of lives for several decades. The core region of this communist insurgency lies between Hyderabad and Kolkata. Who thinks communist rebels, thinks Che Guevara – and a key role for idealist motives rather than hopes for material gains. Yet communist groups also need to pay their rebel soldiers, and it turns out that natural resource rents are key determinants of the longevity of this political warfare in the east of India. When studying the drivers of armed conflict in the Indian subcontinent, Belgian economist Oliver Vanden Eynde has been puzzled.[9] He started from the premise that bad income shocks would drive up fighting, as desperation pushes new recruits into the arms of scrupulous rebel leaders, in line with the aforementioned results detected in other contexts. Strangely enough, he found that this link is extremely strong in some regions, while in others it is weak at best. When digging deeper, he started to understand what was going on: Poverty alone is not a sufficient condition for armed violence, as in very poor areas the would-be warlords also lack the cash for conflict. In contrast, widespread poverty in the farming population owing to adverse weather shocks becomes a time bomb when funding for fighting is added – from resource windfalls. In the context of the Naxalite conflict, Vanden Eynde's research documented that bad weather only led to eruptions of violence in mining areas, while not affecting the scope for conflict elsewhere. Put bluntly, if the population at large is suffering from bad harvests but the rebel leaders can dispose of mining cash, the potent complementarity of capital and labor emerges and enables the building of a powerful rebel force.

To sum up, to foster peace we need to keep in mind both how to prevent the outbreak of hostilities, as well as reducing their duration. While natural resource abundance is often a major motivation to start a rebel movement in a given setting, it hits humanity a second time by helping armed movements to entrench themselves and fund the armed struggle. Put differently, oil, gas, gold, diamonds and other minerals not only make conflict onsets more likely, but they also mean political violence is longer-lasting and harder to stop.

This effect is particularly detrimental in the presence of further adverse shocks (e.g., a generalized drought putting great numbers of agricultural laborers out of work) and if outside powers meddle in a given civil war. Foreign intervention may itself become more likely when the spoils of nature abound, and lead to a very complex web of armed groups that may spur escalation and make for dimming prospects for peace.

As shown in the book so far, building peace is not easy, as powerful forces may push states into chaos and violence. Yet there is no choice: Not acting against political violence would make us accomplices of it and can make things go from bad to worse, through a series of powerful vicious cycles. Thankfully, there is hope, as recent evidence highlights a set of promising concrete policies that can help to set foundations for peace. This is what the remainder of the book is all about.

PART III Give Peace a Chance!

Getting Incentives Right

6   **Power to the People**

Inclusive Democracy and Power-Sharing

Real liberty is neither found in despotism or the extremes of democracy, but in moderate governments.

Alexander Hamilton

The ballot is stronger than the bullet.

Abraham Lincoln

If we are to keep our democracy, there must be one commandment: "Thou shalt not ration justice."

Sophocles

Picture Joe Biden, freshly reelected in the White House and announcing his new cabinet. Now imagine that he unveils key positions allocated to none other than Republicans Ron De Santis, Nikki Haley and Mike Pence.... Such a radical decision would certainly leave the public dumbfounded, and almost enter the realm of science fiction, right? But why? Well, the reason for this absence of 'Grand Coalition' in the United States is that the country has a long history of democratic politics and stability and does (at least up to now) not need to engage in bipartisan power-sharing. However, throughout history and in many other countries today the stars align differently –with society being divided between ethnic or religious groups and power-sharing being required to play a key role. One of them is Northern Ireland.

FROM BLOODY SUNDAY TO GOOD FRIDAY: HOW POWER-SHARING TRANSFORMED NORTHERN IRELAND

When asked in an interview about his violent past in the Irish Republican Army (IRA), former Deputy First Minister of Northern Ireland, Martin McGuinness stated:

> I come from a community that has been discriminated
> against for far too long, not just treated as second-class citizens
> but third-class citizens in our own city. As a result of that, there
> was a conflict, and I was part of that conflict, but I have also for
> the last, more than twenty years, been part of a very important
> peace process that is held up as a beacon of hope for many other
> conflicts around the world.[1]

While his statement may be interpreted as an attempt to white-wash his own role in the "Troubles," McGuinness has a point when stressing that unequal treatment has been one root cause of the Catholic uprising in Northern Ireland and that the recent peace process can serve as an example for other countries.

Indeed, much of the history of Northern Ireland since World War II is symptomatic. Major ingredients of the typical blend of civic discontent are present, and the start of the Northern Irish "Troubles" were no surprise – if anything it is surprising that the violence started only at the end of the 1960s. In this period, social tensions and civil unrest were prevalent around the world. The Prague Spring ended in bloodshed, student protests swept through Paris, Woodstock wrote rock history and mass protests against Vietnam took place in Washington. In this climate of awakening, Northern Ireland was not spared by civil rights movements and calls for freedom and equality. In particular, the Catholic minority voiced grievances about under-representation in electoral politics, in industry and in military and police forces. While the protests were initially peaceful, they rapidly turned violent. After the events of Bloody Sunday in 1972 –when British soldiers killed fourteen unarmed civilians – hopes for a peace-ful reconciliation were lost and the gates of hell were pushed wide open.[2] The point of no-return had been reached and Ulster's descent into chaos seemed unstoppable.

So how did Northern Ireland get back on track? While escalation had been abrupt, de-escalation took longer and was at first less eas-ily perceptible. An important foundation for reconciliation was local, bottom-up cooperation and trust building. Short of a majority, local politicians in several of Northern Ireland's district councils started to –expressly or subtly – share government duties across sectarian boundaries. In some instances, cooperation between Catholic and Protestant parties became even (implicitly) codified, with the two factions altering their hold of the top job (mayor) and deputy position (vice mayor). When real people work together to solve real problems, they start understanding that they may be less different than they initially thought. Or, putting it in the words of Sting, "the Russians love their children too."

But how can we be sure that it really was the sharing of local power that helped Northern Ireland get a grip? While biologists have argued for centuries about which came first, the chicken or the egg, economists have long been troubled by cause-and-effect relationships. After all, maybe the local politicians sharing power with opponents are simply the most open-minded fellows, and power-sharing was not the cause of open-mindedness but simply its product. A way of testing the actual impact of shared government responsibilities is to focus attention on district councils with hung parliaments, that is, where any sectarian block lacks a majority and is forced to reach out to rivals – independently of open-mindedness. Focusing on these kinds of situations, in a recent study with my coauthor Hannes Muller, we showed that in these settings, working together at the local level has helped to save close to 1,000 lives![3] Put differently, forced cooperation owing to electoral arithmetic managed to cut the death toll by roughly half in the places and years under consideration.

Besides the immediate localized impact of sharing power, these successful bottom-up initiatives of joint government have also paved the way for a comprehensive power-sharing agreement at national level. Following the fall of the Berlin Wall in 1989, a "wind of change" swept through Europe. Northern Ireland was keen to capitalize on the positive outcomes shown by local-level power-sharing and began to formulate a comprehensive peace deal. Bringing ancient foes to the negotiation table proved to be a lengthy process, but in 1998 year-long bargaining and trust building had finally given birth to a peace agreement. On Good Friday, April 10, 1998, British prime minister Tony Blair and his Irish counterpart Bertie Ahern proudly emerged in front of the world press to announce that a deal had been struck. This deal, thereafter known as the Good Friday Agreement or Belfast Agreement, created the Northern Irish Assembly and a devolved government with both Protestant and Catholic parties present alongside one another in the Northern Irish government. This agreement was then ratified on May 22, 1998 in both Ireland and Northern Ireland.

Did this power-sharing agreement immediately generate lasting peace? Of course not: We are not living in a fairytale. Scars do not heal at once and decades of oppression cannot be forgotten overnight. Throughout history change has been met with resistance, which is often violent and carried out by the most extreme groups in society. Northern Ireland was no different. For example, in August 1998 the so-called Real IRA – a splinter group from the IRA detonated a bomb that killed twenty-nine people in Omagh, and every year during the "marching season" of the Orange Order and other Protestant groups grievances and tension arise afresh.[4] Despite Northern Irish peace remaining a fragile flower needing care and attention, actual political violence has virtually disappeared in the aftermath of the 1998 Good Friday Agreement, leading Northern Ireland to twenty years of peace and economic renewal. Although new rain clouds have arrived with Brexit, the power-sharing agreement of 1998 is widely seen as a big success.

BEYOND NORTHERN IRELAND: A VOICE FOR EVERYBODY
ALSO MATTERS IN THE SNOWY ALPS AND AROUND
THE WORLD

Is Northern Ireland an outlier where sharing power leads to peaceful progress? To answer this, we will step in a time machine leaving the green plains of present-day Ireland to arrive more than 150 years ago in the midst of Europe's mightiest peaks, covered by eternal snow.

Switzerland in 1847, a country poor by any standards, and so destitute that its citizens had to emigrate in great numbers to Russia and the New World. It is in this year, right at the end of the Swiss civil war (the so-called Sonderbundskrieg) between Protestants and Catholics where the foundations were laid for a success story making Switzerland a global champion of prosperity and peace today. The Catholic cantons (states) in this civil war fought the Protestant ones, with the former wanting to maintain a loose defensive alliance and the latter desiring to create, in the spirit of the time, a nation state. The war was short and easily won by the Protestants. At that point the victors broadly faced two choices: crush (and enslave) the defeated opponent (which in those days might well have been the default option) or write a new constitution sharing power between the different components of Swiss society. Perhaps it was the fresh Alpine air inducing wisdom or worries about future repercussions and grievances, but the fact is the victorious Protestants made, in 1848, the historic choice to share power with their foes. Even more remarkable, the new institutions in many accounts actually favored the defeated and gave them a whole artillery of veto powers. For example, in the new bicameral parliament, representation in the upper house (that has extensive powers in Switzerland) was, by the constitution and as in the US Senate, allocated to each canton equally, despite very unequal canton sizes. With the Catholic areas being on average much smaller, the defeated were significantly overrepresented in the legislature. This striking generosity of the winning camp has opened the road to new heights of peace and stability, which has persisted until today. While in contemporary Switzerland the nature of cleavages has somewhat shifted from religion to language, a deep-rooted culture of power-sharing and consensus still permeates Swiss politics and society at all levels.[5] For now, it has been more than fifty years that the Swiss government has been composed of a grand coalition encompassing (in almost unchanged composition) all major political parties and regions of the country.

To better understand the pacifying effect of sharing political power we must expand our focus beyond small European countries and consider a much larger sample. To begin, we will remain in Switzerland but fast-forward to the twenty-first century. We are now in Zurich, one of the world's financial hubs and the ancient headquarters of Protestant forces in the aforementioned war of 1847. A small army of researchers, led by Lars-Erik Cederman, has collected data on the inclusion in government of over 800 ethnic groups in political processes around the world since the end of World War II.[6] Analyzing the data reveals that somewhat less than half of the ethnic groups worldwide have been associated with political power, while the remainder have been excluded. A striking conclusion arises by splitting the sample and assessing the likelihood of taking up arms against one's government. Among the groups with access to political power, armed rebellion is a rare event: The likelihood that a given group in a given year is involved in a civil war with its government is less than a quarter of a percentage point. In contrast, the rattling of the AK-47 is much more frequent, with excluded ethnic groups. The risk is three times higher for excluded groups in general, and when focusing on excluded groups with separatist autonomy status, in one out of twenty-five groups and years the government was militarily targeted.

WHY DO PEOPLE CARE ABOUT DEMOCRACY?

Such a drastic difference requires explanation – how can it be that people seem to care so much about having a voice? If there is something economists love, it is to express ideas with equations and formulas. Similar to the musician who aims to express feelings through graceful melodies, the economist, while arguably less elegant and romantic, employs standard economic models of rational choice and strategic interaction, to paint us the following picture:

> A person in the drawing room ponders "To fight or not to fight," maybe holding a human skull in her hands like Hamlet. What are the benefits of conquering power (money, power, graft) and what are its costs (money, but also blood, sweat and tears)?

While each person may weigh the costs and benefits of fighting differently in such a computation, a major factor in deciding to share power is that the benefit of being the dominant party in the country drops. Take contemporary Switzerland: Winning or losing an election makes not a lot of difference, as the runner-up also has a proportional representation in the grand coalition government. This makes Swiss politics very predictable and, as the stakes are relatively low, political competition remains rather civilized and gentle (yet a bit too unspectacular for some Swiss observers, who in numbers turn to watch French politics or the likes of Donald Trump for more drama and strife). In summary, in a country such as Switzerland, where all major forces are involved in collective decision making, nobody would kill to be the number one, as the benefits of being number one are dismal.

In contrast, being one of the two main contenders in a very polarized political landscape, as recently in, say, Bangladesh, or Ivory Coast, leads to huge stakes, as the narrow runners-up may face long prison sentences or worse. In such situations, losing an election comes with a dear price tag, and the temptation to leave the realm of politics and abandon the ballot for the bullet is palpable. To quote *Braveheart* and the famous Scottish leader William Wallace, "They may take our lives, but they will never take our freedom!" Put differently, having a voice matters, and representation of all political forces is a precondition for lasting peace, as in the absence of shared power, electoral losers may have powerful incentives to engage in armed confrontation. Why bother running around with an AK-47 with the perspectives of an uncertain battle outcome and high costs, if staying in the political arena offers you a secure share of political power?

While this logic of power-sharing-as-hedging-bets is compelling, there is more to democracy than that. One common – yet controversial – claim is that democracy may champion economic growth. The argument goes that the Sword of Damocles of the next elections disciplines the ruler, and that government accountability and rule of law create an environment that makes business thrive. Well, this sounds quite intuitive, does it not? Even a five-year-old child will be less tempted to misbehave when parents are watching than in the face of impunity – and the same applies to grown-up politicians. And living well under democracy makes it less appealing to give up a good life and join a rebellion to overthrow a democratic regime.

Unfortunately, it is quite tricky for social scientists to study these causal relationships, as obviously the decision to democratize may depend on a variety of factors linked to economic growth. So just comparing the gross domestic product (GDP) of democratic countries with the economic output of undemocratic ones won't teach us much. Think of the popular observation that in places with more storks there are on average more babies. Does this mean that storks deliver babies, as happens in various fairy tales? No, of course not. It simply means that in more rural places there are both more wildlife and higher birth rates. Applied to our democracy-growth relationship, the United States being more democratic and richer than North Korea may not be necessarily owing to differences in government; rather, some underlying differences in, for example, social norms or education may have pushed the United States to grow and to democratize, and have held North Korea back.

HOW THE BRITISH AGE OF REFORM TRANSFORMED THE UNITED KINGDOM INTO A PROSPEROUS DEMOCRACY

Sometimes scholars are lucky and find some historical episode that allows them to get around this methodological roadblock. So it was when some years ago, my colleagues Andrea Marcucci, Alessandro Saia and I struck gold.[7] Picture yourself in the United Kingdom during the Victorian period of the nineteenth century. It was an extraordinary time, with both grandiose political development –the era is called the British Age of Reform for a reason – and a substantial amount of civil unrest. Skirmishes and outright fighting between Conservatives and radical partisans were commonplace, and the mob riots and crowd violence of the 1850s and 1860s revealed social tensions that could have threatened the very survival of the monarchy (as in neighboring France half a century earlier). The British political establishment, however, had the good sense to gradually extend the electoral franchise and give a democratic voice to an ever-increasing number of its citizens. We focused our research on the Second Reform Act of 1867, as this particular reform offers a unique opportunity to study the impact of democratization. Notably, it is widely seen as *the* milestone of the Victorian Age of Reform – leading to an almost doubling of the number of eligible voters. According to the American historian Gertrude Himmelfarb, "The Reform Act of 1867 was one of the decisive events, perhaps the decisive event, in modern English history. It was this act that transformed England into a democracy [...]."

The 1867 reform focused on giving additional political rights to urban workers. By comparing towns with a greater level of enfranchisement (i.e., extending the right to vote to a greater number of citizens) to places with more dismal franchise extension, we are able to quantify the reduction in violence brought about by making politics more inclusive. The effect is spectacular: Franchise extension accounted for reducing the risk of a violent event in a given town by almost half. The cherry on the cake is that the one main reason for which we find this drop in violence is that greater enfranchisement has led to higher local economic growth. Unsurprisingly, when the local economy is booming and living conditions improve, citizens are, on average, less keen to raise their arms against the government. After the Reform Act of 1867 citizens benefited from alternative means of expression and had –amid the booming economy – fewer motives for discontent.

A key question is whether this finding can be generalized. After all, one can find modern examples where democracies do not necessarily outperform autocracies. Think of China, which has grown faster in the past decades than India (although there is no shortage of sceptics doubting the robustness and sustainability of Chinese growth in the long run). It turns out that the China/India example is rather the exception than the rule. Daron Acemoglu from MIT and coauthors have recently studied the worldwide link between democracy and economic growth in the last few decades.[8] Their judgment is univocal: Democratization increases GDP per capita by about a fifth in the long run! And this higher affluence is typically a force of political stability, as citizens pleased with their living condition cannot easily be convinced to take up arms for an uncertain cause.

DICTATOR'S DILEMMA: HOW DEMOCRACY MAKES THE FOG OF BAD INFORMATION DISAPPEAR

Beyond boosting business, consolidated democracy has a series of other virtues that promote peace. A key problem faced by all dictators is bad information, which Ronald Wintrobe termed "the Dictator's Dilemma."[9] If stating your honest opinion leads you straight to a gulag, you may prefer to keep your point of view to yourself. If citizens abstain in voicing grievances, the authoritarian junta has difficulties estimating the level of popular discontent and support for opposition forces. In such situations large-scale revolutions can hit a dictatorship by surprise and sweep the leading cast away. The Persian shah may have been as surprised by the rapid unfolding of the Iranian Revolution in 1979 as was East Germany's Erich Honecker in 1989 when the Berlin Wall started to crumble. It is every despot's nightmare to see, without warning, a mighty fortress of authoritarian rule turn out to be a fragile sandcastle instead. This lack of reliable information on opposition support leads authoritarian regimes to make mistakes. Thinking that they sit firmly in the saddle, they may misread the extent of popular discontent and omit putting in place the necessary reforms in hours of great danger. Had the French king Louis XVI and Marie-Antoinette, in 1789, had accurate information on popular discontent, they probably would have implemented more wide-ranging concessions that might have helped them save their crowns in place of losing their heads.

As shown in recent research together with my Geneva and Lausanne-based coauthors Jérémy Laurent-Lucchetti and Mathias

Thoenig, democracies have by their very nature significant information advantages over dictatorships.[10] Holding frequent free and fair
elections, with actual stakes for voters, reveals to the government
what the people want and how strong the opposition is. This in turn
allows the government to know what concessions are necessary to
avoid revolution, making sure that the opposition is always better
off embracing electoral politics than going astray and trying to win
control of the state by force. Fine-tuning of policies guarantees incentives for peace and allows consolidated democracies to lessen any
risk of upheaval and political violence.

If there is a clear case for integrating all communities in politics
and sharing power between different groups, in addition to organizing
free and fair elections, what about other aspects of democracy, such
as free speech and the rule of law? Are these of secondary importance,
and is simply running free elections enough to lay the cornerstone for
building peace? Why bother to rack one's brain about group representation and civil liberties, when organizing any kind of vote will do
the job? As you might expect, things are more complicated than this
and running competitive elections alone is not enough to secure lasting peace. While there is a pile of arguments and statistical evidence
that mature power-sharing and consolidated democracies are associated with more peaceful and prosperous societies, these virtues of
democracy can only persist in the long-run with the presence of free
speech, the rule of law and democratic norms in society. However,
building up such civil liberties and civic culture requires time, and
the road to stable democracy may in many cases be a bumpy ride.
Hence, it is not sufficient to ponder the effects of full democracy –
once established – and equal attention must be given to the strategies
to get there in the first place.

TRICKY TRANSITION

To see why, let us move to Berlin on November 9, 1989. Late at night,
after days of protests, the Bornholmer Strasse border crossing finally
opened, enabling free passage between East and West Germany. Once

the first brick in the wall came tumbling down, there was a sense of excitement, as the whole world watched the Berlin Wall fall in the hours to come. At the beginning of the 1990s a wind of change was in the air, optimism everywhere, and some scholars, such as Francis Fukuyama, (wrongly) predicted the "end of history." A wave of democratizations swept through the world and competitive elections were on the menu in countries as diverse as Hungary, the Czech Republic, Poland, Bulgaria, Romania, Mongolia, Nepal, ex-Yugoslavia and Rwanda, as well as many others. In various cases the transition to democracy was a rather smooth ride and the last thirty years have been an overall success story of democratic consolidation and rising incomes. Take the Czech experience, a country freed from Moscow's sphere of influence and, after the fall of the Berlin Wall, rapidly turned into a functioning democracy, led from 1993 onward by Vaclav Havel as first president of the newly founded republic. It has since become a member of the European Union, successfully carried out a series of free and fair elections and is ranked 32nd out of 203 countries in the 2021 UN's Human Development Index.[11]

Unfortunately, not all transitioning countries fared as well, and in some cases dreams descended into nightmares. The problem is that running competitive elections for the first time after decades of authoritarianism can be a recipe for disaster if wrongly managed. Take ethnically divided countries such as Yugoslavia or Rwanda for an example. In the 1980s, under dictatorship, ethnic group sizes did not affect the political power of groups directly, as people did not have much say in politics. Put bluntly, being Serb or Croat did not matter much in the old days of Yugoslavia, as all power was concentrated in the hands of Marshal Tito and his inner circle of cronies. However, once the population was freed from their grasp, cynical group leaders, such as Slobodan Milošević and Radovan Karadžić in ex-Yugoslavia or the Interahamwe commanders in Rwanda, started to stir up ethnic tensions. They conveyed to their followers the notion that ethnic group sizes mattered for grabbing power and political rents, and that by pushing out or killing political opponents the political power might be all theirs. This ended in a bloodbath, with the 100 Day Genocide in Rwanda and large-scale "ethnic cleansing" in Bosnia and other former Yugoslavian areas being powerful reminders of the horrendous levels of cruelty and evil humans are capable of – even in phases of nascent democratization. This is what UCLA-sociologist Michael Mann has called "the dark side of democracy."[12]

The Italian economist Massimo Morelli, the Spanish scholar Joan Esteban and I have systematically investigated the drivers of extreme political violence by focusing on fifty episodes of mass killings.[13] We found that a strong predictor of such violence was the presence of natural resources – the cold-hearted logic being that when most money comes from oil and diamonds, the country's output is less dependent on the availability of labor. Digging the riches out of the ground is a capital-intensive rather than labor-intensive process; that is, a mechanical drill can do twice the work of 100 miners with shovels in likely half the time (and frequently natural resource extraction is outsourced to multinational firms that pay royalties). Now consider that if there are fewer and/or smaller rival groups, a bigger share of the pie would be up for grabs. In this situation, where political violence allows one group to win an edge in distributional struggles without resulting in significantly reduced output, attacking other groups is lucrative (to cynical minds). Can democratization tame these evil spirits of greed and rivalry? In the long run yes (as many studies have found), but in the short run not necessarily. Indeed, we have uncovered that the risk of massive political violence is *larger* in the first five years of democratization. This outcome may surprise but there are multiple reasons: First of all, democracy (rightly) insists that no citizens can be too severely discriminated against and exploited. While these restrictions to the "tyranny of the majority" are morally just and beneficial in the long run, in the short run they imply that the ruling group –which now faces some limits to the oppression it can inflict – may find it in its cynical self-interest to substitute discrimination with elimination. In other words, as democracy forbids the most extreme forms of exploitation, to satisfy unlimited greed, now-constrained despots may want to push out or kill rival groups as an alternative means to increase their share of the cake. However, scholars from various universities and disciplines have shown that, once consolidated, democracy powerfully counters crimes against humanity. One major reason is that democracy comes with a protection of the rule of law which restrains power abuses. Or, in the words of Rudolph Rummel, a Hawaii-based political scientist, "power kills, and absolute power kills absolutely."[14]

As Oxford don Sir Paul Collier and I argued in an article, another reason why new democratization bears some risks is the fact that democracy by its very nature champions free speech.[15] While freedom of expression constitutes undoubtedly the right moral choice and serves societies well in the long run, in the short run it can be exploited by would-be rebels and warlords who can more easily organize upheaval. Essentially, as democracy leads to a fairer and more predictable society, it reduces the *reasons* for revolt, but as it guarantees freedom of assembly and speech, it boosts the *means* for rebellion. While we labelled the first implication of democracy the so-called accountability effect, the latter can be referred to as a regression-in-repression effect. Put bluntly, while in a Stalinist dictatorship, the population has many reasons to rebel; the iron-fisted repression leaves its citizens no chance to have their voice heard. In contrast, in, say, Switzerland forming an antigovernment group would be much easier, but there are hardly any (serious) reasons to be unhappy with the government, and hence no sizable radical movements have emerged in the last 100 years.

The magnitude of these effects of democracy on stability varies for every country in every time period. What we have uncovered is that the beneficial virtues of democracy carry greater weight in the presence of a large and strong state. Quite naturally, in rich and complex societies the state plays a fundamental role, and hence having an irreproachable level of accountability and efficient public services is key. The newfound gains of democracy are so sizable that they outweigh the somewhat facilitated coordination and recruiting of extremist groupings offered by free speech and assembly. However, in regions characterized mostly by subsistence farming and oppression from a distant and feeble state, the tables are turned. Unsurprisingly, competitive elections bear significant risks in countries such as Libya, South Sudan and Somalia.

Does this mean that democracy is a concept reserved for fortunate and rich Western states, while the likes of Somalia should be content with competing warlord factions for the decades to come? Is democracy a Ferrari-like luxury good, reserved for the lucky few? By no means! Remember that nineteenth-century Switzerland shared many characteristics with poor and unstable places today and still made it to the top –in terms of achieving sound politics, peace and prosperity. Nevertheless, the essential lesson is that blossoming democracies in poor countries without a long civic tradition need our help. Some countries make it on their own, some require a gentle nudge, but for others large-scale and lasting international support for restoring the economy, building up state capacity and preserving public security is vital if they are to persevere on the path to consolidated democracy.

This has not always been properly acknowledged, and sometimes Western powers have given the impression of overoptimism in the aftermath of having vanquished a "rogue" regime. Think of George W. Bush's (in)famous "Mission accomplished" speech in 2003 after landing on aircraft carrier USS *Abraham Lincoln*. While Bush did not actually voice the words "mission accomplished" (these were only featured on a banner), he still stressed that "major combat operations in Iraq have ended. In the battle of Iraq, the United States and our allies have prevailed."[16] In the coming days and weeks, the mantra of the imminent transformation of Iraq into a stable democracy was ever-present and once more put forward by Bush in June 2005 in a speech given at Fort Bragg, North Carolina:

> In the past year, we have made significant progress: One year
> ago today, we restored sovereignty to the Iraqi people. In January
> 2005, more than 8 million Iraqi men and women voted in

elections that were free and fair and took place on time. [...] And together with our allies, we will help the new Iraqi government deliver a better life for its citizens.[17]

Well, have we witnessed the rise of Iraq to the club of rich and stable democracies within the last fifteen years? Sadly not. The reality is incomparably grimmer: In 2021 Iraq ranked –despite considerable oil reserves – a mere 125th out of 203 countries in the UN's Human Development Index.[18] Similarly, the Economist Intelligence Unit ranks Iraq 124th among 167 countries in the 2022 Democracy Index, and the country still suffers from shockingly high levels of insecurity and political violence.[19] We obviously do not know the counterfactual, and maybe without US intervention the Iraq we know today would be in even worse shape. It is impossible to know. But clearly, organizing the first free elections does not mark the end of the road toward peace and prosperity; it is just the first landmark on a long and winding odyssey packed with ambushes and roadblocks. One had better be prepared, realistic and patient enough to invest a lot of time, money and effort to foster lasting democratization.

SUCCESS STORIES: WHAT CAN WE DO TO HELP?

Nascent democracies can fail in a series of ways. Some of them plunge rapidly into ethnic violence and mass killings such as Rwanda and Bosnia in the early 1990s, while others such as Iraq and Afghanistan may avoid the worst excesses of violence but remain poor, instable and to a large extent undemocratic. So what can we do to help countries get on track for lasting democratic change? Success stories of democratization helped by outside sources include, among others, Germany and Japan after World War II or Portugal and Spain in the 1970s. What these cases have in common are (the promise of) massive economic help in the case of successful embracement of democratic values. While Germany benefited at a large scale from the cash of the Marshall Plan, Portugal and Spain cherished the perspective of obtaining the attractive (and lucrative) membership of the European Union. Such economic spoils naturally provide prevailing incentives for ordinary citizens to support forces of democratic change as they are win–win situations for the public and the powerful. In addition to the spoils, restrictions to power abuse have been put in place and have included security guarantees and arms control by democratic outside forces. For example, in Germany, American army involvement has taken the form of a very large-scale and long-lasting military presence (the Ramstein Air Base in Kaiserslautern is still open today).

So, to summarize, what have we learned about the appeal of power-sharing and democracy for building a peaceful society? Clearly, having a full consolidated democracy with free and fair elections and all groups having access to political power is a winning jackpot. By fostering prosperity, hedging the bets of the losers and providing detailed information of preferences, it allows the government to make sure that the opposition groups are kept happy enough to not challenge the state militarily. Giving all people a voice in a mature democracy gets the incentives right for peace: We don't need to assume that people are angels; even if some of them are selfish and cruel, they will stick to peace when it is in their (economic) self-interest to do so. The relevant policy question is of course how to get there. It's one thing to declare that paradise sounds fun; it's another (typically more complicated) thing to gain access. A substantial number of countries achieve democracy on their own. Others are less lucky and require outside assistance if they want to stay on the path of peaceful democratization. This requires substantial financial investment. US help through the Marshall Plan was instrumental in contributing to the thirty years of unprecedented economic growth in Germany's postwar period, which helped to shift public opinion from supporting fascism to supporting democracy. Again, from the Iberian Peninsula to the Balkans and Eastern Europe, the perspective to join the economically attractive European Union gave support to democratic forces. At the same time, establishing state capacity and guaranteeing public security is a must. During the Arab Spring, Western public opinion was pleased to see grassroot democracy activists at work, promoting liberal values and embracing human rights and democracy. The problem was that these likeable pro-Western bloggers were not actually the ones with arms, military training or a well-structured party organization, and they were rapidly swept aside by more radical groups that could draw on more political and military experience. Thus, in most countries of the Arab Spring no consolidated democracy has emerged (so far), and authoritarian rule (Egypt under Al-Sisi) or civil war (Syria under Al-Assad) were rather the rule than the exception. Thus, for nascent democracy to succeed, democratic forces need enough popular backing and a strong enough state. The promoters of democracy need to show to the population that they are able to deliver public safety, efficient state services and economic growth, and improve lives. As detailed in more depth in Chapter 7, guaranteeing state capacity and public safety are key ingredients for the prevention of civil war.

7 State Capacity for Stability

[The state is] a human community that successfully claims the monopoly of the legitimate use of physical force within a given territory.

Max Weber

Qui desiderat pacem, praeparet bellum. ("Let him who desires peace prepare for war.")

Vegetius

When interviewed in 2009 for the British newspaper *The Guardian*, the infamous Somali pirate captain Abdullahi "Boyah" Ashir laid out the story of his life. This highlights well how state capacity, together with (the lack of) economic opportunities and environmental degradation, shapes incentives for leaving the regular economy for the life of an outlaw. Ashir had been a lobster diver until 1994 – a sector of activity in which it has become increasingly difficult to make a living off the coast of Somalia during the last decades, owing to overfishing, particularly driven by an armada of foreign commercial vessels fishing illegally.[1] With it being increasingly hard to make ends meet, and a large number of international ships romping about in Somali waters, it is easy to imagine that the odd unemployed fisherman might come up with the idea of reinventing himself as a pirate. And that's where state capacity comes in: When out of luck and desperate, disenchanted youth around the globe come up with sometimes creative and sometimes illegal plans for moving from rags to riches. Picture an unemployed young woman or man in the southern Spanish town of Tarifa, right next to the Strait of Gibraltar – a place of similar strategic importance for international shipping as Somalia's Gulf of Aden. If you wanted to become a pirate and get into the business of extorting ships travelling through the Strait of Gibraltar, it would be virtually impossible to carry out these plans, and the would-be Captain Hook would finish up very rapidly in a Spanish prison. The reason is that Spain has a much higher state capacity than Somalia and is able to rely on efficient public service provision and on a potent army and police.

Unfortunately, Somalia is by far not the only "failed state" featuring an uneasy blend of lacking economic opportunities and a government that has lost control over major parts of the territory. This has in recent years been similarly the case for many other countries including Sudan, the DRC, Afghanistan, Syria and Iraq. Yet even among rich and democratic nations with generally high state capacity there can be stark regional differences. While admittedly Italy is rather different from Somalia in many respects, the story of the rise and consolidation of the Mafia highlights well how initial lack of state capacity in certain regions can give rise to violent groups trying to perpetuate the status quo in which they benefit from a power vacuum.

HOW (LOCAL) STATE WEAKNESS PERSISTS OVER TIME

Picture an economist glued to the screen while the Mafia boss character played by Marlon Brando in the *Godfather* trilogy makes "an offer one cannot refuse." While most spectators would admire this catchy line penned skillfully by the screenplay writers, the economist would typically be rather intrigued and start thinking about bargaining models and how it can be that offers cannot be refused. Yet it may not be entirely due to the likes of *The Godfather*, *Scarface*, *Goodfellas* and others that dozens of economists have been drawn to study the root causes of the rise of mafias for many years. In fact, analyzing this phenomenon is much more scientifically relevant than just catchy. First of all, scholars investigating the rise of the Mafia in Italy can delve into historical data from the distant past, given that, besides the recently founded Sacra Corona Unita in Apulia, organized crime in Italy has been operating for centuries. In particular, the Campanian Camorra's origins date back as far as the seventeenth century, the Calabrian 'Ndrangheta has been active since the eighteenth century, and the Sicilian Mafia's roots are in the nineteenth century, with Italian administrations, statistical services and archives providing access to high-quality data. Second, and more importantly, various extents of weak state capacity are pervasive, not just in fragile states but even at regional level in rich and powerful nations, not just in Italy: Think of the Spanish state's struggle in the Basque country or the so-called no-go zones in Northern Ireland at the peak of the "Troubles."

While various teams of scholars have pinpointed particular aspects and factors, there is a general notion that the rise of the Sicilian Mafia took place at a time when the state was only weakly implemented in Sicily and there was a lack of publicly provided security against roaming bandits, pushing landowners to turn to "hired guns" for protection. As Italian economist Oriana Bandiera pointed out, areas with high land fragmentation provided partic-ularly fruitful breeding grounds for the mercenaries to establish themselves gradually as an organized crime syndicate.[2] When land is sliced in many small plots, "buying protection" mostly deflects bandits to the next plot (which economists would call a "negative externality"). This, in turn, raises the neighbor's need for protec-tion and thereby provides further opportunities for benefits for the emerging mafia. What was also claimed to have helped the rise of the Sicilian Mafia was the booming demand for citrus fruits and for sulfur, which occurred in a context of dismal state capacity and fur-ther fueled the need for private protection and helped the Sicilian Mafia to tighten its grip on the peninsula.[3] Again, as mentioned in Chapters 4 and 6, we see that an uneasy blend of weak institutions and abundant spoils of nature can fuel violent appropriative behav-ior. An additional factor highlighted in economic research is the rise of the socialist Peasant Fasci organization in various parts of Sicily, which spread panic among landowners and local politicians and drew them into the arms of the Sicilian Mafia in a quest for protec-tion against this perceived "red threat."

Now, of course, we know that "hired guns" may have their own agenda and turn their barrels against those who hired them (as recently illustrated by the recent Wagner mercenaries' challenge of the Kremlin). While it is quite easy to grasp how private militias hired for protection may evolve –in a context of weak state institutions – into the Mafia, it is maybe more surprising how this can still manage to persist until the twenty-first century, especially given that Italy as a whole is a rich democracy with substantial state capacity. MIT's Daron Acemoglu and coauthors stress that the Mafia presence systematically hollowed out political competition, and that once organized crime is deeply entrenched in a given town or area, the state's track record in terms of public education and service provision starts to crumble.[4] This of course makes it harder for the state to fill any power vacuum and establish the Weberian monopoly of legitimate violence that is needed to guarantee the security of all citizens.

Again, nothing in the aforementioned mechanisms is unique to southern Italy. Around the world armed nonstate actors thrive on weak state capacity, and many of them have understood that it is in their (selfish) interest to hold the state's service provision back (while of course not in the interest of the rest of society). Consider the entirely different context of the Sahel zone, which has in recent years hit the headlines as the current front line in the global fight against jihadism. The Sahel is also a semiarid region that is hit particularly hard by climate change, which fuels tensions between nomadic cattle herder groups against sedentary crop farmers. In particular, we focus on Niger where my Swiss coauthor Patrick Premand and his World Bank team have been involved in a large-scale cash transfer project.[5] This massive program, dubbed "Filets sociaux" by Niger's government, has helped countless families to make a living and has overall had very beneficial effects on the local economies. It has been designed as a so-called randomized control treatment, which means that the scarce resources have been distributed to a pool of villages drawn by lottery, while other a priori identical villages have not been drawn and constitute a control group. The logic follows that of drug trials, where of, say, 100 patients half receive the new medical drug, while the other half obtain a placebo pill that looks the same. Of course, the goal is – once beneficial impacts have been demonstrated – that the control group also benefits from the treatment. We were able to piggyback on this existing program and study the nonintended impacts of the program on conflict proneness at village level, using very detailed conflict data on all incidents of armed violence throughout the whole country over recent years. Our findings came as a surprise: While the program does much economic good at a local level and we didn't detect any impact on conflict behavior by local groups, in villages benefiting from the cash transfers there is –if anything – a *surge* in attacks perpetrated by *foreign* groups. This is especially the case for transnational jihadist groups such as Nigeria-based Boko Haram. It is not entirely clear whether their motives are mostly about stealing or if they engage in deliberate sabotage of promising programs to prevent the rising effectiveness and popularity of services provided by the state. Yet when digging deeper into the background of particular fighting incidents, it is striking to discover that in various instances state institutions were very deliberately targeted. This may well suggest that at least part of the rising violence could be carried out with the goal of deliberately delegitimizing the state and keeping its capabilities weak.

SECURITY FIRST

After having described how a country can become entrenched in persistently defunct state capacity, the natural next step is to think about how to remedy this. Like a doctor after the diagnosis, the plan is to come up with a cure. Following in these footsteps, we shall first consider "foreign" solutions before presenting "domestic" recipes. As has become clear from this discussion, once a country is in a state of meltdown, it is nightmarishly difficult to get it back on track. The policymaker's task gets complicated by the fact that the situation is riddled by vicious cycles. For one, a lack of infrastructure and public service provision depresses economic perspectives, which fuels insecurity, and this in turn further renders it difficult for the state to honor its key functions. To get a handle on this Gordian knot, the University of California's Eli Berman and coauthors crunched wide-ranging and fine-grained data provided by the US Army covering various locations in Iraq from 2004 to 2009.[6] For Iraq in 2004, picture a country that had been invaded a year earlier by a US-led coalition, resulting in the fall of former dictator Saddam Hussein. In 2004 the country was ruled by a transition government, heavily supported by American troops, but facing a large-scale anti-Western insurgency, as well as heavy sectarian violence between different religious and ethnic groups. The US military rapidly established funding for service provision and provided a large number of grants for various projects that were supposed to help the local population and step up support for the new government in place. The statistical analysis of the Berman team uncovered some unexpected and maybe puzzling findings: It turns out that a "buying hearts and minds" approach is ineffective, when implemented in the midst of heavy fighting, but that infrastructure construction and service provision can be powerful tools for peace when the state forces and their allies have already managed to significantly decrease fighting. Put differently: As already highlighted in Maslow's famous hierarchy of needs, safety is –together with physiological needs such as water and food – the very basic need for any human society. When insecurity reigns, no public policies and initiatives can really gain great traction.

A ROLE FOR MILITARY AID?

If the massive and yearlong US involvement in Iraq has (so far) failed to transform the land of Euphrates and Tigris into a prosperous and peaceful democracy, does this outcome represent an exception or the rule? Sadly, the track record of Western military aid to regimes under stress from insurgency is overall rather bleak, to say the least. Military support from a Western democracy can come in all shapes and forms, ranging from US and British involvement in Afghanistan and Iraq to French soldier deployments in the Sahel. Yet in terms of the big picture, a "typical" case would see –especially during the Cold War – the United States militarily supporting a pro-Western regime challenged by insurgents, where the regime in question may or may not be democratic, and the insurgents often communists (during the Cold War) or jihadists (in recent decades). A salient case matching this "playbook" is US military aid to Colombia, which a New York-based duo of scholars, Oeindrila Dube and Suresh Naidu, studied some years back.[7] Colombia has indeed been a major focal point of US involvement, as the Fuerzas Armadas Revolucionarias de Colombia, together with other Marxist militias, such as Ejército de Liberación Nacional, posed a formidable challenge to the Colombian state. These well-equipped communist rebel groups had a comparatively high military capacity, with a sizable troop strength and stable access to funding. To keep them in check, Colombia's rulers counted on the fighting power of the regular army, as well as various (right-wing) paramilitary groups that supported the government militarily. To further raise the stakes, there was the widespread perception that if Colombia –one of Latin America's economic and political heavyweights – went communist, there might well be a domino effect, turning the whole continent red. Dube and Naidu were able to work with very detailed data on US military aid to particular Colombian military bases and compared political outcomes of municipalities with and without bases. Their findings were as spectacular as they were chilling: If deterring the communist guerrillas was the goal, it backfired, as US military assistance did not have any effect on attacks by Marxist rebels. In contrast, there were (unintended) side effects: Homicides by right-wing paramilitaries surged during election years in "swing municipalities" with uncertain majorities. Put differently, US military aid led to an empowerment of far-right thugs going after left-leaning politicians, thereby undermining local political institutions.

Sadly, these results extend beyond Colombia. To get the big picture, a team of German economists went global – studying 174 countries worldwide from 1968 to 2018, covering world politics ranging from the midst of the Cold War to the post-9/11 fight against terrorism.[8] Their question was simple: Has US military aid helped to make America a safer place, by keeping its foes in check? As for the study on Colombia, the global big picture painted by their study with the telling title "Paying them to hate US?" must come as a blow to the Pentagon. It turns out that more American military aid led to an increase in anti-American terrorism in the given recipient country, where US embassies, citizens or companies could all be on the radar of Uncle Sam's enemies. But the study did not stop there. Uncovering facts is good but understanding them is better. In this spirit, the statistical analysis captured the underlying mechanisms at work, pinpointing a surge in corruption and exclusionary politics. As in the case of Colombia, US cash was pocketed and misused. It ultimately helped some politicians to enhance their political clout against domestic rivals who see themselves increasingly marginalized and excluded from the honeypots of public spending. And that is the moment they lift their Kalashnikovs against the regime in place and their foreign sponsors, the United States. As policy-relevant as these findings are, obvious questions remain. In particular, not a few of the recipient countries are ruled by autocratic regimes of cronies, kleptocrats and gangsters, and handing money on a silver platter to crooked politicians can hardly result in much good. Now, maybe US support for truly democratic regimes that use funds to homogeneously raise safety throughout a territory may have a less detrimental effect? This is still something we do not know, and addressing this question may be able to help us finetune our arsenal of policies at hand. Food for thought.

Another riddle is why the United States and other powers continue to provide military aid despite the dismal track record. Are they understaffed in terms of analysts? This seems hard to believe – watch any action movie or Netflix series portraying the CIA and Ministry of Defense and you will see great numbers of specialized analysts crunching data. Political scientist Navin Bapat has pondered over the same paradox and has reached a conclusion that is not flattering for neither the United States nor the recipient governments.[9] Bapat argues that the (often shady) regimes on the receiving end do not have any incentives to root out terrorism, after which US aid would cease. Hence, their antiterror campaigns are pursued half-heartedly at best. At the same time, the United States knows that its military support contributions are misused and neither buy peace nor democracy. Yet, the cash is potent enough to keep the recipient's current pro-US regime in place, which the United States prefers over the anti-Western insurgents (who may be, for example, Marxist rebels or jihadists). Put differently, according to Bapat's study, the United States knowingly continues to pop up bad regimes to keep even worse folks out of power.

WHAT ABOUT BLUE HELMETS?

If a failed state is too fragile on its own to control its territory and provide vital services to its population, and Western military aid backfires, is there anything the international community can do to help? Thankfully, yes. In search for the answer, we find ourselves in the scenic Swedish town of Uppsala, just north of Stockholm. This sleepy student city, where in winter one can go to work on cross-country skis, hosts one of the world's leading hubs for studying conflict. Together with its partner institution, the Peace Research Institute Oslo, the Uppsala Conflict Data Program is one of the main providers of detailed information on conflicts around the world. Information on any conflict episode, with exact location, precise date, armed groups involved and various other specific information is just a mouse click away. In this peace researcher's paradise Lisa Hultman and several colleagues have investigated the role of UN blue helmets.[10] It all started with an intense data collection effort. Without knowing exactly where peacekeeping troops are deployed and how they are composed, we would not be able to say much about their effectiveness. Or, to put it in the words of Sherlock Holmes, "Data! Data! Data! I cannot make bricks without clay!" But as challenging as it was, collecting the data was not even the greatest obstacle. The most formidable roadblock was distinguishing causality from correlation. Just comparing places without UN blue helmets (say Switzerland) with places with UN peacekeeping troops (say Mali), one will inevitably reach the conclusion that there is more violence in spots where blue helmets operate. Yet it would of course be misguided to conclude –based on this correlation – that UN peacekeeping missions lead to instability, as the association between peacekeeping and chaos may simply reflect the fact that you don't send blue helmets to peaceful places. Hultman and other scholars tackled this statistical difficulty by analyzing spikes in blue helmet deployments owing to local variation in the exposure to changes in the global peacekeeping budget. Put differently, the international peacekeeping community sometimes has good years (when key countries elect leaders committed to international cooperation) and sometimes has bad years, when funds are scarce (e.g., when candidates with isolationist platforms get elected or when a global recession squeezes budgets). And some countries are hit harder in bad years than others, which provides some random variation in the presence of blue helmets. After having put in place this and similar statistical wizardry, spectacular conclusions emerged: UN peacekeeping troops do not only help to prevent the breakout of future hostilities in postconflict settings, but also save lives during war, both on the battlefield and among civilians. This is among other reasons owing to a shortening of conflict episodes and the protection of civilians against abuse from rebel forces. The effect is quantitatively big. Take an area of roughly 50 by 50 kilometers, which corresponds to roughly a third of Bahrain. Putting a contingent of 3,000 peacekeepers there would cut the risk of attacks on civilians by about half. In a nutshell, in contexts of great insecurity and endemic political violence, UN peacekeepers provide the necessary security and stability that allows people to get back to their businesses and enables the state to fulfill its basic functions.

BETTING ON HOME-GROWN STATE CAPACITY

While UN peacekeepers are part of the solution, there is unfortunately only so much that they can do, and it has often proven difficult for the United Nations to field enough troops necessary for their peacekeeping missions. The recent demise of the blue helmets operating in Mali is a telling example. Hence, much state capacity building needs to take place domestically. State capacity is not only central for peace but also for development and for a variety of socioeconomic outcomes, it has unsurprisingly attracted the attention of various scholars in recent years. A particularly important contribution has been made by the British-Swedish duo Tim Besley and Torsten Persson.[11] They start by revisiting and formalizing, in a game-theoretic model, classic arguments on the roots of state capacity differences across countries. One first element they highlight is the abundance of natural resources. If Mother Nature blessed a given region particularly well, the riches of the earth suffice for keeping the state household going, and there is –at least in the short-run – no need to put in place an efficient public administration and fiscal capacity to raise taxes. Paradoxically, the generosity of the local soils can backfire in the long run. It is a bit like a gifted athlete who gets to regional elite status without much training, but then lacks an efficient training regime once she wants to step up her game and qualify for the world championships. Similarly, living off royalties from natural resources (the extraction of which may be outsourced to a multinational enterprise) fosters neither incentives for a frugal management of public money nor for democratization. Remember that in many cases around the world a rise of tax rates has been accompanied by greater democratic rights, as well synthesized by the slogan "No taxation without representation!" from the American Revolution. Well, if autocratic rulers can get by solely using oil, gas or mineral money, their (selfish) incentives to share power with the population are rather dismal, which can lead to "rentier states" where personal rule, kleptocracy and mismanagement reign. If resource cash can allow a despot to stay in power for a long time, a lack of public scrutiny and a focus on blind loyalty rather than competency for civil servants can result in a crumbling of state institutions and the bad regime being brought down like a house of cards facing a light breeze. Remarkably, the same thing that helps dictators cling to power in the short run can lead to their fall further down the road. Of course, to every rule there are exceptions, and in fact the timing of resource discoveries is key. As shown some years back by a team of Norwegian scholars, if a state is already strong and democratic at the time when the spoils of nature are discovered, they may end up being a blessing rather than a curse.[12] It is surely not a coincidence that Norwegian scholars came up with this research idea, as the land of the fjords is a persuasive example of well-managed oil wealth. Much of the fossil fuel cash flows directly into the coffers of a Sovereign Wealth Fund that has engaged in diversified investments across thousands of companies.

Another factor highlighted by the legendary sociologist Charles Tilly is accounted for in Besley and Persson's framework: the (threat of) external wars. Or as Tilly puts it, "wars made the state, and the state made war."[13] This means that –maybe paradoxically – in the hours of greatest danger, different factions in a country manage to close ranks and rise to the challenge. This is well illustrated by France in the aftermath of its 1789 revolution. Picture yourself in Paris in 1798, almost a decade after that epochal shift in world politics. The last nine years could have hardly been more tumultuous, as not only were French philosophers championing modern democratic institutions, but also Revolutionary France had originated the term "terror," stemming from the French word *terreur* that defines the 1793 and 1794 period. During these times, revolutionary zealots were running the show, the guillotines were in full occupation and thousands of French citizens were perishing in internal purges. Add to this the external threat: France was isolated and surrounded by hostile powers, with the Napoleonic Wars starting only a few years later (in 1803). Hence, unsurprisingly, in 1798, when the French government wanted to step up its military capabilities, it was in need of new ideas. And, indeed, the "Directoire" government pioneered a military innovation which would change warfare forever (yet not necessarily for the better): the universal military conscription of all young, unmarried men in the so-called *levée en masse* enshrined in the 1798 Jourdan Law. This large-scale army needed much management and required the French bureaucracy to modernize in various ways. Similar increases in the size and scope of the state and its capabilities were seen across the world during and after the two world wars. More recently, comparable mechanisms related to a closing of ranks have been observed in Europe since the annexation of Crimea by Russia in 2014. As shown in the statistical analysis made by German economist Kai Gehring, there has also been an increased enthusiasm for the European Union in various member states.[14] Conspicuously, the surge in European identity has been bigger, the more geographically exposed a given EU member country is to the reach of Russia. And this surge in cohesion and institution building has been –if anything – accelerated both at EU and NATO level since the full-scale invasion of Ukraine by Russia in 2022. In a nutshell, while war is overall disastrous, as amply shown here, one side effect is that the *threat* of interstate war may lead to administrative reforms and the building of state capacities. Obviously, if the threat of war ends up materializing, then the destruction of fighting also destroys part of this state capacity, at least in the short run.

There is a series of other factors that affect state capacity building, documented by various scholars in recent decades. A similar effect to external war threats can be sometimes observed when crucial challenges are of an economic, rather than geopolitical nature. Put differently, times of economic crises have often been propitious for major reforms. This was the case, for example, in the aftermath of the 1929 Wall Street Crash, as discussed further in due course. When it comes to major health shocks, the disastrous COVID-19 pandemic had the side-effect of spurring digitalization not just in the private economy but also in the state apparatus.

Last but not least, it has been documented that in more homogeneous communities the formation of a common identity and the willingness to finance public goods is easier and more rapidly achieved.[15] Yet this ease of nation building and state capacity development comes at a steep price, as Ekaterina Zhuravskaya and I have highlighted in recent research.[16] Strikingly, when plotting all countries worldwide on a scale of ethnic homogeneity, it hits the observer that all states with large-scale fascist movements in the 1930s and 1940s are comparatively homogeneous, and that on average linguistically or ethnically more heterogeneous countries such as, for example, the United States, Canada and Switzerland displayed much lower popular support for fascist ideologies. Again, this underscores the fact that ethnic homogeneity is a double-edged sword: While it eases the road towards a nation-state, it also entails a slippery slope towards fascism if the nation's path is not secured by democratic checks and balances and the protection of minority rights.

The factors enumerated so far are typically external constraints and opportunities over which the domestic government yields little power. It can neither immediately determine the extent of external threats, nor global recessions, nor the geology of the soils or the composition of ethnic homelands. Yet this is only part of the story, as there are several powerful feedback loops. If a country is lucky enough to benefit from favorable starting conditions for building state capacity, the establishment of a powerful administration supports economic development. In turn, peace is more likely in the presence of a well-run state that holds the "monopoly of legitimate violence" over a territory and in the presence of high incomes that raise the opportunity cost of leaving the legal economy and "going rogue." Further, peace yields the much-needed political stability that supports state functions and democratization, and that helps the economy to develop. Hence, this powerful virtuous feedback cycle of high state capacity, democracy, high income and peace leads to a cluster of powerful, democratic, rich and peaceful nations. Sadly, on the grimmer side of the scale, there looms an analogous vicious cycle triggering a cluster of failed states suffering from weak state capacity, kleptocracy, poverty and conflict. But are our destinies mechanically determined by powerful feedback loops that are not unlike particles in physics experiments? Put differently, is whether a given country ends up in a good or bad equilibrium a foregone conclusion or can clever domestic public policies make a difference? It turns out that they can.

A NEW DEAL

It is important to realize that we are not in a predetermined world, but that countries and their politicians and citizens can make the right or wrong choices at critical junctures of their journey. This is maybe best illustrated by the 1930s where around the world millions of people were hit hard by the Great Depression in the aftermath of the 1929 stock exchange crash on Wall Street. Livelihoods and savings of a lifetime in some cases evaporated overnight and left bankrupt shareholders with nothing but grief. As in other times of acute economic crises, governments around the world had basically three choices: 1) do nothing (which was hardly an option, given the extent of the crisis), 2) go after minorities and steal their wealth or 3) step up inclusive welfare state institutions and show solidarity with those hit hardest. Sadly, in several countries politicians, such as Adolf Hitler or Benito Mussolini, selected option 2 and played the fascist card, leading to humanity's darkest hours, with millions and millions of people dying in the Holocaust and on the battlefields of World War II.

While thankfully there have been some positive developments over the last seventy-five years, for example the rise of democracy in many countries (including in nations formerly governed by fascist regimes), the strategy of scapegoating minorities in times of crisis is sadly not off the table and regularly resurfaces in new forms and brands of populism and politics of hatred. Yet there is a (infinitely) better way to go, the aforementioned option 3, where in times of crises and grand challenges a country deliberately embraces diversity and aims at strengthening state capacity. Take the key critical juncture when Nelson Mandela came to power in South Africa. After having lived all his life under the cruelest regime of apartheid and after three decades of imprisonment, it would not have been surprising for Mandela to have sought revenge and expropriated the slim white minority's assets, controlling as they did virtually all land and enterprises. Yet, in contrast to neighboring Zimbabwe's ruler Robert Mugabe's divisive politics, Mandela showed an incredible strength of character and engaged in a dialogue with his former torturers, aiming to build a "rainbow nation" with strong, democratic institutions from the ashes of the former rogue regime.

There are various other historical examples that show –at a critical juncture and in the face of formidable challenges – leaders choosing inclusion rather than exclusion and a strengthening of democratic state functions rather than their demise. Another striking example is the one of Franklin D. Roosevelt's New Deal. America was in a shambolic state in the early 1930s, with the stock exchange crash having contracted US gross domestic product (GDP) by a fifth and unemployment rates skyrocketing to 25 percent. After his election in 1932, the Roosevelt administration implemented the so-called New Deal program that massively strengthened the role of the federal state, more than doubling the share of federal public spending in GDP (previously, federal nonmilitary spending accounted for less than 1 percent of GDP). The program had many facets, but among the most visible, millions of citizens benefited from direct payments from the federal government, the Works Progress Administration was, at its peak, the largest US employer and substantial agricultural support payments were made to farmers, as well as emergency relief being given to homeowners and businesses. These poverty relief efforts not only contributed to the stabilization of the economy but also led to a significant long-term strengthening of (federal) state capacity. A maybe less well-known effect of the "New Deal" was that it led to a sizable surge in patriotism and national cohesion.

In a recent article by the Switzerland-based economists Bruno Caprettini and Joachim Voth, they have exploited (arguably random) local variation in the scope of the New Deal measures to estimate their impact on various dimensions of patriotism.[17] Notably, citizens who benefited to a greater extent from New Deal support, bought more war bonds in World War II, volunteered more often and, as soldiers, won more medals for bravery. Overall, the example of the New Deal highlights that building a solid welfare state can in times of crisis increase national cohesion and a sense of belonging, and prevent the risks of political radicalization among the losers from grand societal disruptions such as the Great Depression. Building a stronger social safety net and better service provision by the state prevents a power vacuum from emerging in which armed thugs can thrive.

MIND THE GAP (IN SECURITY WARRANTIES)

What these studies illustrate is that there is a great human need for security and basic services. If the state is not strong enough to cater for these necessities, the emerging power vacuum will be filled by armed groups that thrive on insecurity and defunct state functions, and try as hard as they can to sabotage any progress, development and institution building. Put differently, the overall strength of the state is a key determinant of political stability and public safety, as illustrated by examples stretching from Africa (Somalia, Niger), over Asia (Iraq), Europe (southern Italy, France) and Latin America (Colombia) to North America (the United States). While successful public good provision fosters public support and social cohesion in the long run (as illustrated by Roosevelt's New Deal), addressing safety concerns in the short run is the basic condition for progress in other dimensions. Hence, being feared (by extremist groups) may be (in the short run) more important than being loved (by the population at large). In order to win the hearts and minds of the population, it is essential that public safety is guaranteed and basic services are delivered efficiently. Such security warranties are a key component of a virtuous cycle featuring state capacity, democratic institution building, development and peace, all mutually reinforcing each other.

8 Plenty Makes Peace
Education, Health and Labor Market Policies

> If we are to reach real peace in this world and if we are to carry on a real war against war, we shall have to begin with children.

Mahatma Gandhi

When the US Secretary of State George C. Marshall approached the podium at Harvard University on June 5, 1947, he knew that the challenge he faced was formidable. He was about to write history – or fail miserably. The argument he wanted to bring home was that the United States had to help all of Europe on humanitarian grounds – with funds directed to both former allies and foes. While allies received larger amounts according to what was later to be known as the "Marshall Plan," its transfer recipients still included the countries that started World War II and whose fascist regimes were responsible for the mass murder of millions and millions of innocent lives. How to explain to the US taxpayers that they now had to pay sizable amounts to the same Germans who killed their boys some years earlier? While in human history the concept of "reparations" paid by the loser (such as for example after World War I) was well known, Marshall's inverse notion of the winner wiring money to help the loser was rarely heard of and all but revolutionary.

Now, of course, in hindsight we know that the Marshall Plan – which brought its architect the Nobel Peace Prize – was a phenomenal success. This help package, together with security guarantees (think of US troops in Ramstein and other bases) and large-scale denazification policies in Germany and beyond, helped to transform some of the most cruel and evil regimes in history into well-functioning democracies. Europe's new democracies have also since become pillars of a rules-based world order, as well as major global economic powers. The reparations of the vital infrastructure and well-designed investments led to a boost in productivity and unprecedented economic recovery throughout Europe (called the *Wirtschaftswunder* in Germany and dubbed the *trente glorieuses* in France).

This was complementary to another key policy innovation arising from the ashes of World War II: European integration. Again, if history is full of examples of enduring rivalries between foes or large multiethnic empires arising under the domination of one particular power, it is rather rare that a number of sovereign nations freely agree to give up a substantial part of their self-determination to build a new supranational body with rotating leadership. This being said, it is not unheard of – for example, Swiss cantons did something rather similar when forming an ever more integrated defensive alliance some seven centuries earlier. On a larger scale, the post-World War II European integration really took off with the European Coal and Steel Community in 1952, which integrated these key strategic industries of France, West Germany, Italy, Belgium, the Netherlands and Luxembourg. From this ignition it gradually evolved into the European Union, which has been a warrant for peace and democracy in Europe, as well as an engine for the continental economy.

LEARNING TO MAKE PEACE

But is the story of Europe since 1946 representative of the power of public policies to foster incentives for production instead of predation? Or is it the exception rather than the rule? It turns out that there is a strong case for the peace potential from a series of particular public policies, one of which is education. Some years back I had the opportunity to team up with a group of World Bank economists interested in education policies in resource-rich economies.[1] We rapidly realized that the first order effects of any education programs are not necessarily confined to the realm of strictly economic considerations and outcomes. One can of course compute the narrowly defined returns to each dollar invested in education, focusing on future salary gains. By the way, these turn out to be huge in many countries, providing a powerful rationale for subsidizing education, scholarships and student loans to counter cash constraints. Yet that is by far not the end of the story, as the sum of direct and indirect returns to schooling are substantially larger. In terms of social values, education not only reduces the incentives for crime and boost civic engagement, but it also constitutes a very potent and strong rampart against political violence! Following in the footsteps of the "beautiful mind" of Nobel prize winner John Nash, we aimed to translate the scope for violence into the logic of a game-theoretic framework. Turning words into mathematical variables and arguments into equations helped to analyze manifold mechanisms that can account for the nexus between education and peace.

First of all, as trivial as it sounds, the time spent in school is not spent elsewhere. Put differently, it is quite straightforward that a child on a school bench is less at risk of being abducted or hired to become a child soldier. This mechanical effect is stronger the better the guarantee of school security. The second mechanism is that a good education offers opportunities down the road to make a decent living with a regular job, driving down the temptation for enrolling as a rebel soldier. If these first two virtuous effects of education are unambiguous, the third way in which schooling affects the prospects of conflict is more of a double-edged sword: Education transmits values. These can be positive values of tolerance, open-mindedness and embracing diversity; and, overall, in many countries this seems to be the case. In various contexts one indeed observes that on average more educated citizens less frequently vote for populist parties and are in general more civically minded.[2] Yet there is no rule without an exception, and in some contexts, studies have demonstrated that the state curriculum can inculcate divisive nationalist ideas and resentment against minorities or foreign nations.[3]

Now on top of these fairly intuitive links between education and peace, which apply similarly to all countries, there is a further one that has been all but ignored and that is particularly critical for resource-rich nations. Picture two lucky winners of a lottery, say Amy and Betty, both winning 50,000 USD or Euros. Amy puts the money under her pillow and tells everybody about it, while Betty invests all the cash into the college education of her daughter (and obviously also brags about it widely). Which of the two is more likely to get robbed? It seems obvious that Amy is a more attractive victim for the greedy burglar, as all of Betty's cash has gone. Well, actually it has not gone – it is simply that through education, "physical capital" has been transformed into what economists like to call "human capital" (which boils down to knowledge and skills). It turns out that the story of Amy and Betty is not very different from the tales of resource-rich countries that spend the manna from Mother Nature very differently. For instance, Amy could be Angola and Betty Botswana. Investing natural resource cash into schooling not only allows for raising productivity in the medium run, but it also allows for getting rid of appropriation incentives in the short run. There are of course various shades of grey, and the easier the money can be accessed by whoever runs the state, the more powerful are the incentives to grab power. Put differently, it is of course better to have a Norway-style sovereign wealth fund than just hoard banknotes in the treasuries of the Central Bank. Yet even if sovereign wealth funds are useful, their contents are still not fully out of reach of kleptocrats, and hence it is still advisable to invest a sizable portion of windfalls into education.

SCHOOLING OR RULING – WHAT DO THE DATA SAY?

As compelling as the aforementioned arguments may seem, the real test of their validity lies in scrutiny of the data. Easier said than done. Existing research has documented well that there is a strong positive association between educational expenditures, school enrollment and literacy, on the one hand, and peace on the other hand.[4]

The problem is, of course, that better regimes spend more money on forming their pupils (rather than, say, for getting the nuclear bomb). So if, say, South Korea invests more in education and is less belligerent than North Korea, then it may be erroneous to attribute this to schooling alone, as the two countries may differ across a variety of dimensions (e.g., political regime and economic structure, to just name two). Thus, studying mere correlations between education spending and peace will not be enough to allow us to conclusively deduce that the former causes the latter.

Hence, answering the question at hand conclusively across the globe may prove a hard nut to crack. Yet for specific countries and context there may exist what economists like to call "natural experiments," where for some random reason similar places obtain different levels of education. Alessandro Saia and I came across such a unique historical case, Indonesia's INPRES program, first studied by Nobel-Prize winner Esther Duflo in the context of labor-market outcomes.[5] In particular, the Indonesian government put in place in 1973 one of the most ambitious school construction programs that has ever been implemented across the world, raising enrollment rates among children aged seven to twelve from 69 percent in 1973 to 83 percent by 1978, and it has attracted the attention of various leading economists in recent years. One of the reasons for all this interest, besides the sheer scope of the enterprise, is that the numbers of schools constructed followed a simple bureaucratic rule that resulted in comparable places seeing many more or way fewer new facilities built. The kind of stuff economists love: random variation! Given that conflict data was not available for Indonesia so far back, the school construction had only been linked to several other economic and societal outcomes, but political violence had remained untouched. As in other projects, we have addressed this shortcoming by assembling our own conflict data, based on coding newspaper articles. The fruit of our work is still preliminary, but we have so far found quite a salient link between more schools and fewer instances of fighting, exactly in line with the aforementioned predictions.

While this study design is statistically cleaner than associations between countries that can be as similar as apples and oranges, the natural concern could of course be that the results are confined to Indonesia only. Although let's not forget that Indonesia is of interest on its own thanks to its sheer population size, being the world's fourth most populous country and home to about 280 million people. Still, we are of course very keen to know if similar virtues of education programs deploy in other contexts. Thankfully, a similar random school variation exists in another, even more populous, Asian country, India. A fresh piece of research by a UK/Switzerland-based team has studied a related question, investigating the impact of school construction on domestic violence.[6] In particular, India launched the District Primary Education Program in 1994; this built around 160,000 new schools, targeting districts below the national average female literacy rate of 39.3 percent. Put differently, a district with a literacy rate of 39.2 percent saw new schools popping up like mushrooms, while an almost identical district with the slightly higher literacy rate of 39.4 percent received no new schools through the program. This allows us to benefit from the ideal comparison group and to get any statistician excited about the clean statistical investigation. What they find is no less spectacular: The program increases women's education by almost a year and decreases several forms of domestic violence, such as emotional domestic violence (13 percent less), less severe physical domestic violence (drop by 27 percent), sexual violence (reduction by 9 percent) and injuries owing to domestic violence (a 10 percent decrease). When exploring potential mechanisms, the study documents the key role of altered gender beliefs and attitudes. Moreover, women benefiting from stepped up schooling are found to find "better matches." In particular, on average they form couples with men who embrace more progressive gender norms, and they can rely on easier access to information and potential help from law enforcement authorities.

Strikingly, these findings are consistent with evidence from an entirely different context on another continent, where a very different program took place.[7] Not unlike the situation in India, females are subject to shockingly high levels of domestic violence in Kenya, where around the time of this study women were severely underrepresented at parliament (with only 10 percent female representatives) and three-quarters of women had shared experiences of abuse in reports. Within this hostile environment, in 2001 the Dutch nonprofit organization ICS introduced a merit scholarship program in the West Kenyan district of Busia. This was designed as a randomized control trial in which a lottery decided which thirty-four primary schools were eligible for the program from a pool of sixty-nine comparable facilities, hence relegating the remaining thirty-five schools to the control group. In the selected schools the top 15 percent of girls in grade six received an award that covered school fees and other school-related expenses for the following two years of primary school. It was found that exposure to the program altered attitudes, and in particularly drove down young women's acceptance of domestic violence and political authority, as well as reducing the likelihood that parents were involved in choosing their daughters' spouses. While the program also led to increased political interest and knowledge, the effects were more of a mixed bag in other dimensions. No increase in community participation or voting intentions was detected and there was even suggestive evidence that the perceived legitimacy of political violence increased. The latter result may not be so surprising in a context of large-scale discrimination and disenfranchisement of women, pointing out that education programs may be best stepped up in parallel with efforts for better representation of all parts of society.

MEDICATION AGAINST CONFLICT

When economists talk about "human capital," they are in some sense digging their own grave. First of all, many noneconomists find the term a bit strange and overly complicated, and not a few are offended by its neoliberal and capitalist "feel," which can be perceived as degrading humans to mere factors of production. To be fair, in economic models of production the concept of "human capital" does indeed have a heuristic use and fosters prediction power, as it can help us understand how education affects productivity and that we lose skills when not using them regularly, a bit like depreciation of capital and infrastructure (think, for example, of the butterfly swimming style that we learnt in school as teenagers but cannot master anymore when trying to impress our kids during our midlife crisis...). Still, it is not clear how useful it is to employ this jargon, as even economists are often confused by it. In particular, "human capital" is often simply used as a synonym of "education." Yet, broadly defined, "human capital" encompasses so much more than that, and productivity (and hence salaries) not only depend on years of schooling but also on a healthy, well-trained mind and body. Hence, not only education but also public health policies may have an impact on economic productivity and the opportunity cost of fighting, and thus in turn on the likelihood of conflict. Importantly, health should not only matter through productivity, but also being in good health results in a longer time-horizon, making it relatively more attractive to engage in schooling and economic investments yielding gains far into the future. In contrast, when poor health squeezes the time horizon, risky activities with substantial short-run gain (such as violent appropriation) may become relatively more attractive. Yet, strangely enough, despite its obvious relevance, the role of health has been all but ignored by scholars when studying the root causes of war.

Thankfully not completely forgotten, though! An Italo-German team of academics has in recent years strived to uncover the nexus between health and peace.[8] This is, again, a task of formidable difficulty, as correlation does not equal causality. Consider Helsinki and St. Petersburg, two cities that are a mere 300 kilometers apart and on roughly the same latitude, and hence typically face a similar climate and disease environment. If life expectancy is significantly higher in, say, Helsinki than in, say, St. Petersburg, and at the same time the recent history of Russia has been much more conflicted than that of Finland, does the former imply the latter? Not necessarily, as the political regime and governance both affect health outcomes and conflict proneness. Hence, just comparing countries may lead to wrongly attributing any difference in peace prospects to health while other factors may actually be at the root of it. Similarly, if worldwide conflict events surged during the global COVID-19 pandemic, there would not necessarily be any causal link, as the pandemic was accompanied by grand economic challenges in many countries. And it is not farfetched to think that it is ultimately the economic turbulences that triggered political turmoil. Hence, as for the previous Gordian knots described in this book, the solution to these intractable dilemmas is to find some random factor that leads to unexpected changes in health that can then be exploited for the statistics.

To start with this endeavor, a health economist will have to read up on the determinants of infectious disease environments. Most of us last learnt about malaria and mosquitos sometime in high school and we vaguely remember that in some countries one should avoid mosquito bites, and that is pretty much it. It turns out unsurprisingly that things are more complex. To cut a long story short, there is a class of infectious diseases that public health specialists call multihost vector transmitted pathogens (where the animal transmitting the disease is indeed often a mosquito), and they are notoriously difficult to eradicate. These include, for example, malaria, dengue and yellow fever, and they cause major public health challenges in the affected countries. For some of them vaccine protection is available, but often incomplete, and some of them have been successfully eradicated in certain regions, by draining swamps for example. Yet in many places several of these deadly diseases remain present or even endemic, and the threat from them varies with weather conditions. Specifically, the onset of the raining season often provides ideal breeding grounds for mosquitos, which triggers an infection wave. The fact that within a given country different regions are affected unequally by pathogen exposure and that health risks vary over time depending on weather shocks yields exactly the kind of statistical variation over space and time that economists cherish. Exploiting these heterogeneous effects

of the caprices of Mother Nature allows us to estimate how deterioration in the disease environments may fuel the scope for armed
fighting. The findings are chilling: An intermediate range surge in
pathogen exposure can drive up the risk of conflict by half!

When the authors of this study first told me about these
remarkable results, it became rapidly clear that –as spectacular as
it was – this was only half of the story. To start with, pinning down
the mechanisms at work is not so easy when most of the action
comes from weather wizardry. And even more importantly, what
about "reverse engineering"? If bad weather shocks in places with
endemic pathogens fuel political turmoil, can medical innovation do
the reverse? Can a sound public health policy kill two birds with one
stone, at the same time healing patients and providing medication
against conflict? On the same day of that conversation, we started
frantically reading up on potential medical innovations, ranging from
drug discoveries over vaccine developments to public health measures. The quest was not an easy one, as to have enough statistical
power, one needs both a medical discovery that is of large enough
scope to be a real game changer and one that affects various countries
and regions differentially over a substantial period of time. Again,
we need credible random variation in treatment over space and time.
After many long evenings in front of books and computer screens,
we finally found what we were looking for: The development of antiretroviral drugs to combat acquired immunodeficiency syndrome
(AIDS).[9] Developing a powerful drug to combat the AIDS epidemic
was indeed one of the most crucial medical breakthroughs of recent
decades and has had a lasting global impact, although differentially
for each country, depending on their level of initial exposure to the
human immunodeficiency virus (HIV).

HIV impairs the function of white blood cells in the immune
system and replicates itself inside these cells. Consequently, infected
individuals experience a weakening of the immune system, making the body vulnerable to infections and some types of cancer. In
advanced stages, the infection turns into AIDS, which ultimately

leads to death. The spread of HIV started on a regional scale in the 1970s and then accelerated ever more threateningly, becoming a global pandemic by the 1990s. By 2000, an estimated 26 million adults and children lived with HIV/AIDS in Africa, constituting more than 70 percent of the global infections. Governments and media worldwide were alarmed and there was no end in sight. Newspaper headlines speculated that this new disease might completely destabilize, to its foundations, the African continent and beyond, and the UN Security Council held a debate on the impact of AIDS on peace and security in Africa. Then, in the late 1990s, finally good news arrived: The identification of the main receptors of HIV led to the development of combination antiretroviral therapy (ART), reducing morbidity and mortality and restoring immunity in infected people. Growing public pressure culminated in the introduction of much cheaper generic drugs for ART in 2001, leading to rapidly expanding ART coverage throughout the world.

In our study we made use of the fact that in the early 2000s, when the groundbreaking therapy became available, some countries were in a more dire state than others. The hardest hit from AIDS also benefited the most from the arrival of ART treatment, which has allowed the statistical analysis to exploit fine-grained variation in health improvement over both space and time. The findings are clear-cut: Various types of violent events get curbed both at the national and local level, ranging from demonstrations to riots, linked to both economic and human rights grievances. When digging deeper into the mechanisms at work, it turns out that what seems to be going on is that better public health provision is a key driver of government legitimacy, and that prompt and competent provision of crucial treatment raises trust in institutions such as parliament and local government. Put differently, successful public health interventions not only deter armed conflict by raising the opportunity cost of leaving paid work and extending the time horizon of people (thus making risky short-termist behavior less appealing) but also boost the government's legitimacy and attenuate popular grievances.

WORK NOT WAR

But what about other economic interventions, such as, for example, labor market policies? Remember that we have encountered ample evidence that bad economic shocks and poverty carry the seeds for political turmoil through a reduced opportunity cost of fighting among others. As spelled out previously, large parts of the population being out of luck and desperate constitutes a fertile breeding ground for rebel recruiters. The natural idea is to see whether once again "reverse engineering" is possible. If unemployment and poverty trigger conflict, can employment and welfare policies bring peace? This one million dollar question has in recent years attracted the attention of various scholars around the world.

One pioneering study was set up by Chicago's Chris Blattman and Jeannie Annan from the International Rescue Committee.[10] They teamed up with the nonprofit organization Action on Armed Violence that ran an employment program in 2009 in postwar Liberia. At the time peace was only half a dozen years young, and the country was still very much haunted by the ghosts of the last war. The so-called Second Liberian Civil War lasted from 1999 to 2003 and opposed warlord-turned-president Charles Taylor against several rebel groups. This brutal war gave rise to a whole generation of young men without job perspectives but with fighting experience. Given that the peace after the First Liberian War was short lived, experts rightly feared that Liberia was sitting on a time bomb ready to explode if ignited by some mounting social tensions. In this context, the natural idea arose to put in place an employment program that helped to get "high-risk" young men off the streets into jobs that would allow for a better future.

In particular, this program provided several months of residential agricultural training, counseling and life skills classes, and farm inputs to high-risk men, many of whom had previously flirted with illegality by occupying rubber plantations or illegally mining or logging. Of the 1,100 high-risk men recruited by the nongovernmental organization roughly half were randomly offered participation in the program. The impact of this was quite striking: Those benefiting from the program showed an interest in farming and were much less involved in illicit activities. They were also less easy prey for mercenary recruiters, as measured by several proxy questions. An interesting and maybe unexpected angle of the results is the complementarity between capital and training. Expected future farming input transfers played a key role in getting the treated high-risk men to walk the line. At the end of the day the findings highlight how elastic the choice between illicit and legal activities is and how relatively small differences in relative returns can prevent high-risk individuals from leaving work for war.

As catchy and well designed as this Liberian study was, the skeptical economist, of course, asks the usual question about how representative and applicable this would be to other contexts (referred to as "external validity" in the jargon). Thankfully, further evidence is available for again very different contexts. Let us move first to India, where a recent study investigated to what extent negative weather-driven income shocks could be attenuated. As mentioned earlier, in countries such as India where agriculture plays a major role, erratic weather conditions represent key determinants of the scope for armed conflict. Bad income shocks lower the bar considerably for the eruption of organized violence, among other factors owing to the relatively greater ease of fielding a combat-ready crowd. But if one could somehow insure vulnerable peasants against natural hazards, could clever policy design not get a handle on these adverse meteorological side effects?

It turns out that India's National Rural Employment Guarantee Act of 2006 goes exactly in this direction. Interestingly, the legal entitlement of 100 days of public work per year at the official minimum wage makes this job guarantee differentially attractive, depending on whether this amount is relatively sizable or not compared with local average wages and prices. It turns out that this employment guarantee has made a considerable difference in places with poor outside options, where the introduction of the scheme has all but broken the link between poor weather and poor prospects of peace.[11] The results again echo the previous findings that if people are offered decent legal perspectives, most actually prefer to work than to fight (besides maybe a tiny minority of sadists or ideologues). This confirms that boosting productivity and providing jobs are first order tools for tranquility and lasting peace.

Not only can access to work deter full-blown armed war, but also weaker forms of violent behavior can be tackled. As mentioned in Chapter 3, we have found in a recent study that asylum seekers in Switzerland exposed to armed conflict during childhood showed a much higher propensity for violent behavior in their new host country.[12] Yet also for this dilemma public policy is not devoid of solutions. After establishing the childhood conflict exposure/adult violent crime link, we have made use of the fact that Switzerland is a federal state with large variations in institutions and public policies across its twenty-six cantons. While the area and population size of this Alpine democracy is some magnitudes smaller than of the United States, the heterogeneity in local politics is arguably similarly large in the Swiss Confederation. When it comes to migration policies, in some areas of Switzerland asylum seekers can rapidly work in all sectors of the economy while in other cantons work access is barred for longer and/or restricted to some sectors of activity only. Given that the newly arrived asylum seekers are randomly allocated to cantons, this wide intercanton heterogeneity allows us to obtain suggestive evidence on how strongly labor market integration matters. And, indeed, it matters massively: We found that fostering prospects for the labor market integration of asylum seekers can reduce the effect of conflict exposure on future crime propensity by two-thirds! More specifically, the opportunity to apply rapidly for jobs in all sectors together with the promotion of labor market access are driving this landslide mitigation of childhood trauma. Related to this, we also uncovered that social integration measures, such as civic education courses, may well constitute ramparts against the long-lasting side effects of childhood conflict exposure. Note that while these findings are based on migration waves to Switzerland some years back, they could hardly be more topical. In fact, when it comes to the large numbers of Ukrainian refugees currently fleeing from the Russian invasion to various countries, the message is clear-cut. Providing rapid labor-market access and promoting access to local language teaching may be policies that are win–win for everybody.

Last but not least, let us consider other types of economic policies, beyond education, health and labor market programs. A natural candidate is social spending, and in particular cash transfer programs. As mentioned earlier, the track records of (unconditional) cash transfers and food aid are mixed at best, which intuitively is in line with the logic that boosting productivity raises the opportunity cost of fighting, while in contrast distributing valuable goods or cash may represent attractive prizes that motivate appropriation and rent seeking. This being said, one needs of course to keep in mind the key humanitarian role of cash transfers, and it is also important to stress that there have been contexts in which cash transfer programs do not augment the risk of conflict. Again, the devil lies in the details of their design.

Yet there is a related policy that we have omitted to discuss so far: conditional cash transfer programs, for which the cash disbursement is tied to meeting a series of conditions. While this kind of policy has again proven a bit of a mixed bag in some contexts, where local governments were firmly entrenched in the implementation of the program, it has delivered encouraging results concerning peace promotion in settings where the conditionality was geared towards household actions. In particular, a very revealing study was conducted some years ago in the Philippines, which, like Indonesia, is rich in population and geographically very scattered, making it a difficult task to keep the country together. In the case of the Philippines, over 100 million people occupy an archipelago stretching over some 7,000 islands and islets. In past decades the Philippines has suffered from a great deal of political violence, associated with the insurgencies perpetrated by various rebel groups, including, notoriously, the

New People's Army, the Moro Islamic Liberation Front and the Abu Sayyaf Group, among others. In this challenging environment, it seems natural to set up programs that strengthen the incentives to work rather than fight.

A team of US scholars has examined the effects deployed by a large-scale conditional cash transfer program, the so-called Philippines' Pantawid Pamilyang Pilipino Program.[13] Under this scheme, household eligibility hinges on having income below the regional poverty line and raising children below the age of fourteen. For eligible households to receive the cash transfers, they are required to ensure school attendance for the children, as well as the receiving of a series of vaccination and deworming treatments. In 2009, in a randomized experiment, 130 villages were randomly assigned to either receive the treatment (i.e., conditional cash transfers from 2009 onwards) or be part of the control group that did not get transfers until 2011. The impact of the program on conflict has been stunning: The treated villages that benefited from these conditional cash transfers experienced a substantial drop in conflict in the first year of the program, as well as a reduction in insurgent influence. In line with the aforementioned evidence, the combination of policies that target improvements in education and/or health with capital inputs has the potential to lift households out of poverty and nudge their incentives away from illicit activities.

To wrap up, let us of course never forget that the devil lies in the details and that well-intended but ill-designed programs can, and do, backfire. Yet with this caveat in mind, the evidence of this chapter points towards public policies having a key role to play in getting (economic) incentives right and steering potential rebel recruits away from mercenary fighting towards legal employment in the labor market. While productivity and returns to work are not sole guarantors of peace, well-designed education, health, labor market and other welfare state policies are clearly part of the policy mix that can transform an uneasy blend of distorted incentives into a healthy cocktail of pacifying ingredients.

9 Forgiving Not Fighting

Fostering Trust and Reconciliation

They who do not trust enough, will not be trusted.

Lao Tzu

The air was heavy on April 6, 1994 in Kigali, Rwanda. Political tensions had been mounting for years. The autocratic pro-Hutu government, led by officer-turned-president Juvénal Habyarimana, who had seized power in a coup in 1973, was ruling with an iron fist a country that had become increasingly close to catastrophe. Militarily there was an ongoing conflict between the Hutu-dominated government and the Tutsi-led Rwandan Patriotic Front (RPF) rebels, who had started invading northeastern Rwanda in 1990. While the 1993 Arusha Peace Agreement had officially ended the three-year Rwandan Civil War, and foresaw a broad-based transition government, much of the agreement had not been implemented (yet) and the ceasefire was fragile. On the economic front, there was still widespread poverty and the track record of the two-decades of Habyarimana rule was –to put it mildly – far from stellar. Finally, there had been surging radicalization among Hutu extremists who opposed the peace process with the RPF. Their preferred arm of anti-Tutsi propaganda and hate speech had become the Radio Télévision Libre des Mille Collines (RTLM), a widely listened-to radio station founded in 1993.

In the calm before the storm the presidential jet prepared to land at Kigali International Airport on the evening of April 6, 1994, carrying among others Rwandan president Juvénal Habyarimana and his Burundian homologue Cyprien Ntaryamira. Nobody knows (nor will ever know) what the two Hutu politicians and the fellow passengers and crew were talking about when suddenly the evening sky was torn apart by surface-to-air missiles that hit the plane. In the ensuing explosion all twelve crew members and passengers perished. This dramatic event provided the ignition that Hutu extremists had been hoping for desperately for several months. Speculating that the plane had been shot down by Tutsi rebels, they now had the pretext they hoped for to put their plans for wide-scale massacres into action (note that the exact circumstances of the attack on the plane have still not been elucidated).

The same night of the plane crash, the organized mass killings of Tutsi and moderate Hutu people started, giving rise to what became known as the Rwandan genocide during which, over about 100 days, over 800,000 killings took place.[1] After the assassination of the moderate Hutu prime minister, Agathe Uwilingiyimana, and her ten Belgian UN bodyguards the next day, the Hutu extremists took control of the state. One of the chief organizers of the massacres was Colonel Théoneste Bagosora, who would later be convicted by the International Criminal Tribunal for Rwanda (ICTR) for genocide, crimes against humanity and war crimes, and the interim presidency was assumed by Theodore Sindikubwabo, known for his infamous inflammatory hate speeches and who died in exile. The fact that lists of addresses of prominent Tutsi and moderate Hutu politicians and personalities had been readily shared among the involved murder squads, who rapidly killed them, corroborates the notion that the massacres had been planned way in advance.

After the aforementioned initial killings of UN peacekeeping troops, the UN forces pulled back. On April 21, the UN decided to reduce the United Nations Assistance Mission for Rwanda troops in the country from about 2,500 to 270 (while revising their decision in May).[2] This, with hindsight incomprehensible, choice opened the gates of hell even further. Wider-scale massacres spread throughout the country, with the army, Hutu Interahamwe and Impuzamugambi militias bringing brutal death and devastation to

Tutsi and moderate Hutu communities, fueled by Radio RTLM's escalating hate speech, encouraging listeners to kill their Tutsi neighbors who were referred to as "cockroaches."

The mass killings only came to a stop once the Tutsi rebels of RPF had militarily won against the Hutu interim government. By early July the RPF had gained control over most of the country and Kigali fell by July 4. Later that month a transitional government had been sworn in and the genocide had ended. In the aftermath, many of the estimated 200,000 perpetrators fled to the DRC and the ICTR took up its work. The Rwandan political landscape has since been considerably shaped by Paul Kagame, the leader of the RPF, who became vice president and minister of defense in 1994 and president in 2000, a position he still occupies today (2024).

THE RADIO OF DEATH

In the aftermath of this heart-breaking tragedy a great deal of academic research has strived to make sense of how it was possible that the Hutu extremist spin doctors managed to mobilize great masses –an estimated 200,000 perpetrators – to join in their evil deeds. Obviously, analyzing never means condoning – the bloodshed of Rwanda's hundred days of massacres can never ever be excused or forgiven. Still, understanding the mechanisms behind the madness is key to avoiding history repeating itself and to finding policies that can mend a society in complete meltdown.

A key element that has crystallized scholars' attention has been the role of hate speech and propaganda (which sadly is as topical and timely as ever). Now, of course, it is not straightforward to measure this and to get a handle on causality. If extremists are more likely to listen to extremist radio programs, it is not obvious whether hate speech really made a difference or whether listeners were already radicalized to start with. While around the globe scores of social scientists were struggling with this methodological roadblock, a Swedish doctoral student, David Yanagizawa-Drott, suddenly came up with a brilliant idea that built up on previous work in media economics: Reception of Rwanda's notorious hate radio RTLM varies considerably given Rwanda's hilly terrain.[3] In the state that is sometimes dubbed "country with the thousand hills," this irregular landscape necessarily means that dozens of villages may have been affected less by the hate speech, which should be reflected by the local death tolls. Taking into account the location of the two transmitters of RTLM (on Mount Muhe, one of the country's highest mountains, and in the capital, Kigali), as well as drawing on detailed topological maps, it was possible to compute the radio reception strength for each of Rwanda's villages. The ensuing findings are chilling: One moderate increase in radio signal strength (called a "standard deviation" in the jargon) leads to 10 percent more killings in a given village, underscoring the devastating impact of the propaganda issuing from the radio of evil.

CONTACT NOT CONFLICT

If the Rwandan genocide constitutes one of the darkest hours of humanity, it is sadly not a lone outlier: Similar mechanisms of interethnic violence have occurred at various scales in many countries around the world. Think, for example, of Bosnia, or of the current ethnically motivated attacks on civilians that are currently (2024) taking place in Darfur. It goes without saying that in Rwanda, as well as in other postconflict settings the task of rebuilding destroyed intergroup trust and reconciliation could hardly be more daunting and the stakes hardly higher: If these tasks fail, a revenge war or new outbreak of interethnic killings is an all too real threat. As in the previous chapters, the natural question an economist may ask is the one about reverse engineering. If wars fuel hatred and destroy trust, could we then prevent follow-up wars by putting in place policies that deliberately foster trust and reconciliation?

One key concept here is what psychologists have dubbed "the contact hypothesis." Put simply, the idea is that when you meet somebody from another community and this interaction is fair and non-discriminatory then you start to know the other group better, understand their social norms and values and build mutual trust. Think of the magic encounter in *The Little Prince* by Antoine de Saint-Exupéry in which the fox explains to the little prince that before knowing each other his encounter would just have been with one fox among dozens, yet once they created a bond they would be unique and important to each other. This being said, of course, "negative" encounters that lack respect, equality and where one party dominates or exploits the other will –if anything – backfire and fuel mistrust between groups. As is typical for many peers in economics, I could not only admire the beauty and depth of this concept in psychology but also felt the urge to "translate" it into our own language – game theory. For this endeavor, Mathias Thoenig, Fabrizio Zilibotti and I teamed up.[4]

Picture a society with two large groups – it could be Hutu and Tutsi or Hindu and Muslim, for example. Individual members of the two communities meet every day, and often quite randomly, to engage or not in business. If half a century ago most economists thought about business solely in terms of capital, labor, prices and quantities, in recent years it has become clearer and clearer that key ingredients for economic interaction are also located in the realm of institutions, rules, norms and, ultimately, trust. Yet when people don't personally know someone they meet for the first time, they often tend to try to infer trustworthiness from group membership. If you have had great experiences with people from Switzerland and love our chocolate and watches and are a fan of Roger Federer, maybe you are positively inclined to do business with a Swiss person. In contrast, this may be less so if last time you were in Zurich your wallet was stolen at the classy Bahnhofstrasse. As misplaced such prejudices may be, they are all too often observed in reality.

The trouble is that they are self-reinforcing, leading to vicious cycles. Imagine that both Democrats and Republicans are not fundamentally bad people and believe that their ideas will eventually help society. Now let us further presume that there is a misunderstanding of some sort, in which each party starts to perceive the other as untrustworthy. This will push members of each group to interact less with the group members of the other faction, so there are fewer foregone business rents at stake in case of an all-out conflict. Put differently, the lack of ties makes conflict "cheaper," which in turn may lead to more frequent disputes. This will further crowd out trust and interaction, and so on. Luckily there is an analogous virtuous cycle, in which peaceful reaching out at community level fosters individual trust of outgroup members, which will result in more business and greater opportunity costs of conflict, which may become prohibitively expensive – further cementing honest intergroup dealings and peace. Fascinatingly, the potential for trade-related virtuous cycles did not escape Baron de Montesquieu centuries earlier, making him notice in his magnum opus *The Spirit of the Laws* that "commerce is a cure for the most destructive prejudices; for it is almost a general rule, that wherever we find agreeable manners, there commerce flourishes; and that wherever there is commerce, there we meet with agreeable manners."[5]

These feedback loops are so stark that a society may get pushed into "mistrust–lack of intergroup interaction–frequent conflict" without there being any fundamental reason for it. You could call this a war trap. Groups may just have been drawn into a self-perpetuating fight despite being initially positively inclined and cooperative – just because of an initial misunderstanding that set in motion destructive dynamics. This is not unlike what may happen to couples, as highlighted in a few dozen romantic comedies every year: The stars of the movie love each other dearly, yet there is a misunderstanding of some sort that pushes them apart and escalates their discord. While in romcoms the heroes typically end up together in the end, the world is neither a fairy tale nor a romantic comedy. Hence, it is not infrequent that different groups or countries can get into decades-long feuds, which political scientists sometimes call "enduring rivalries." Think, for example, of the India–Pakistan conflict over Kashmir, which is already more than seven decades old.

While understanding disastrous vicious cycles of mounting mistrust is important, it may be even more capital to understand how to put in motion positive virtuous cycles of building trust. Hence, various of the brightest minds in the profession have focused their efforts on investigating instances of how positive "contact" can yield lasting trust and cooperation between communities. Our first stop on this journey is India, a country that has sadly suffered from extensive intercommunal violence over the past decades.

SEARCHING FOR THE ROOTS OF PEACE IN MEDIEVAL INDIA

Cities come and go and so do ports and islands. Global warming has in recent years accelerated the reshaping of worldwide shorelines, and rising sea levels menace hundreds of cities around the globe, with the list spanning Venice and Bangkok to New Orleans and Basra in Iraq. Yet before human-made climate change kicked in and made things way worse, Mother Nature has regularly redistributed the cards, with trade ports emerging and ceasing to exist. Could these natural changes in exposure to trade help us to understand the deeper conditions for fruitful contact? Yes, indeed! Stanford's political scientist Saumitra Jha came up with the brilliant idea of going back in history and studying the legacy of ancient trade between communities –even in places without any accessible or active port today.[6] Picture two comparable cities with a similar economic and population structure but just one having a long legacy of world trade. Comparing the recent history of communal violence between Hindus and Muslims may allow us to understand the impact of trade, and contact more generally on the risk of conflict.

To dive deeper into Jha's underlying hypothesis, we need to take a step back and look at medieval trade in India. From at least the eighth to the seventeenth century, Muslims had an edge in world trade, as pilgrimages such as the Hajj opened up various trade routes across the Indian Ocean. This led to fruitful complementarities between Hindus and Muslims in India's medieval trading ports. They had a constructive business interaction and mutually needed each other to thrive. Under the tightening grip of the British in the eighteenth century, cards were reshuffled again and medieval trade routes lost their capital importance. The basic idea for disentangling pure causality from pure correlation was to find a determinant for medieval trade ports that played less of a role for colonial and ulterior ports. After all, it could have been that medieval ports were simply located in places that were peaceful to start with or that trust plays no role, and it is simply today's commercial wealth that fosters peace. Again, Mother Nature provides the solution to this statistical challenge: It turns out that the location of medieval ports was strongly driven by which coastal indentations and bays provided so-called natural harbors at that time, and this proved fairly unrelated to the location of colonial era ports or commercial shipping hubs today. The reason is that sand segmentation and other slow-moving changes reshape the shoreline continuously, and today's perfect harbor is very different from an ideal one two centuries ago. Or, as Heraclitus said, "no man steps in the same river twice."

Did the aforementioned prosocial norms survive the demise of commercial wealth and prosperity when fortunes reversed and Indian Ocean trade declined in some medieval trade ports? Yes: Even when the ancient business bonds weakened, there was still enough accumulated trust between Hindus and Muslims in these places to guarantee a much lower risk of communal riots than elsewhere. Crucially, it turns out that intergroup relations were not only relatively peaceful throughout medieval times but also that local intergroup trust persisted under British rule. Jha found that places with medieval trade ports were roughly five times less likely to see Hindu–Muslim riots between 1850 and 1950 than similar cities without a trade port history. Even in the post-World War II period, there remains a measurable effect, reducing the incidence of rioting by more than half.

FROM LAGOS TO ABUJA AND FROM GRANADA
TO BARCELONA: LOVE THY NEIGHBOR

Now the skeptical reader will certainly ponder whether we learn much from medieval India about the virtues of contact with strangers in our hyperglobalized world of today. Can similar effects be detected in the twenty-first century, and if yes, how would you typically do this? Two recent studies took the bull by its horns and investigated this question. First, a team of Spanish scholars discovered a unique "natural experiment."[7] As in many other countries, some areas of Spain are major tourist destinations, while others are all but unknown. To foster a fair allocation of recruits in the then mandatory military service and to warrant that all had the same chances of hitting the jackpot of being located in a prime location (e.g., the air base at Palma de Mallorca), the Spanish military set up a lottery determining between 1987 and 1991 which conscript served the service in which military location. This, of course, led to the kind of random variation that economists adore so much. It is indeed pure luck whether the person is located far from home and hence exposed to contact with people from a very different area or instead assigned to service in the home region.

It turns out that a quarter of a century later the effects of this lottery allocation were rather spectacular: Consider comparable men (with similar characteristics) from regions with a "weak" Spanish identity. The regions classified as such are the Basque Country, Catalonia and Galicia, which all speak languages that differ from Spanish and have seen the rise of separatist movements, as well as Navarra, where a sizable share of citizens share the Basque identity and self-identify as non-Spanish. Those men from the four regions who were allocated to serve their military duties outside their home region were more likely to self-identify as Spanish, than those staying at home. The magnitude corresponds to a huge seventeen percentage points rise, which marks a very fundamental shift. Those who experienced living in other areas of Spain also participated more in Spanish elections, again by a game-changing margin of eighteen percentage points. Finally, they also tended to vote less for regionalist parties and were more likely to report having friends from another region, which highlights the key role of intergroup contact.

Another continent, a similar lottery, again with stunning results: Let us set sail to Nigeria, where World Bank economist Oyebola Okunogbe scrutinized another "natural experiment."[8] She examined the impacts deployed by the Nigerian National Youth Service Corps program which has been running since 1973. This government scheme has dispatched various cohorts of university graduates to all corners of Africa's most populated country for a year of national service. Participation is mandatory for all graduates of tertiary institutions, and the program is a heavyweight in terms of scope, featuring over 200,000 participants per year. Beyond the aim of fostering development needs by relocating highly educated youths to places with shortages in skilled labor, the goal of this initiative was from the onset to promote national integration and curb prejudice and discrimination.

The results are nothing short of spectacular. Having been randomly allocated to serve outside their own ethnic region makes participants five times as likely to live outside their home region seven years later. And this is not just confined to staying in the place they were allocated to: The experience of living in an unknown environment also appears to instill a general thirst for travelling and adventure, making these participants more likely to discover other parts of the country in which they have never previously set foot. Further, participants living outside their ethnic area also step up their general knowledge about Nigeria, as tested by answering factual questions about governors and capitals of states in other regions. Again, the effect is not confined to the host area. So, for example, a participant from Lagos deployed to the northern state of Yobe would not just acquire better knowledge of Yobe but would at the same time show a surge in general interest for the country, reflected also in better factual knowledge about, say, the eastern state of Taraba. Exposure to a different ethnic environment also deploys a series of further effects, such as higher reported willingness to migrate to another region of Nigeria in search of a better job, as well as greater national pride, a greater likelihood to having dated someone from a different ethnic group and an increased appreciation of diversity.

But, maybe at first sight surprisingly, this does not crowd out ethnic pride and identification with a home ethnic group, suggesting that you can have your cake and eat it. The idea is that exposure to new social norms and ideas both increase one's horizons but at the same time trigger a sweet sense of nostalgia and homesickness. Or, to phrase it in terms of psychologists' social identity theory, immersion in a foreign culture fosters the salience of a person's group identity. Everyone who has lived abroad for some years may relate to a sense of double identification, at the same time enjoying learning more about the new place, while missing home. If I were to run a survey among the fellow Swiss who studied at the same time as I did in Cambridge, it is likely that most would agree with my claim that never before or after our years in England did we eat as many fondues and raclettes: every time one of us went home, we would bring back large amounts of Swiss cheese (and chocolate) for our ex-pat community, to indulge in traditional cheese feasts.

In a nutshell, the aforementioned results are encouraging, as they highlight the potential to embrace differences and broaden one's horizon, while not at the cost of reneging on one's origins. Put differently, when handled cleverly, ethnic and national identities are not substitutes, but complements!

DOUBLE PASS, DRIBBLING, BICYCLE KICK AND ...
INCREASED TRUST AND NATIONAL IDENTITY

Now, sadly, not so many countries routinely have programs and initiatives that promote interregional mobility and between-group contact. To address the scarcity of natural experiments of random relocation as in Spain or Nigeria, Yale's Salma Mousa has made a virtue of necessity and has simply created her own intervention (although so far only on a small scale).[9] In this recent research project she worked with Iraqis displaced by violent assaults from the Islamic State (ISIS). Specifically, amateur Christian soccer players were randomly assigned to either an all-Christian team or a mixed soccer team also featuring Muslims. While the stakes of amateur soccer are –to say the last – not very high, these kinds of informal contacts in a relaxed setting, where all players are a priori treated equally, may actually be exactly the kind of environment that is conducive to rebuilding war-scarred trust. The results suggest that indeed exposure to the unknown may reduce fear, as participants randomly assigned to mixed teams were more likely to state that they would not mind playing in mixed teams in future years. They also showed much less in-group bias in awarding sportsmanship prizes and were more likely to engage in mixed training sessions after the intervention. While the intervention was a success when it came to fostering trust and friendships on the soccer field, the results were weaker for off-pitch behavior and attitudes. Various measures of generalized trust towards people from the out-group did not move, suggesting that the effects were mostly confined to the personal ties built with specific people met on the soccer pitch. Even though the findings for Iraq may be somewhat less spectacular and weaker than the previous results for Spain and Nigeria, they nevertheless remain remarkable, as of course the situation could hardly be more challenging. If you can mend social interactions among people victimized by the notoriously brutal ISIS assaults, you may be able to rebuild trust in almost any environment.

The soccer results prove to be not a one shot finding; there is more to come. In fact, if you strive to nudge your teenage kids into studying economics, which they may (wrongly) judge as boring or nerdy, there is a simple remedy. You could talk about one of the catchiest papers in the profession in recent years, which also turns out to be about soccer and national cohesion![10] An international researcher team, drawing on a sample consisting of sub-Saharan African countries, recently studied how the victories of national soccer teams impact on nation building efforts. Who does not know these moments of collective euphoria, such as in 2022 in London when the Three Lionesses won the European Championship at home, in the famed Wembley stadium, with people chanting in the streets that "football is coming home" (yes, we all know that the British invented it, as so many other sports). Popular perception does indeed stress the surge in national cohesion and tackling of societal cleavages and tensions in moments of these national triumphs. But of course, as we have now seen ample times, anecdotal evidence does not necessarily hold up to the scrutiny of cold-hearted statistics, and the effects may not be long-lasting. Maybe on the same day, after the chanting in the streets of London, the post-Brexit gloom of many has swiftly returned. Well, to answer such questions is indeed part of the job of social scientists, requiring a statistical analysis.

For this purpose, the study team drew on a rather clever research method that has now become increasingly popular in various fields. Its starting point is that the usual opinion polls and surveys take quite some time to implement, and during this time span things may happen that influence the later respondents but are ignored by the earlier participants. If you asked people about their stand on nuclear energy on March 9, 2011, that is, two days before the Fukushima nuclear disaster, their answers might have systematically differed from answers given to the same survey questions on, say, March 13, 2011, right after the catastrophe took place. Well, the approach is the same here, comparing answers to the same survey questions on ethnic identity and national cohesion that were asked immediately before or after important matches of the national squad. Note that the scholars did not have to run new surveys to implement this cool idea, and could just build on existing survey data. As there is a substantial number of regular surveys already, there will always be some running by chance around the not-so-infrequent national soccer games. This shows you that one can put in place a really fascinating research design without wide-ranging financial needs or fancy statistical innovations – a great idea suffices!

The findings of the study are rather telling: Respondents interviewed right after an important victory of their country's national squad were 37 percent less likely to primarily self-identify with their own ethnic group and 30 percent more likely to trust people from other ethnicities, as compared with those interviewed right before the event. Furthermore, when switching to a more aggregate level of analysis, the research team found that 9 percent fewer violent episodes were recorded in the following months, when a country secured qualification to the Africa Cup of Nations in a knife-edge last-minute thrill, as compared with failing the qualification by a small margin. These results are nothing short of spectacular and underscore the tremendous potential of intergroup cooperation in sports, as a parable for working together in society to tackle not just attacking goal getters but also more serious societal issues. Obviously, the key remaining question is how long-lasting these effects may be. To find the answer, more research is desperately needed.

FLAMES OF FORGIVENESS?

In the aforementioned studies the increased intergroup contact is built-into programs focused on other activities. Spanish conscripts are primarily there to be trained as soldiers, the Nigerian program has a key development goal, and the soccer player's main motivation is likely to be to ... well, play soccer. An alternative approach is to address intergroup tensions head-on rather than indirectly. This is the approach privileged by a US-based team in a recent study. As mentioned previously, Sierra Leone's civil war from 1991 to 2002 was particularly bloody, and much of the violence was neighbor on neighbor, with victims and perpetrators often belonging to the same village or region. These features make it very difficult to move on and engage in reconciliation, especially if every day on the market square you bump into the killers of your defunct family members.

While national truth and reconciliation commissions had been set up by central government, they often failed to reach people living in remote rural areas. In order to address this shortcoming, the nongovernmental organization (NGO) Fambul Tok (which translates to "Family Talk") started to organize – five years after the end of the fighting – community-level reconciliation forums. The goal was to encourage both victims and perpetrators to talk openly about what happened during the war. The end of the process was a two-day bonfire ceremony during which the perpetrators asked for forgiveness. The study in question drew on the work of the NGO and provided an evaluation of its impact.[11] For this purpose, the expansion of these reconciliation forums was set up as a randomized control trial: Among a pool of 200 villages, half of them were "treated" with these forums, while the rest constituted the "untreated" control group.

The results turned out to be a mixed bag. On the one hand, societal healing was clearly fostered by this initiative, but at the price of psychological suffering. In particular, the researchers found that the reconciliation forums led to greater forgiveness, strengthened social capital, enlarged social networks and increased public good provision. Yet on the other hand, it also led to a worsening of psychological health, increasing depression, anxiety and Post-Traumatic Stress Disorder. And these positive as well as negative effects of the intervention persisted over two years after the end of the ceremony. Overall, the results of the study convey the notion that while leaving the past behind may, under some circumstances, foster individual psychological healing, at the same time thematizing past atrocities may be a necessary step on the road towards national reconciliation. More research is needed, but there is the hope that cleverly designing these reconciliation processes may be able to deliver societal benefits while keeping the individual psychological side effects to a minimum.

REVERSE INDOCTRINATION?

If all of these studies tackle the issue of missing intergroup trust by fostering direct contact between people from different groups, it may be conceivable to follow a wholly different approach, targeting beliefs and attitudes directly. The idea could be to reverse past indoctrination, by subjecting people to positive messages of tolerance and critical thought. Obviously, if you are a liberal, all alarm bells will immediately go off. Can everlasting good come from deliberately targeting people's beliefs, even with good intentions? Is this not a slippery slope preparing the terrain for evil indoctrination, once it has been proven that influencing works and when an ill-faithed despot has grabbed power? While the dangers of systematically meddling with people's beliefs are all too apparent, there are studies that also describe the potential upsides of belief targeting. The trade-off between risks and potential benefits lies in the eye of the beholder.

A first telling study of altering attitudes using the media was the work by Arthur Blouin and Sharun Mukand.[12] Focusing on postgenocide Rwanda they asked a daring question: "If the deeply evil radio propaganda of RTLM fueled the massacres, could an inverse, tolerance-fostering media content reverse the ethnic cleavage?" Rwanda is an ideal place to study this, not only because of the tragic history of ethnic violence but also because the new postgenocide government under Paul Kagame rapidly understood that to prevent future atrocities it was key to build a stronger national cohesion and to reduce interethnic hatred and prejudice. To take on this top priority of reconciliation, the government established the National Unity and Reconciliation Commission, expressly mandated to build interethnic trust and support national identity formation. Besides a new legislation against "genocide ideology," a rewriting of schoolbooks and compulsory ethnically mixed collective work programs, the authors of the study documented substantial media indoctrination and a crackdown on what the government judged were dangerous content. This went as far as that the mere mention of ethnicity was forbidden and that the country in the current 2023 World Press Freedom index of Reporters without borders is only ranked 131st among 180 (with the top five scores all attributed to Northern European countries).[13] You get the message: Rwanda's Kagame government has put in place the rare experiment

of authoritarian indoctrination that replaces the usual divisive populist rhetoric with a reconciliatory message. Can this go well?

Three decades after one of radio's darkest hours – the RTLM
hate campaign – this media form is still by far the key channel of
communication in Rwanda. In particular, the government-owned
station Radio Rwanda plays a crucial role in the regime's communication strategy, spreading the official ideology of an ethnicity-free
society (there are no more Hutus, Tutsis and Twas, just Rwandans)
and national reconciliation. Conveniently, the authors of this study
stood on the shoulders of giants and could simply, off the shelf, make
use of the random variation famously used in previous studies: the
hilly topology of the "land of a thousand hills," which implies that
some places have much better radio coverage than others and hence
are more exposed to government ideology.

The results of the study suggest that Radio Rwanda's propaganda offensive "works": Those exposed to the government's nation
building rhetoric were over ten percentage points less likely to cat-
egorize others based on ethnicity in lab experiments. Radio Rwanda
exposure also led to an over fifteen percentage points higher likelihood of teaming up with someone from another ethnicity for a
cooperative task, as well as resulting in increased intergroup trust.
Taken together, these sets of outcomes suggest that tolerance can
be instilled as much as intolerance. This astonishing efficiency of
propaganda highlights that it is of even greater importance to have a
political system characterized by enough checks and balances.

THE DANGERS OF DEMAGOGY

Unfortunately, though, checks and balances are not enough to always
avoid horrifying consequences when reconciliation propaganda
derails. A Lausanne-based team has recently studied the impact
of the infamous movie *Birth of a Nation* in the aftermath of the
American Civil War.[14] This was released in 1915 – five decades after
the end of the war – and became a major Hollywood blockbuster.
If in terms of cinematographic techniques and special effects it was

very catchy for that period, it spread the historically wrong and hate-promoting narrative of the "Lost Cause," a revisionist retelling of the history of the American Civil War. In its account of the war, African-Americans were portrayed in the role of scapegoats and defamed as a common enemy, while the former Unionist and Confederate foes were invited to reconcile and unite to restore white supremacy, which the movie argued to be threatened by the enfranchisement of African-Americans. While there cannot be any doubt about the fact that the movie was morally repellent, one still open question investigated by this study was whether the evil propaganda trick "worked" or backfired. Knowing this is not unimportant: If using the racist card to foster reconciliation between two opposing political camps was effective, then maybe the risk of the future use of such dirty tactics may increase, and knowing what we are up against in terms of such ill-faithed propaganda helps to best counter it.

Exploiting the timing patterns of when and where the movie was shown, the statistical analysis uncovers shockingly large effects. It turns out that the screening of the movie led to a semantic shift in the public discourse, to the benefit of a more nationalistic and less divisive rhetoric in terms of Unionists versus Confederates, as shown by a large-scale text analysis of 3,760 newspapers. Further, there was a surge in patriotism, as measured by enrollment in the US Navy. And finally, cultural convergence occurred between former Civil War foes as proxied in terms of baby name choices – Confederates were increasingly likely to select traditional Unionist first names and vice versa. Yet, sadly, this reconciliation came at a terrible price: There was a steep surge in discrimination against African-Americans in public discourse and in the labor market. Scholars went as far as quantifying the relative sizes of the effects, and found that slightly above half of the movie's impact on reconciliation was precisely through this worsening discrimination. All in all, the chilling results of this study stress that propaganda is – at best – a double-edged sword, and that generally, the destructive side of the blade cuts much deeper.

AND WHAT ABOUT INSTILLING CRITICAL THOUGHT?

Given the dangers of propaganda interventions as slippery slopes towards authoritarianism and scapegoating, are there any interventions where such hazards are relatively well contained? One may be tempted to refer to initiatives that nudge participants into stepping up critical thinking. Well, it turns out that an American duo of a psychologist and a political scientist studied exactly this kind of intervention, focusing on a country where ethnicity has proven in the past tragically salient: postgenocide Rwanda.[15] In particular, they studied a randomized experiment in which the treatment group was presented with a radio program that discouraged blind obedience and following authorities, instead fostering independent thinking and teaming up collectively to solve problems. The comparable control group of participants was randomly assigned to another radio program centered around dealing with HIV.

The experiment found quite striking results in line with the expected impact: The radio audience belonging to the treatment group was more likely to express dissent with peers and was less inclined to chiefly rely on local officials for problem-solving. Instead, an increased sense of collective responsibility and local initiative emerged. These findings highlight how critical thinking and questioning of authorities may be much more promoted at various stages of the life cycle, starting obviously in the school curriculum. A short glance at any history book rapidly highlights the danger of "being a lemming" and blindingly trusting authorities without independent thinking. Together with democratic checks and balances, free media and a level economic playing field, critical thought and independent civic mindedness are key ingredients of the cement that holds a peaceful society together. As argued in Chapter 10, there is indeed a role for each one of us to play to support peace.

10 A Role for All of Us?

Smart Idealism, Global Public Opinion and International Support for Peace

That this nation, under God, shall have a new birth of freedom; and that government of the people, by the people, and for the people, shall not perish from the earth.

Abraham Lincoln

The greater the power, the more dangerous the abuse.

Edmund Burke

Many of the policies highlighted in Chapter 9 are by their very nature domestic, making national governments and domestic civil society key actors. However, this does not mean that international stake-holders – and all of us – cannot get involved and play positive roles. As seen before, however, the effectiveness of the broad set of peace-related policies varies very widely, and even well-intended initia-tives can backfire if ill-designed or in the presence of nonintended by-products. Think, for example, of the aforementioned negative side effects on political violence of US food aid. It follows that it is paramount to pair good intentions with evidence-based policies that work. Figure 10.1 illustrates two basic dimensions of policymaking. On the vertical axis we have the extent to which a leader or citizen is open to scientific evidence. Somebody completely stuck in simplistic beliefs of how the world works and dismissing any rigorous scientific evidence would score low on this dimension. Examples include cli-mate change deniers or people believing that vaccines cause autism, despite solid scientific evidence showing that this is not the case. On the upper part of the scale, you have those academics who are completely open to the scrutiny of new scientific evidence, which they are easily willing to accept –without fighting back – even when new evidence rejects famous results.

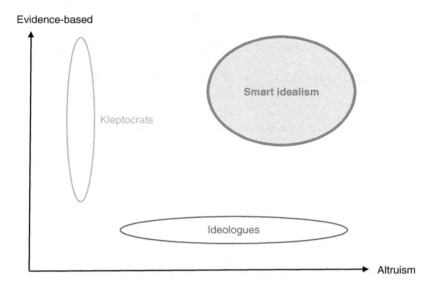

FIGURE 10.1 The scope for smart idealism

A second key dimension in this space is plotted as the hori-
zontal axis. It is about whether a given person is altruistic enough to
have good intentions for society or is above all concerned with her
or his personal gain. Low values pinpoint the egotist, while scoring
high on this dimension captures a strong will to improve society,
even if it demands heavy personal sacrifices. If examples at the lower
end of the scale include various warlords and arms traffickers, on the
upper end of the scale you have people who are willing to forgive and
reach out to former foes even after having suffered from unbearable
injustice and pain, an example being former South African president
Nelson Mandela.

This space contains three regions. On the very left, in the region
dubbed "kleptocrats," are those people whose focus lies to a large
extent on filling their pockets. The list is long, and finding examples
is as easy as spotting green grass in Ireland. Years ago, *The Guardian*
attempted to create a "who is who" ranking of the biggest personal
fortunes amassed by heads of states. Overall, when looking at the
whole list, it is striking that the richest heads of state on average

come rather from poor than rich countries, suggesting that to some extent the richer the leader, the poorer the country. In the *Guardian* ranking the top spot goes to Indonesia's Suharto with 15–35 billion USD, followed by the Philippines' Marcos with 5–10 billion USD, and in third place the DRC's Mobutu Sese Seko with about 5 billion USD.[1] What these three countries have in common is a long history of several wars and conflicts taking place over recent decades. So, to put it mildly, to be ruled by a leader in the left-hand corner seems to hardly be a promising policy for peace and prosperity.

What about the lower part of the graph, labelled "ideologues"? Well, these come in all shapes and sizes. Some ideologues truly believe that they do the right thing, while others may be bloodthirsty or corrupt – think of the pigs that are "more equal" than the others in George Orwell's *Animal Farm*. While overall it may be safe to think of academics to be at the more open-minded end of the scale, there are of course a few exceptions we all know: those who found some now famous result twenty years ago and devote the rest of their careers, with remarkable stamina, to argue that it holds broadly, despite increasingly shaky evidence; or those who write grant proposals while so convinced of the validity of their hypotheses that they sketch the conclusions of their studies before actually conducting them (which leaves one to wonder what the point of research is if you already know in advance what results you are supposed to find). These extreme examples of what psychologists call confirmation bias are thankfully not too frequent.

Yet, of course, ideologues, sectarians and dogmatics can have more tragic impacts than dubious grant applications. When studying comprehensive datasets on mass killing episodes in the post-World War II period together with my coauthors Joan Esteban and Massimo Morelli, it was striking that in quite a few instances these atrocities were perpetrated by ideologues and fanatics who had the delusional belief of doing a good thing for a better, utopian society.[2] One particularly sad example is the one of the Khmer Rouge, which devastated Cambodia from 1975 to 1979. Starting out as a radical communist movement, its military campaign under the lead of the infamous Pol Pot gained control over first the countryside and then the capital by 1975. In the words of the Holocaust Memorial Day Trust, in terms of ideology "the Khmer Rouge's interpretation of Maoist communism drove them to create a classless society, simply by eliminating all social classes except for the 'old people' – poor peasants who worked the land." The effects of pursuing this sectarian dogma were terrible. As put by the Encyclopedia Britannica, "the Khmer Rouge's rule over the next four years was marked by some of the worst excesses of any Marxist government in the 20th century, during which an estimated 1.5 million (and possibly up to 2 million) Cambodians died and many of the country's professional and technical class were exterminated."[3]

Obviously, many utopian movements do not turn violent, and of the ones that do the perpetrators of the atrocities always contain not just zealot ideologues but also a mix of thugs, sadists and power-thirsty opportunists. Still, the aforementioned discussion highlights the extreme dangers of the fanatical pursuit of an ideology while being immune to any adverse evidence demonstrating its harmfulness. It is not because somebody really believes in a cause and is willing to make substantial personal sacrifices that we should stand in admiration and follow her or him like a lemming. Devotion without reflection may carry the seeds of destruction rather than enlightenment. Or, to put it in the words of French writer Jean-Paul Sartre, "the road to hell is paved with good intentions."

So where does this leave us? The best solution for fostering peace (and other welfare improving policies) is to aim at the upper right corner of the space, labelled *smart idealism*. This pairs both the altruistic idealism of not just thinking about oneself but trying to improve lives for the multitude around the globe, together with the willingness to support policies that are evidence-based. This means that the choice of policies should not be guided by ideology without any regard for the actual consequences of the choices. And at the same time, the goal should be to foster the happiness of the multitude. In economist jargon, this would boil down to an altruistic objective function where the welfare of others has a positive weight.

When students ask me which fellow social scientists I find most impressive, I reply to them that –maybe surprisingly – they are not necessarily the best published ones, those who win the most prestigious prizes, and even less so those with most followers on social media. While I of course very much respect fundamental research without immediate policy-relevance, I am personally particularly inspired by colleagues who try to have an evidence-based positive impact. When they have uncovered new policy-relevance evidence, they do not content themselves with sending the paper to a prestigious academic journal and moving on, but try to think hard about how these findings could be applied to improve the world and what they personally can contribute.

The list of these admirable scholars is too long to mention, and there are literally hundreds of fellow colleagues who have succeeded in making a difference by putting rigorously researched evidence into practice. So let us stick to one single example: Princeton's Leonard Wantchekon. Together with Marko Klasnja and Natalija Novta, he has been able to show the wide-ranging positive effects of the first regional schools in colonial Benin.[4] They found substantial positive returns, not just for the first generation of students but also their offspring, ranging from higher living standards to civic mindedness. And the cherry on the cake is that even the uneducated in villages with schools, as well as extended family members, benefit from positive spillovers. The paper was rigorously researched and well written, and finally ended up published in one of the best five journals in economics (the so-called top five constitute a bit of a holy grail for many economists, to put it mildly). Most of us would have stopped there and moved to the next research question, while Leonard paused and asked himself, "Based on these findings, what can I personally do to help?" The answer was to team up with others and play a decisive role in the foundation of the African School of Economics (building on a research institute that he had previously created). This renowned institution has since then done a marvelous job at training and promoting brilliant young scholars. This is just one example of what I would call "smart idealism."

AMBUSHES AND ROADBLOCKS ON THE AVENUE TOWARDS SMART IDEALISM

There are plenty of pitfalls threatening the scope of smart idealism. The first is *hypocrisy*, which comes in all shapes and sizes. If somebody hides behind some abstract principles to look the other way, fully knowing that some will face dire consequences from the unwillingness to help, then the person follows the path of that biblical persona Pontius Pilate, who claimed that "I am innocent of this man's blood" while knowingly triggering the painful death of Jesus. Historically, this accusation of hypocrisy can also be targeted at a (rapidly shrinking) community within economics who believe too much in markets always being right. To give an extreme example, a misguided economist could argue that somebody selling an organ is entering willingly into a business transaction. Yet of course we know that a world in which people are so desperate that they consider selling their organs necessarily features inequality levels that are unacceptably high and leave millions of people without any real chances and freedom of choice in life. Obviously, if you are so destitute that in most areas of life you, de facto, do not have any real choice, then by definition you cannot really willingly enter into any business transaction – instead your poverty and deprivation dictate your whole life and you are easy prey for the ruthless. Disregarding such coercion, looking the other way and not trying to tackle this shocking inequality and exploitation would be hypocritical and reveal a total lack of compassion. (This being said, this is a bit of a "strawman argument," as the percentage of economists thinking like that may lie somewhere in the low single digits.)

Another common threat to smart idealism is *paternalism*, with leaders claiming that they know better what people want and need than the citizens themselves. Think of the Nazi fanatics celebrating their idol Hitler as savior of Germany and the world. Did it occur to them that in the last free and fair election on November 1932 the NSDAPs vote share dropped by four percentage points to 33 percent, with two-thirds of voters rejecting the party? Rather than pondering about the meltdown of approval ratings and the increasing evidence for the disastrous consequences of fascism in all dimensions, they first rigged and then abolished multiparty elections.

Or think of those civil servants of the German Democratic Republic (DDR) who actually believed in the project and were convinced they were building a better society (while of course many others marched with them out of fear or opportunism). Why did they never consider the reality of people voting with their feet? Did they never ask themselves the question why – if the DDR was so much better than the Federal Republic of Germany – thousands of East Germans put their lives at risk by fleeing, while not so many desperately tried to get out of West Germany to travel east? And why do the (few remaining?) true believers in North Korea not ask the same question? It appears that incomparably more people try to flee from North Korea to South Korea than the other way around. If you need to build walls around your country to keep your citizens from emigrating, shouldn't that raise a few questions?

In the past, welfare analysis in economics was a rather abstract and theoretical endeavor. While it is useful, it seems important to supplement this classic tool with easy-to-communicate empirical evidence. Thankfully, a group of scholars have put into practice the rather natural idea of simply asking people how satisfied they are with their lives and trying to see what factors are positively associated with life satisfaction. One fruit of these efforts is the annually published "World Happiness Report," which contains a ranking of the happiest countries worldwide and tries to disentangle the major contributing factors.[5] It goes without saying that these findings need to be taken with a pinch of salt, as one can think of reporting bias and various other behavioral biases that may influence differences reported between countries. Imagine, for example, that people from country A moan much more than those of country B, which may render comparisons hard. Still, the results are rather telling: The top ranked countries in the 2023 edition of the report are all peaceful and prosperous democracies with a well-functioning welfare state and broad access to higher education and a high-quality health sector, and largely free from widespread corruption. Gold goes to Finland, followed by Denmark and Iceland. Now, of course, if you are one of the leaders of the Taliban, you may well try to argue that your theocratic rule is exactly what Afghan people want – yet the happiness statistics speak another language: Afghanistan is ranked last (137 out of 137 countries, where data is available). Despite all its imperfections, there is still a fundamental virtue to these statistics, as it allows us to debug phony claims of dictators, fanatics and kleptocrats who claim that they are acting in the interest of their people.

Beyond the aforementioned political spin to combat smart idealism, the toolbox of bad politicians also contains several violent means of *repression*. In various countries around the world, it has become rather clear that the vast majority of the population want a more democratic and less corrupt regime in place, yet the population at large is gagged by a much less numerous yet well-armed and ruthless junta engaging in brutal repression. As argued later, in such situations you need –as the Beatles sang – a "little help from your friends."

Last but not least, consider the question of what "smart" means in "smart idealism" when existing evidence is limited. I would argue that the "smart" stance is to pair open-mindedness with a *healthy critical thought* that may at times border on skepticism about the motives of those proposing given reforms. This mindset characterizes quite well a typical way of approaching problems in the field of political economics. The premise is that not just consumers and producers but also politicians, civil servants and all of us respond to incentives, and that it is reasonable to at least ponder about what the self-interest is of the person taking an initiative. If I go tomorrow to the provost, rector or vice chancellor of my university and propose to increase the salaries of the economics professors in order to raise the attractivity of our institution for future hirings and sketch the potential to build a world-class department that raises abundant third-party funding, I may well, at least in part, hope to also increase my own salary by this initiative. This does not mean that my proposal is necessarily flawed, but it simply means that the "smart" provost would keep some healthy skepticism and would not wholeheartedly believe in the relevance of all elements of my sales pitch.

Similarly, if a colleague of yours proposes a reorganization of your institution, dropping buzz words such as "leaner," "better structured," "modern" and "responding to emerging key challenges" it is not unreasonable to start from the assumption that the person may have some personal skin in the game (increasing power, securing a legacy, pushing some ideology?), and to carefully question the stressed motivation for change. This of course does not mean one should drift into conservatism and reject all change from the outset. Instead, it simply means remaining critical, asking the right questions and requiring solid data for key claims and selling arguments.

BLIND TRUST IN POLITICIANS WOULD BE FATAL

Related to this, one key thing to realize is that we cannot simply rely on our politicians to do the right thing, as either of the two components of smart idealism may be missing. Ideological bias may result in policies falling short of being smart or failing to be idealist, namely when politicians' incentives are distorted. First of all, electoral terms typically of four years result in a bias towards short-run policies (at the detriment of the lengthy but crucial task of building peace), and often there are personal benefits for politicians that distort their decisions. When it comes, for example, to fostering peace, mediating politicians sometimes have distorted incentives that push them to cut shady deals with despots (e.g., allowing them to secure a position on the board of a state-owned company after political retirement). To get the incentives right, public pressure must ensure that the reelection chances of our politicians crucially depend on fostering peace at home and abroad. If voters care about this, then politicians will as well – whether out of intrinsic motivation or purely to get reelected.

If you think that the last paragraph reads a bit too much like an op-ed and would like to hear about actual empirical studies backing this up, here you go: There has been a growing literature in media economics studying what determines the political agenda of elected officials. To cut a long story short, to a substantial extent politicians react most decisively to problems that allow them to score points with key voters or the public at large, and those suffering in silence somewhere in the shadows are all but forgotten. For example, two decades ago the British economists Timothy Besley and Robin Burgess performed a large-scale statistical investigation on the drivers of food aid and calamity relief in the face of natural disasters.[6] And that is where –as expected – politicians' incentives come in: A quantitatively sizable determinant of the scale of government help is the level of newspaper circulation in a given region! Or, as the cynical politician may think, "Why do good if nobody notices it and if doing good does not help *you* do well?"

Similar findings have been recorded in various other contexts around the world. Another telling example is the allocation of funds in a major New Deal relief program in the 1930s. As mentioned in Chapter 7, in various respects this major US welfare state initiative was a great success, yet even for an overall very remarkable public policy, the biases in cash disbursements were sizable. As shown in an influential study, this time by Stockholm's David Strömberg, US counties with many radio listeners received more relief funds than comparable counties where the expansion of radio was still at an earlier stage (even when controlling for sociodemographic factors).[7] By the same token, areas with a higher voter turnout were also more generously served by Uncle Sam.

Beyond media implementation, the attention of public opinion also matters. Follow-up work has investigated how US government response is influenced by whether the public eye is staring at emergency relief efforts or blinking distractedly.[8] Drawing on a large-scale dataset of about 5,000 natural disasters between 1968 and 2002, the authors collected information on whether newsworthy events such as the Olympic Games took place during the same time period. They found that these unrelated headline events led to a squeezing of available news coverage, which crowded out the reporting on natural disasters with harmful consequences. A given disaster was 5 percent less likely to receive relief when taking place during the Olympics! Considering another metric, a natural catastrophe occurring during highest news pressure levels would have to feature six times as many casualties to benefit from the same chance of receiving relief as a comparable disaster taking place in times of lowest news pressure, when journalists are desperate to find something to cover. While this media economics literature has focused on emergency relief and general public spending, the impact of public attention is also very salient when it comes to the realm of conflict behavior, as discussed in what follows.

PROTECTED BY THE PUBLIC EYE

Few are the intellectuals who are as gifted as German poet and playwright Bertolt Brecht for penning a punchline. His following quote from the *Threepenny Opera* says it all: "Denn die einen sind im Dunkeln. Und die anderen sind im Licht. Und man sieht nur die im Lichte. Die im Dunkeln sieht man nicht" ("There are some who are in darkness. And the others are in light. And you see the ones in brightness. Those in darkness drop from sight").[9] As pointed out in this statement, those suffering from poverty and mistreatment are often less visible to the public eye than those enjoying privileges. And let's not be fooled – this lack of transparency and visibility of human suffering is often to the benefit of the despots who rob and enslave their citizens.

History abounds with examples of transitions to peaceful democracy for which the main credit of course goes to domestic activists fighting for their rights, yet where the scrutiny of international public opinion has put pressure on politicians of various countries to support these prodemocracy movements. As mentioned in Chapter 1, the largely "home-grown" democratic transition in South Africa was helped by the fact that after cowardly turning a blind eye for decades, finally international public opinion and the political establishment concluded that the inhumane apartheid state needed to be stopped. They got their act together and put considerable economic pressure on the thug regime in Pretoria, to push it towards prodemocratic reforms.

Related to this, consider the Latin American cases, also touched upon in Chapter 1. When Uruguay's people finally freed themselves from the military junta led by Gregorio Conrado Alvarez in 1985, when Chile's population escaped the autocratic dictatorship of General Augusto Pinochet in 1990 and when the citizens of Peru finally got rid of the autocratic regime of Alberto Fujimori in 2000, it was obviously the domestic population that did the heavy lifting. Still, the mounting discontent across the globe about the human rights violations may well have helped the demise of these three repressive rulers.

Another continent and another time, yet a related pattern: In December 2010, when widespread protests meant that the dictatorial regime of Zine al-Abidine Ben Ali started to crumble, the leading actor was, again, the domestic population, with the supporting role, again, taken by international public opinion, supporting prodemocracy activists. One could add many more examples to this list, stressing the importance of an attentive public eye at home and abroad. The trouble is, however, that politicians have closely followed the powerful action of international public opinion in the past and try nowadays even harder to keep unpopular actions undercover, as discussed in the next section.

ATTACK AND HIDE WHEN THE WORLD IS NOT WATCHING

Some politicians are more skilled and others less, but what defines many of them, is to be as sly as a fox. If it took economists a while to figure out that media attention for major developments such as natural disasters declines in the face of news pressure, politicians seem to have figured it out ages ago and have often timed unpopular measures to take place when the world is distracted. To give two examples, think of Italian prime minister Silvio Berlusconi's emergency decree aimed at freeing imprisoned corrupt politicians, which was adopted on the very same day when the Bel Paese celebrated a qualification for the 1994 FIFA (Soccer) World Cup final. Or think of the sending of Russian troops into Georgia that took place on the opening day of the Summer Olympic Games of 2008. Beyond such examples, a recent study has analyzed systematically the link between news pressure and the timing of military operations for the case study of the Israeli-Palestinian conflict, over the time period 2000–2011.[10] It draws on data of fatalities in this conflict at daily level and confront them with measures of news pressure in the United States, as measured by the relative time devoted on a given day for the first three news stories (that are unrelated to the conflict at hand) in the evening news of three major national channels, NBC, ABC and CBS. Anticipating worries about potential confounders, they focus on the spikes in news pressure that can be attributed to anticipated events announced in advance. These push up the news pressure and span everything from political events, such as presidential inaugurations, general elections and State of the Union addresses, to sport events, such as the FIFA World Cup. The findings are telling: Israeli attacks are more likely to occur when US news the following day is dominated by important predictable events. The idea is that the generals have their plan for attacks readily available but wait for the most politically opportune moment to put it into action.

If from time-to-time you watch spy movies or political thrillers, it won't escape to you that Israel can hardly be considered an average country in terms of military and intelligence capabilities. With Mossad being probably the most famed secret service in the world and unrivalled in several domains of high-tech military weapon development, it is obviously a stronger candidate than many for sophisticatedly timed military attacks taking place according to the media calendar. Any country with average military power may typically have a much harder time at fine-tuning the schedule of attacks, as it will lack the precise intelligence that informs it at every point of time the exact location of enemy targets and will also not have advanced enough arms to carry out targeted first strikes on any desired day. Take, for example, the governments of the DRC or the Philippines, which are already struggling to keep their country from disintegrating in the face of various rebel groups and striving to conquer their share of the cake. It seems hard to conceive that their national armies would be able to carry out such precisely timed attacks as Israel, and hence it seems a priori unclear how representative the aforementioned results are for a country with a more average military power (or, in an economist's jargon, what the so-called external validity of these results is).

To study more broadly the link between international public attention and domestic political violence, I teamed up some years back with a group of University of British Columbia economists, Siwan Anderson, Patrick Francois and Rogerio Santarrosa.[11] "Standing on the shoulders of giants," we have followed the path of the previous paragraphs' study for Israel, but broadened the sample of events studied considerably, to cover the whole African continent and to consider various major international actors, and not just the United States. To illustrate the basic idea, imagine that you recently gained power through a coup in Niger and are at present ruling the country (as happened in July 2023). A nonnegligible part of the state budget stems from foreign aid and the main donor countries typically also matter heavily in terms of foreign direct investment, trade and military cooperation. Hence, like the Israeli army considering strikes against Hamas, the rulers of Niger may also be keen to time unpopular crackdowns at moments when key donors are distracted, for example if there is a major flood in the United States or a presidential election in France. Yet we expect things to be fundamentally different in Niger than in Israel, as Niger – like almost all other countries – lacks the virtually unrivalled secret service and military capacity of Israel. Not just the current military junta, but also the previous elected government has had a hard time to militarily control the entire territory of the state and keep hold on the monopoly of violence perpetrated within Niger's borders. While the current rulers may be tempted to jump on international inattention to repress political opponents and demonstrators asking for democracy, their ability to initiate such crackdowns may be limited by the military's capabilities. This offers a window of opportunity for the opposition to "go undercover" during periods when the public eye is distracted and potential government crackdowns may hence be more threatening.

Drawing on very fine-grained data about conflict events at the daily level of all African countries, bilateral donor link networks between each recipient state and various international donor countries, as well as both natural disasters and elections taking place in the donor states, we benefit from various puzzle pieces to assemble the overall picture. And the patterns that emerge from the statistical investigation of these data is that public inattention matters considerably. When public opinion in key donor countries is not watching, we indeed observe that opposition forces recognize the danger of the hour and scale down all forms of manifestations, peaceful demonstrations and riots. In line with the key premise of economics, the citizens react to incentives and go into hiding when the cameras of the world do not protect them from government crackdowns. Importantly, in some scenarios we also observe a surge in violent actions by the opposition, such as targeted killings. This is consistent with the notion that for murderers the public eye does not offer protection. The higher relative risk of peaceful demonstrations (vis-à-vis the unchanged consequences of engaging in violent actions) may lead to some actors substituting peaceful means of expressions with violent ones, fueling polarization in political deeds.

Overall, the consequences of public inattention are bleak, as the scope for peaceful prodemocratic political expression is severely circumscribed and the civil society is denied the opportunity to benefit from the protection of the international public opinion when hoping for constructive political change. When voting is barred or rigged and social movements are limited in their ability to express themselves, desperation leads many to cling to the last hope: voting with their feet, hoping to find real chances and freedom of choice in greener pastures.

And, actually, when scrutinizing repression events around the world, the statistician crunching these data may substantially underestimate the problem, as the (what game theorists would call "out-of-equilibrium") threat of repression owing to public inattention crowds out much peaceful expression of discontent, and what the data show may only constitute the tip of the iceberg of repressive politics. So when the statistician happily points out that the frequency of violent government repression is still somewhat limited, this may hide a much more dire state of affairs, where the relative calm hides the despair of people who are too frightened to speak up. Thankfully, there is a role to play for all of us, as the recent evidence highlights that scrutiny and attention from the world press and the public at large is a powerful rampart against repression. And conversely, attacks and self-censure happen when the word is distracted by other major news. Thus, next time we hesitate about spending an hour watching grumpy cat videos on social media or, alternatively, reading up on world news and getting involved in public debates, we know what to do.

11 Global Coordination to Curb Conflict

> The structure of world peace cannot be the work of one man, or one party, or one Nation. (...) It must be a peace which rests on the cooperative effort of the whole world.
>
> Franklin D. Roosevelt

> If you want to go fast, go alone. If you want to go far, go together.
>
> Proverb

If in the last few years a handful of wars (e.g., the ones in Syria and in the Ukraine) have received some regular media attention, the same cannot be said for numerous conflicts that have been all but forgotten. While now, for several years, the peace researchers from the Uppsala Conflict Data Program have recorded every year over fifty ongoing conflicts around the world, most of us are, at best, able to name a handful. One particularly gruesome war that is almost completely under the radar of mainstream media has been unfolding for more than a decade now in the Central African Republic. Many people do not even know that this country exists: Some mix it up with the DRC and only few outside Africa would be able to name its capital city (it is Bangui, by the way). This landlocked country that is slightly bigger than France is home to a population of about 5.5 million people and is one of the poorest countries in the world (ranking 188th out of 191 in the 2022 Human Development Index).[1] After gaining independence in 1960 from a brutal and destructive colonization by France, the country has been held back by political instability, ethnic violence, repressive governments and coups. The fifth coup, in 2013 by the mainly Muslim rebel coalition Seleka, ousted President Francois Bozize – who had himself seized power ten years earlier in a coup – and led to an increase in the amount of atrocities committed. This also triggered the establishment of a competing, mainly Christian, armed faction, the anti-Balaka, which itself has a terrible track record when it comes to respecting human rights. Ethnoreligious conflicts have further surged in the Central African Republic over the past years, involving over a dozen rebel groups, and large parts of the country are currently (2024) controlled by bands of thugs armed to their teeth. One factor making a bad situation worse is the tightening grip of Wagner Group mercenaries over various areas in the country. More than a thousand Russian mercenaries are operating at various bases in the country.[2] They have been accused of playing key roles in an ever longer list of brutal massacres, targeting countless locals, Chinese miners, UN peacekeepers and international aid workers. If atrocities happen with chilling frequency, the few reported by international media represent, at best, the tip of the iceberg, as most mass killings of civilians in remote areas never get covered by the media. Anjan Sundaram's new book *Breakup: A Marriage in Wartime* gives a compelling account of how so many lives lost and so much suffering happens in total isolation from the rest of the world.[3]

As has been the case in other countries, such as, for example, Sierra Leone, the DRC and Angola, diamond mining has been at the center of fighting. Controlling these lucrative gems is a key stake, and according to research by the nongovernmental organization (NGO) Global Witness, both the large-scale armed factions of Seleka and anti-Balaka have systematically plundered mining wealth and financed fighting using cash from "blood diamonds" (rough diamonds sold to finance civil wars). The mercenaries of the Russian Wagner Group have also been alleged to be heavily entrenched in the diamond business of the Central African Republic and to be directly involved in killings taking place in and around mining sites.

MONITOR MINING!

But wait, how is this possible? Isn't there a diamond certification scheme, designed to tackle precisely the issue of "blood diamonds"? Yes, there is. The road toward international cooperation to ban sales of conflict diamonds took off in the year 2000 with a meeting between representatives of Southern African diamond-producing countries in Kimberley, Northern Cape province, South Africa. As a next step, ministers from thirty-seven countries and the European Union met in 2002 in the scenic Swiss Alpine town of Interlaken – which links Lake Thun with Lake Brienz and offers a breathtaking view of the mountain massif of Eiger, Mönch and Jungfrau. There they adopted the so-called Kimberley Process Certification Scheme, which spells out the minimum requirements for verifying that rough diamonds are "conflict-free." The Kimberley Process has now been up and running since 2003, with forty-eight individual states and the European Union on board.

Does the continuous presence of the blood diamond trade mean that this certification scheme is a paper tiger? Brand new research from German economists suggests that –while improvable – the Kimberley Process makes an important difference.[4] It is a bit like locking your front door: If a burglar really wants to get in, she or he will find a way, but this will take time and is often not worth the effort. Hence, locking your front door will prevent some but not all burglaries. It is similar for the Kimberley Process. The aforementioned research focuses on conflict occurrences in Africa over recent years and distinguishes between diamond producing and nonproducing areas. They find that not much has changed in the control group of diamond-free regions since the certification scheme's adoption. In contrast, conflict has, relatively speaking, significantly declined since 2003, when the Kimberley Process was introduced. The effect found is massive: Violence has dropped by more than half in diamond areas once the certification scheme was in place.

Yet this good news should not bar our view of the numerous persistent challenges to combat blood diamonds. NGOs and specialists point out that at all levels of the diamond production and cutting process loopholes persist, and that more frequent and stringent controls are needed at various levels to further tackle the fact that our engagement rings may finance the acquisition of AK-47s by warlords and their brutal squads of fighters. Or to go back to the comparison with your front door: Locking it is good, yet maybe you should acquire a stronger lock.

Now, of course, diamonds are only one particular mineral, and many further valuable minerals and metals have been linked to armed conflicts, as discussed earlier. What about them? Can traceability also play a role beyond diamonds? As mentioned in Chapter 4, together with three French colleagues I studied the impact of mining price increases for a variety of minerals and metals, finding that the price spikes of the "commodity supercycle" can account for up to a quarter of the violence in Africa in the early 2000s.[5] In the second part of the article, we tried to go beyond this gloomy conclusion and investigate what the international community can actually do to remediate this sorry state of affairs.

The first question we asked was about the monitoring of multinationals in extractive industries. Would more stringent rules on corporate practice and responsibility (either in the host or home country or internationally) make a difference? It turns out that the answer is "yes"! The detrimental consequences of price booms are much attenuated when mines are exploited by firms that are members of the International Council on Mining Metals, a network of companies promoting corporate social responsibility in the mining industry.

Now, what about traceability and transparency initiatives for other metals and minerals that are comparable to the Kimberley Process for diamonds? We looked at two country-level transparency initiatives, the Extractive Industries Transparency Initiative and the Mineral Certification Scheme of the International Conference on the Great Lakes Region. The former requires its member countries to fully disclose taxes and payments made by mining companies to their governments, while the latter traces the origin of a number of metals and aims to identify mines that are linked to conflicts (through illegal control, taxation and extortion). In the statistical analysis we coded the corresponding variables for the two initiatives, taking into account which countries and minerals were covered from what year onwards. Consistent with the diamond results from earlier, we found that indeed mining transparency is a game-changer, reducing substantially the risk of conflict. These findings call for a step up in international transparency efforts, covering more metals, associating more countries and putting in place more stringent controls.

A CLOSER LOOK AT MULTINATIONALS

While this evidence makes a compelling case for monitoring the international mining sector, what can we say about the multinational firms operating in other sectors? Is their impact good or bad and is there a case for monitoring them as well? Estimating the impact is not easy, as they self-select by investing in places where they expect highest profits. Imagine, for the sake of the argument, that weak domestic institutions and high corruption levels may offer multinationals an edge in negotiations to circumvent stringent environmental rules, but at the same time make it difficult to achieve the stability and predictability required for complex industries. This would mean that the high-tech semiconductor and pharma R&D plants crave strong, democratic institutions, while firms producing primary commodities at the cheapest price using dirty technologies may, under some circumstances, prefer to operate in weak states. This would imply that any correlations between conflict and the number and types of firms may well be spurious and not reflect any causal relationship. Bologna-based Tommaso Sonno has found a smart way to deal with this roadblock.[6] He exploits the fact that some firms have a higher share of outside capital and are hence hit harder by global recessions and banking crises than others. This yields a quasi-random variation in firm growth across space and time, providing fertile ground for a novel statistical inquiry.

If you are a libertarian politician, you may not like his results: Multinational activity is found to significantly raise the risk of conflict. The effect is quantitatively important, as one more affiliate of a multinational firm in a given local area increases the conflict risk by roughly a third. This finding is driven in particular by firms active in land-intensive industries that require large-scale land acquisitions. Beyond conflict, follow-up work also finds that an expansion of multinational activity causes severe loss of forest cover, erodes biodiversity and increases air pollution.[7] In a nutshell, for both ecological as well as conflict-related reasons, it seems important to step up the monitoring of multinational firms, not just domestically, but also in the home country of the firm's headquarters, as well as internationally.

TOGETHER AGAINST TRAUMA!

Growing up among bombs, gun fire and violence is a very traumatizing experience, and this victimization leaves scars years after the shooting has stopped. As we see in Chapter 3, war experience during childhood is reflected in a substantially larger likelihood of engaging in violent crime later in life.[8] As the sample for that study consisted of asylum seekers in Switzerland, it becomes clear that these detrimental effects of childhood victimization even persist in surroundings where crime rates are lower than almost anywhere else in the world. In addition, in the same chapter we reviewed a body of mounting evidence that wars lead to a very salient loss of years of education, with schools either being destroyed or becoming unsafe to attend. Sadly, these lost years of schooling are never really caught up, and result in a lasting loss of productivity and chances in life (call it "human capital" in economist jargon). In turn, being out of luck makes someone an easier prey for rebel recruiters, triggering a vicious cycle of persistent conflict.

The punchline is that there are both immediate and long-run reasons to get children out of war zones as rapidly as possible. In the short run, there is of course the moral imperative to protect them from physical harm. But on top of this there is the long-run threat of childhood conflict exposure leading to trauma and education loss, with the aforementioned feedback loops that make long-run peace harder to achieve. What this means is that getting children out of the immediate theatre of combats is not enough, as even being confined for years in relatively safer makeshift settlements for internally displaced people can lead to serious trauma and may give rise to losing several years of schooling. This is where the responsibility of rich nations comes in: We need to be more generous in admitting more refugees fleeing from war zones and we need to provide them with psychological counselling, free language teaching and immediate school access, to avoid the loss of schooling years. As discussed earlier, the war exposure during childhood/violent crime as adult link can also be broken by offering rapid and wide-ranging access to the local labor market and civic education courses.

DON'T SELL WEAPONS TO BAD PEOPLE

At first sight the maxim of not selling arms to dangerous, cruel and violent people seems a rather intuitive moral imperative. At least, that is what one would think. Yet, very rapidly, counterarguments surge: "Well, we know that this dictatorial country or group does not respect human rights and executes every year scores of innocents, but, you know, it is a valuable ally in fighting against an even greater evil." Or the less refined version of the argument: "Yes, tyrant X is an a.hole, but he is *our* a.hole. Hence, we shall happily sell him arms or train his death squads." A classic example of a rich democracy supporting a group of unsavory characters in the goal of fighting a supposedly even greater evil, is the US involvement in the conflict in Nicaragua. According to the Encyclopedia Britannica, when it comes to the links with the "contras" who fought the left-wing Sandinista government in the 1980s, "the U.S. Central Intelligence Agency played a key role in training and funding the group, whose tactics were decried by the international human-rights community." In fact, the extent of brutal atrocities perpetrated by this counterrevolutionary group was so large that in 1984 the US Congress banned military aid to them.

There are quite a few caveats to this "Realpolitik" reasoning. First of all, one's ally may lose in the fight against the domestic foes, and the arms may be appropriated. That is basically what happened in Afghanistan in 2021 when the United States hastily withdrew their troops. As pinpointed recently in a *Foreign Policy* headline, "The Taliban are now arms dealers," selling left-behind US weapons to anti-Western terrorists around the world. Further, related security hazards include the risk that the dubious ally changes side and suddenly points the received arms against their previous sponsor, or that supporting a bad leader attracts the fury of the disenchanted population. As discussed previously, a large-scale statistical analysis has shown that in recent decades US military aid has on average backfired and fueled anti-American sentiment.

Another set of arguments used to try to justify making money with arms sales to bad regimes or violent armed groups is: "If I don't sell them arms, somebody else will." This reasoning is also flawed. Let's first debug it from a logical point of view: If warlord X buys her or his arms from you, this means that you are the cheapest supplier, and if you are out of the market then switching to a new supplier will typically cost more (hence, leading to fewer or less powerful weapons for the same budget). Furthermore, switching takes time, during which violence may stall, which could give peace talks a welcome window of opportunity.

You find this pure logic a bit tentative and fuzzy? Well, let's try the empirical evidence. It is obviously challenging to understand statistically if weapon exports do fuel violence or whether they are simply the symptom of escalation in a place that turned violent to start with. One could imagine that it is all demand-driven: If you are under threat of a military junta you are keen to purchase arms, while if you are a small democracy surrounded by peaceful neighbor countries your military budget may be tiny. And supply simply serves demand, without having any causal effect. Thankfully, Lausanne economist Quentin Gallea came up with a clever way to investigate this.[9] He drew on a dataset tracking all African countries from 1992 to 2011 and started from the premise that you don't frequently switch supplier (as weapon systems need to be compatible) and that arms exports depend on whether the producer country is involved in an armed conflict. Imagine that you are "hooked" on Russian arms and now Russia has invaded Ukraine and has no more weapons to spare and to sell to you. Or that you traditionally use US weaponry, and the United States tries in a given year to free the world of a dictator (say, Saddam Hussein, Slobodan Milošević or Muammar Gaddafi) and runs low on ammunition to sell to you. One can think of such conflict involvements of arms producers as a random (or exogenous) source of variation in the quantity of arms exported to particular African countries in the study sample. And, of course, supplier networks differ widely among countries. Hence, not all African states face weapon import shortages in the same year. This statistical variation over space and time allows us to estimate what the effect is of selling one more batch of arms.

The news isn't good: Wider arms availability leads to a surge in violence against civilians perpetuated by the state or rogue rebel groups, in battle-related fatalities and in the number of refugees forced to flee their home country. The impact is sizable, as increasing the value of the explanatory variable (log of arms imports) by a bit more than 10 percent yields a rise in the risk of a new internal conflict breaking out by a bit less than a tenth of the baseline risk. And when it comes to refugee flows, the computations suggest that a one-year stop in European arms sales to Africa would result in a half a million fewer people having to flee. To take stock, arms-producing countries have it in their hands to reduce the ability of bad regimes to massacre their civilians. Again, international cooperation plays a major role in this endeavor, as a global tightening of regulations for arms sales would also magnify the impact of the withdrawal of any single supplier, as replacement would be harder and slower to find. Hence, this is a prime example of global cooperation achieving more than the sum of all parts.

MAKE TRADE NOT WAR?

When discussing earlier how microfoundations of the contact hypothesis could be modeled, a key premise was that more joint business between groups makes the break-out of hostilities less likely. Let us now dig deeper into this relationship. The basic idea is that when you rely heavily on bilateral trade with a given partner country, war would be prohibitively costly and thus unlikely to happen. Say, for the sake of the argument, if the United States were to attack South Korea, the disruption of the US economy would be huge, as South Korea produces many components for the mighty US high-tech industry. Similarly, any conflict of Canada with the United States would be badly damaging for both, as Canada–US trade in goods and services represented about two-thirds of Canada's total global trade in 2022, and Canada is the largest trade partner of the United States.[10] The analogous logic was used in the aftermath of World War II to create the European Coal and Steel Community – the precursor of the European Union – to make renewed fighting among Western European powers all but impossible. Pioneering statistical studies have indeed found a strong correlation between bilateral trade and peaceful bilateral relations, and the notion that trade fosters peace has been widely popularized beyond academic circles into the mainstream policy space.[11] Whenever German policymakers were challenged for their soft stand concerning human rights violations by key trading partners, they used to repeat like a mantra: "Wandel durch Handel!" (i.e., change through trade). Or in the words of Immanuel Kant, "It is the spirit of commerce, which cannot coexist with war and which sooner or later takes hold of every nation."

Sounds good, right? Or is there a problem with this? Having made it to the eleventh chapter of this book, you can see the objection coming. Well, the trouble is of course that correlation is not causality. If Switzerland negotiates a major deal with Austria, then this may be rather a consequence than a cause of the peaceful relationships between these countries. Put differently, it may be plausible to think that trade has no impact whatsoever and is simply a reflection of whether relations are good or not – think, for example, about the trade of NATO member states with Russia that collapsed after Putin's invasion of Ukraine.

But isn't there a way to get at causality? Well, there is. Three French economists, Philippe Martin, Thierry Mayer and Mathias Thoenig, investigated some years ago the complex relationships between bilateral and multilateral trade, on the one hand, and peace, on the other.[12] Their article with the telling title "Make trade not war?" uses random variation in the propensity to trade of a given country pair (drawing on the remoteness of the countries in question and the impact of the introduction of the "generalized system of preferences," championed by the UN). Armed with this statistical toolkit they find that trade is a bit of a mixed bag: While bilateral trade reduces the risk of hostilities for a given country pair, the impact of multilateral trade openness is the opposite. Take China and South Korea: If their bilateral trade skyrockets, they are much less likely to go to war against each other, yet if globalization makes both of them much more integrated in international trade with dozens of trade partners, their bilateral risk of militarized disputes goes up! Both of these effects are in line with the aforementioned logic that interdependence fosters peace: Bilateral trade makes China and South Korea more interdependent, while multilateral trade in a globalized world *reduces* their mutual dependence, and hence drives down the opportunity cost of war. To the extent that, overall, the risks of hostilities are greatest for countries within striking distance (say, Russia is more likely to invade a neighboring country than to attack New Zealand), regional economic integration appears to be a key policy for peace, as highlighted by the success story of the European Union in terms of peacebuilding.

As pinpointed in a handbook chapter by my colleague Mathias Thoenig, countries face a delicate geopolitical trade-off when deciding with whom to trade.[13] Increasing interdependence with a potential rival (say, the United States with China) increases the opportunity cost of war and hence makes hostilities a priori less likely. Yet if war still breaks out, it is accordingly much more damaging. In contrast, promoting "America First" and cutting ties with China may reduce vulnerabilities, but could lead to an increase in the risk of war owing to a drop in interdependence. While the Republicans may not like the last sentence, they may be keener on the next one: What this analysis also implies, is that you don't want to have *asymmetric* dependence, where you depend more on your rival than the other way around.

But could there not be an additional geopolitical "footprint" of globalization, in which lucrative world trade fosters the incentives to step up international coordination? This is what my former PhD advisee Quentin Gallea and I investigated a few years back.[14] We started out creating for each point on earth an index value of strategic importance for global trade flows. Among the world's major choke points, there are typically important straits (think of the Strait of Gibraltar or the Strait of Hormuz) or canals (such as the Suez Canal or the Panama Canal). As expected, strategically more valuable spots are, on average, more combated (you may be keener to conquer Gibraltar than a random village in the Argentinian pampas). Yet when investigating as a next step how globalization may have altered the nexus between trade-centrality and conflict risk, we found a startling result: In periods of high trade, strategic hotspots of world trade became – if anything – *safer*! This is in line with the notion that when push comes to shove, there is scope for stepping up international cooperation and coordination. And one hard to capture but rather credible virtue of general interdependence is to create ground conditions for reinforcing international collaboration.

To take stock, and cut a long story short, moving from a world with all countries being autarkic, without any trade, to a world where nations are more interdependent, seems good news overall in terms of peace. However, shifts from regional trade clubs to a globalized planet and back are a mixed blessing that involves a series of complex trade-offs. Still, the best bet for turning worldwide commercial flows into a force for good is international coordination, which may be helped by the fact that working together fosters prosperity.

DEMOCRATIC PEACE

The idea that the global spread of democracy may curb conflicts dates at least as far back as Immanuel Kant's famous book *Perpetual Peace*, first published in 1795.[15] Since then, the idea has intrigued scholars around the world, and in recent decades the availability of better data coverage has allowed scholars in international relations to investigate the democracy/peace nexus statistically. As discussed in Chapter 4, there exists clear-cut evidence that democracies may be no less likely to fight against autocracies (think of the Gulf War of 1990–1991).[16] Yet it is excessively rare to see one democracy fielding its troops against another democratic country. One of the reasons for this is that political prowar bias is on average lower in democracies, as those deciding on war (the population) have also to bear its costs. It follows that strengthening democratic rights worldwide should –at least in the long-run – reduce the scope for fighting. The trouble is that since 2006 global democracy levels have not increased but declined every year.[17] Challenges range from populists within mature democracies to propaganda by autocrats, who explain to their population why they are supposedly better off ruled by a dictator. Incidentally, we know such a claim couldn't be more wrong: Statistical evidence clearly shows that democracy results in peace and prosperity, better health outcomes and greater life satisfaction. We have all been lulled by getting so used to living in a democracy that we fatally take it for granted. We shouldn't. History is full of examples of democracies dying and being replaced by evil regimes that have destroyed generations of people. The fight to keep democracy alive and kicking never stops – and like watering our favored plant, it requires regular attention and care. Checks and balances and free media need to be strengthened for combating the enemy within (populists, antidemocratic demagogues, postfascists, etc.). And democracies need to signal that they are reliable partners to "swing states" flirting with autocracy. One problem of recent years is that the major democratic powers have been regularly seen as hypocrites, preaching human rights abroad but supporting cruel regimes. They have been talking about solidarity and cooperation, while hoarding masses of COVID-19 vaccines until after the expiry date and quibbling about refugee admission quotas. Moreover, policies linked to foreign aid and market access for poorer nations can hardly be described as overly generous.... And the cherry on the cake is that the rich who have caused much of the global warming hope to share the burden of cleaning up the mess.

Don't be fooled: A global strengthening of democracy is the only way forward, and despite all their imperfections (well-run) democracies have been the only regimes in human history that allow people from all population groups to benefit from a wide menu of rights and liberties. Overall, people in, say, Sweden can choose their profession, their place to live, their sexual orientation, their partner, their religion, their political stand and so on, which are freedoms that have been denied to most people in most societies since Antiquity. Of course, not all is rosy, and even in Sweden not everybody can really exercise all these rights (e.g., migrants without a valid permit). Still, we need to realize how comparatively lucky we are to live in a democracy, and we need to actively engage in preserving it. And the best "soft power" available that makes it harder for autocrats to keep afloat is to lead by example: If today's democracies are not only perceived as peaceful and prosperous, but also as kind, open-minded and generous, more people will be keen to deepen peaceful civic engagement to oust their bad regime and join the club. And, similarly, more people in democracies will think twice before casting their vote for an antidemocratic party, realizing that if the demagogues get elected, this may have been their last free and fair vote. Last but not least, small open economies will realize that their interests are best served in a rules-based global order rather than in a world where they are bullied by the closest located superpower in whose self-defined zone of influence they happen to find themselves situated (and their destiny may be even worse if placed at the border of competing zones of influence, which may subject them to being in the combat zone of a proxy war).

HEAT AND HATE

Besides the dire state of global democracy, the world is struggling with another global challenge to peace that requires global solutions, namely fossil fuel dependency and the ensuing global warming. As discussed in Chapter 4, fossil energy rents tend to fuel several types of conflict, from civil wars and mass killings of civilians to inter-state wars. The first best solution at global level is to accelerate the green transition away from fossil fuels. As I highlighted recently in an e-book edited together with Christian Gollier, the way forward is to bet on decentralized clean energy that employs local labor and benefits the local community.[18] This not only contributes to com-bat climate change but also curbs rent seeking and violent appro-priation incentives. And, again, achieving a rapid green transition is only possible with "all hands-on deck," highlighting the scope for international coordination.

Besides preventing as much further global warming as possi-ble, there is the need to cope with the climatic changes that have already occurred in recent decades. And there is already solid sta-tistical evidence that higher temperatures lead to a surge in conflict risk.[19] Various mechanisms are to blame, stretching from reduced opportunity costs of conflict owing to lower harvesting yields and resource competition to psychological explanations (lab experiments have shown that uncomfortable heat may trigger aggressivity – as most parents may have experienced with their kids, even without a lab experiment).

A specific negative effect of more frequent droughts has attracted a fair amount of scholarly attention recently, namely the escalating conflicts between sedentary crop famers and (semi) nomadic cattle herders, taking place with particular intensity in Africa's Sahel zone. In recent work, my former PhD advisee Ulrich Eberle, my colleague Mathias Thoenig and I estimated the impact of temperature shocks on conflict likelihoods at local level throughout Africa.[20] We found that a one-degree Celsius increase in temperature leads to a 54 percent increase in conflict probability in mixed areas (with farmers and herders), as opposed to a 17 percent increase in nonmixed regions. We then put together these local-level estimates with fine-grained projections of global warming (in which some regions such as the Sahel are estimated by geoscientists to warm more than others, owing to soil characteristics, among other factors). This allowed us to simulate how projected global warming until 2040 impacts the risk of war. In the absence of such herder/farmer clashes, the number of conflicts were to rise by a quarter. Yet in contrast, filtering in this additional layer of complexity (i.e., more resource competition in areas that are projected to heat up disproportionally), leads to an upward revision of estimates: We fear a daunting surge of conflict events by a third.

Contrary to some sensationalist media reports brandishing the slogan "the Sahel is on fire," our prime goal is of course to find solutions. As shown in the last part of our paper, besides the best policy of abandoning fossil fuels altogether, a strengthening of formal property rights can help. If in the past informal arrangements have done a good job of keeping intergroup relations peaceful, the mounting heat now drives nomads to travel earlier and further, putting strain on historical agreements. Hence, the need arises for putting in place well-defined and well-protected formal property rights. Further, recent research by Kai Gehring and Paul Schaudt has emphasized another clever policy approach: an index-based livestock insurance scheme.[21] They studied empirically a Kenyan program which provides automated, preemptive payouts to pastoralists affected by droughts. By limiting the scope of desperately moving cattle to far-away, unknown pastures, the insurance cash is found to strongly reduce drought-induced conflict. To the extent that pastoralists and their cattle do not typically just move within but also across national borders, these policy approaches will require international coordination.

To take stock, all the policies showcased in this chapter have in common a distinctively international dimension, in which global cooperation and coordination matter heavily for the prospects of success. The first best option would be to get all countries on board. If this is not feasible, at least the "club" of rich democracies should get their act together and raise their efforts to make progress towards tackling these key challenges. So far, many of these dimensions have been a bit off the radar of the political agenda, as they are not so easy to communicate in the next election campaign. Still, being caught up in short-termism and scoring points with swing voters may prove disastrous. If democracies lose sight of the crucial challenges of our time, including climate change, the crisis of democracy and record-high numbers of conflicts around the globe, they leave the door open to autocracies that do not suffer from short-termism (many despots cling to power for decades) and can shape the international system in a way that benefits their grip on power, yet does not help solving any of the aforementioned challenges, and ultimately means that all of us lose out.

PART IV The Art of Peace

Take-Home Messages

12 Conclusion

There are but two powers in the world, the sword and the mind. In the long run the sword is always beaten by the mind.

Napoleon Bonaparte

What a road trip the book has taken, travelling through various methodological and disciplinary terrain, from the arid drylands of economics to the fertile fields of political science, while even trespassing from time to time into the hidden gardens of sociology and history. The topics covered have been equally diverse and rich. When we set sail on this journey together, we started investigating common misperceptions and studying success stories of policies that worked.

Then we embarked on a difficult leg of the expedition, facing the harsh reality of what wars entail in terms of human suffering. Far from romanticized blockbuster accounts of fighting and from cynical (and false) statements that wars are good business, the bleak reality has emerged. We have been able to draw on the work of courageous colleagues striving to obtain numbers of death tolls that are as accurate as possible for various forms of political violence. This daunting and depressing task yields chilling insights, with the lives wasted, owing to conflict, being in the dozens and dozens of millions. In addition, not just lives are wasted but also livelihoods. As we discussed, wars entail a drastic collapse of economic output, leaving a given country almost a fifth (18 percent) poorer than before the breakout of hostilities, with the recovery being excessively slow and dragging on for decades.[1] If some years ago it was harder to explain how interconnected the world has become, this has tragically changed with Putin's invasion of Ukraine. The shock waves of this catastrophe have not only caused immense pain and suffering for the Ukrainian population but have also had widespread repercussions around the world, including surging inflation in food prices, refugee flows, the fear of World War III and nuclear Armageddon, supply chain disruptions, recessionary pressures in various countries and surging military budgets.

Yet, sadly, misfortunes never come singly, and a conflict is hardly a one-off event. Beyond the immediate deaths, pain and devastation, it also alters, with lasting effect, the track on which a given country progresses – or regresses. It is like having a car accident on a narrow bridge which not only injures the passengers but also destroys the bridge and forces the travelers to wade through muddy water full of vortices, which entails the risk of another disaster. Or imagine yourself in a country without much of a social safety net and defunct public transport when you have just lost your job: If you don't have savings, you may be forced out of your flat and have to sell your only transport option, which makes it harder to find a new job. And the longer you remain unemployed the more you lose your professional skills, adding a further layer of difficulty in getting back on track.

As we noted in some detail, violence today sows the seeds of future fighting through a series of vicious cycles. First of all, persistent poverty creates vicious cycles of deprivation and disputes. Namely, it provides the breeding ground for violence, as the lack of income and perspectives makes it relatively more appealing to join an armed rebellion. This, in turn, further impoverishes the country, which keeps the vicious cycle going. Yet physical reconstruction is not even the hardest part of the road to recovery. Rebuilding houses, roads and bridges is –if anything – more straightforward and quicker than rebuilding trust between previous foes. In fact, wars tear the social fabric of society apart, which in turn hinders postconflict reconstruction. Put differently, hate and distrust in the aftermath of fighting often trigger revenge wars further down the road, taking a country down a spiral of enduring hostilities. And unfortunately, this isn't even the end of the story, as on top of the poverty- and social capital-related vicious cycles there are negative feedback loops at an individual level, where war exposure leads to a loss of schooling years as well as psychological trauma, which both make the person easier prey for being enlisted in violent activities later in life. These various vicious cycles also imply that making peace today yields not only immediate gains but also dynamic benefits ranging far into the future, which one may want to call a peace multiplier.

After this hopefully compelling account of how armed conflict robs people not only of their family members and livelihood but also of their future perspectives, and the need to act decisively and rapidly for fostering peace, we took a step back in the second part of the book and tried to understand the root causes of war. Like a doctor, we need to know what causes a medical condition before being able to administer the best possible treatment. Drawing on numerous recent empirical studies, we first discussed the key role of negative economic shocks that reduce the opportunity cost of fighting and make it easier and cheaper for warlords and rebel entrepreneurs to recruit fighters for their violent cause. What also contributes to an explosive concoction are ethnic rivalries that can be skillfully exploited by cynical politicians and malicious rabble-rousers. Last but not least, the riches of Mother Nature are sadly often more of a curse than of a blessing, with fossil fuels and minerals constituting a cherished bounty to capture.

Yet beyond motivating violent appropriation, natural resource rents also fuel the risk of a civil war dragging on over decades by providing a funding source for both the government and its opponents. While would-be dictators are abundant around the globe, those that manage to keep afloat and constantly feed an (expensive) machinery of armed fighting and devastation need a constant inflow of cash. If one key source of financing is the stolen spoils of nature, in other instances it is foreign funding that leads to proxy wars between fighting factions supported by foreign powers.

After all the diagnostic tests and lab exams, the doctor finally administers the treatment. Armed with the insights of the first two parts of the book, in the third part we were finally ready to examine which institutions and policies are able to reduce the scope for armed conflict. What all the advocated policy approaches have in common is that they require both a balanced consideration of interests of the whole of society, going beyond self-interest, and that they are based on empirical evidence. Put differently, if me, myself and I are the only three people on earth who matter to me or if I am immune to statistical evidence for updating my prejudices and unwarranted priors, I may indeed not have the right mindset for positive change.

After having documented how important it is to pair good intentions with evidence-based policies, I have coined a term for this altruistic open-mindedness, namely smart idealism. And given that many leaders either lack the "smart" or the "idealism," we cannot simply rely on our politicians to do the right thing. Ideological bias may result in policies falling short of being smart, or failing to be idealist, namely when politicians' incentives are distorted. Electoral terms of around the typical four years result in a bias towards short-run policies (at the detriment of the lengthy but crucial task of building peace), and often there are personal benefits for politician when cutting shady deals with despots (e.g., a position on the board of a state-owned company after political retirement).

To get the incentives right, public pressure must make sure that the reelection chances of our politicians crucially depend on fostering peace at home and abroad. If voters care about this, then politicians will as well – whether out of intrinsic motivation or just to get reelected. As we have seen, recent evidence highlights that scrutiny and attention from the world press and the public at large has been a powerful rampart against repression (and, conversely, attacks happen when the world is distracted by other major news). And series of successful transitions to peaceful democracy pinpoint the crucial role of public opinion support and international pressure.

Importantly, your voice does not just matter if you live in a country ruled by a despot or kleptocrat and if you peacefully push for democratic change. Every one of us should care and can make a positive difference. As we have seen, many key policies require international coordination, and even if you are lucky enough to be a citizen of a peaceful and prosperous nation you are a stakeholder of global peace and can help –as a voter and member of civic society – to provide incentives for your domestic government to do the right thing and be a facilitator rather than blocker of positive change.

So far there has been much talking in this chapter about "doing the right thing," "positive change," "evidence-based smart policies" and so on. A bit vague, isn't it? This is why in what follows we shall synthesize a set of key principles, institutions and policies that are part of what one could call the *peace formula*, which has been discussed at length throughout the book.

DEMOCRACY, DEMOCRACY, DEMOCRACY

While democracy on its own is not a sufficient condition that guarantees peace in all circumstances, having a democratic voice is a central pillar without which peace –both domestically and internationally – cannot thrive in the long run. We have seen that having fair political representation drives down incentives for violent insurgency, tilting the trade-off between peaceful voting versus overthrowing the regime in favor of the nonviolent option. Further, democracy champions the scope for peacefully bargaining, by acting as a commitment device, guaranteeing future power access to all groups. Last but not least, elections reveal information on relative group support, which reduces asymmetric information and the fog of uncertainty that can favor the onset of hostilities. One of the reasons why dictatorships often crumble unexpectedly lies in the dictator's inability to gain accurate information of the population's preferences and support – or would you directly tell your ruler that you disapprove of the regime if that gets you sent straight to jail and torture?

Obviously, democracy is a multidimensional concept encompassing, among other things, representation and enfranchisement for electing leaders, as well as a battery of key civic rights and checks and balances. Unpacking this multifaceted black box, studies have stressed a series of key aspects of the democratic rule of law. First of all, fair representation of the whole population and all societal groups decisively reduces the scope for intergroup conflict, for example along ethnic, linguistic or religious lines. We have in particular revisited empirical evidence highlighting the paramount importance of extending the electoral franchise to the whole population. Especially in multiethnic countries, it has been documented that there is key importance in the set of safeguards against a tyranny of the majority, including power-sharing arrangements, coalition governments, proportional representation, bicameralism and adequate representation of all groups for key positions in the administration and police. Beyond case study evidence, ranging from Northern Ireland to Switzerland, where power-sharing has successfully ended long-lasting intergroup struggle, there is systematic statistical evidence for the peace-promoting potential of power-sharing across a large number of countries. While we have also stressed a series of caveats and risks –especially during the tricky transition to a young democracy – the key role of international support and checks and balances has also been highlighted, as illustrated, for example, by the democratization of postfascist powers in the aftermath of World War II.

Democracy also matters heavily beyond domestic politics. The importance of a rules-based international geopolitical order has also been highlighted. Rivalry between major powers can fuel proxy wars in third states and trigger perilous (nuclear) arms races. One key statistical result in international relations is that democracies go much less often to war against other democracies, hence the road to curbing interstate disputes is to boost the share of nations that are adopting democracy. The underlying logic is quite straightforward: If you bear the costs of an unwarranted war –having, for example, to carry your son to his grave – you may be less keen to support hawkish policies than if you and your junta are shielded from personal sacrifices and get their hands on disproportionate shares of potential war bounties. Importantly, democratic major powers can pave the way for fruitful international cooperation when they lead by example. If the world's greatest democracies can show off convincing political, social, ecological and economic performance and fairness, their soft power and international influence will grow, while if they can be accused of hypocrisy and double standards, this is grist to the mill for autocrats who are resisting democratic change.

SECURITY GUARANTEES AND STATE CAPACITY

Drawing on several recent studies, we have seen that Maslow's pyramid of needs is also echoed in the politics of peace. Security is a fundamental human need, and if it is not provided, all other public policies are bound to fail. Moreover, putting in place any peace process requires security warranties – or would you lay down your arms as a rebel leader if this was likely the last free decision of your life? We can think of at least two aspects of security guarantees. The first is that the state holds the monopoly of legitimate violence. If a state is not strong enough, then the vacuum is filled by warlords, rebel entrepreneurs and organized crime syndicates. Examples are numerous and range from historical Sicily to present-day Somalia. Obviously being prosperous helps to step up fiscal and legal capacity and warrant sufficient fiscal revenues that foster the state's control of the territory and a wide-ranging coverage with public services. Yet a key role is also played by clever policy choices, as illustrated by the US New Deal in the interwar period, which both stepped up (welfare) state capacity and promoted national cohesion.

The second aspect is that sometimes you cannot do it all by yourself, and you need a little help from your friends (to combine the evergreen lyrics of Eric Carmen and the Beatles). International support is key, both for rebuilding the economy and state capacity, as through the "Marshall Plan" in the aftermath of World War II, as well as for providing military support directly. While we have encountered ample evidence that channeling cash to cronies backfires, a broad-based international peacekeeping support has been shown to significantly reduce risks of atrocities. Hence, UN blue helmets are clearly part of the major components of the *peace formula*.

PROMOTING PRODUCTIVITY AND PEACE

With the exception of a limited number of sadists who actually enjoy violence and killing, most people choose a quiet, law-abiding life when this option is on the menu. To back up this claim, consider the classic economist "revealed preferences" argument, and apply it to EU member states, in many of which crime rates are, relatively speaking, low and most people never commit a violent crime. Why, then, in other countries –say, the DRC, Yemen, Syria or Sudan – do a substantial number of people join armed militias instead of pursuing a nonviolent professional career? Well, to put it bluntly, it's because the state has failed them, and a "nonviolent professional career" is anything but easy. To borrow Karl Marx's term of a "reserve army," you can think of an always well-stocked reservoir of desperate young people out of luck and struggling to make ends meet who become easy prey for rebel recruiters. Hence, the first best remedy seems obvious: Reduce this "reserve army" of potential rebel recruits, by providing better opportunities in the domestic economy. For this purpose, public policies need to provide more and better schooling, better access to hospitals and medication, and active labor market policies that create jobs. As shown in a series of recent empirical studies, these measures of promoting work are overall very effective at raising the opportunity cost of foregone labor, and thereby reducing the incentives for armed conflict involvement.

Obviously, investing in these core public policies requires substantial financial means, and a cash-strapped country crumbling under foreign debt and suffering from protectionism abroad for exporting its goods may find it difficult to raise the necessary funds. And this holds even if the country is run by a competent government keen to boost the welfare of its people (which, evidently, is not always the case). What may this well-intentioned government do if rich democracies do not help? Well, it may come up with ingenious yet dodgy ways of raising cash, for example by selling passports to shady individuals around the world. Or, even more likely, it may turn to rich autocracies to fund its investments, with often dire long-run effects: lasting dependency and indebtment, crumbling infrastructure imported "off the shelf" that does not create positive spillover effects on the local labor market and an erosion of domestic democratic processes. Are we so cheap and miserly that we want to fuel –by help omission – a world like this? In the light of the evidence in this book, the answer is a clear "no"! Helping a failing state to get back on its feet, strengthen its institutions and promoting prosperity and peace is an excellent investment – both on moral grounds and when following a consequentialist logic of fostering peace worldwide. Now, as always, the devil lies in the details and the exact modalities of each and every program matter. As seen in this book, disbursing cash or valuable goods that can easily be appropriated will under some circumstances backfire, while productive investments in education, health and employment on average prove very successful.

FOSTERING TRUST AND RECONCILIATION

As discussed at length, the contact hypothesis from psychology translates well into game-theoretic conflict models of economists and is in line with various recent empirical findings. The logic is simple but powerful. If both groups have positive "fundamentals," that is, are cooperatively inclined, the main risk of conflict arises from miscoordination and misinterpretation of random events. We know the story from so many "opposites attract" romantic comedies. When the stars of the film start out as foes, their prejudices make them interpret even kind gestures by the other as insults and provocations, while after getting to know each other better they build trust and begin to understand the underlying kindness that directs the actions of their future sweetheart. As cheesy and predictable (yet enjoyable to simple minds as mine) these movies are, the underlying idea of mistrust being self-perpetuating is actually in line with the logic of dynamic game-theoretic models. Further, the fact that (fair and non-discriminatory) contact fosters intergroup trust is consistent with recent scientific evidence. As noted in this book, "natural experiments" stretching from Spain to Nigeria and from India to Iraq show that exogenous surges in exposure to people from other groups tend to reduce prejudice and foster open-mindedness and national identity as opposed to ethnic identity.

While the aforementioned findings have focused on "normal times" in the absence of conflict, we have seen that well-designed intergroup interactions in the context of reconciliation ceremonies have the potential to rebuild depleted trust – even in the aftermath of particularly vicious and brutal intergroup attacks. Now, importantly, reconciliation efforts have not always been limited to reestablishing contact between estranged groups. In several contexts, the government has attempted some kind of "positive indoctrination," or call it "reversed or rewired hate propaganda." While in some cases love and understanding was preached between former foes, in other cases hate speech was directed against a third group that was viciously scapegoated, leading to discrimination carrying on until today. The punchline is that even well-intended propaganda remains ... well, propaganda. Brainwashing people always constitutes a dangerous slippery slope towards autocratic rule. As shown in recent research, the most promising intervention may be –if anything – to nudge people into stepping up their critical thought!

GREEN ENERGY TRANSITION

When first reading about the "green energy transition" in Chapter 1, your first hunch may have been "Wow, what a buzz word green transition has become; it now even appears in books about conflict, to which it is tangential at best." Well, not quite. As we have seen, our fatal fossil fuel addiction is not at all unrelated to conflict but is actually a major driver of wars around the world through a series of mechanisms. First of all, oil and gas reserves have more often than not had detrimental effects on politics. The side effects of the riches of the soil include the rise of autocratic rentier states and soaring corruption (even in democracies), as well as a higher likelihood of civil conflicts, civilian massacres and interstate wars, as documented in a series of statistical studies. Further, the global warming caused by our reckless and irresponsible energy policies has also had direct impacts on political stability, leading to a robustly measurable surge in the risk of conflict. This is due, among other factors, to a plunge in agricultural activities in arid areas and the related resource competition between different groups. The escalating conflicts in the Sahel region provide a sad illustration of this.

So, what can we do? We need to get out of oil, gas and coal as rapidly as possible and bet on renewable energies such as water, solar and wind. They provide a "double dividend": Besides the clear-cut environmental benefits, they also entail a series of desirable political features. If well organized, these modes of energy production are more decentralized, which makes wide-ranging appropriation harder and hence cuts incentives for political rent-seeking.[2] These sustainable energy sources also have the potential to provide local jobs, which drives up the opportunity cost of conflict. Last but not least, these energy sources are not only better in terms of limiting global warming but they also lead to less local pollution than dirty fossil fuel extraction, thereby curtailing the scope for local grievances against the state. Thus, measures to save the environment also help to foster sound politics.

INTERNATIONAL INTERDEPENDENCY AND COORDINATION

Many of the grand challenges faced by humanity in the twenty-first century – ranging from international warfare over the global crisis of democracy to climate change – require international cooperation. The trouble is obviously that the world's superpowers are at each other's throats, in the midst of a new Cold War (which we all hope will not escalate further). Hence, to make progress, beyond wishful thinking, we may want to focus on policy solutions that lie in the interest of all the world's nations, or alternatively, which can be quite successfully implemented even if only backed by a "coalition of the willing."

One first policy dimension that by its very nature exceeds country borders, is international trade. As discussed earlier, an interconnected world is safer than one in complete autarky. Yet switching from regional trade "clubs" to a fully globalized world does not necessarily enlarge the scope for peace, as a very global outlook reduces interdependence with one's neighboring countries, hence reducing the opportunity costs of a bilateral war. Furthermore, when it comes to trade between faraway countries, such as, say, between the United States and China, there are complex trade-offs. More bilateral trade increases the opportunity cost of a major war, which is a priori good news for peace, yet if a conflict were to still break out, its disruption would have a wider range. To balance these countervailing forces, an important geoeconomic lesson is that mutual dependence should ideally be balanced, to avoid being "blackmailed" by a trade partner.

A particular sector of activity is the weapons industry. Recent evidence suggests that a major caveat applies to this sector: Selling arms to bad regimes is not a good idea and leads to soaring violence. As shown in recent research, this association goes beyond a pure correlation, and there is indeed a causal impact. So if you have been selling arms to unsavory individuals, mumbling some bogus justifications, know that Pilate-style washing of your hands does not work for shady arms deals. Another caveat concerns trade in fossil fuels. If we are hooked on cheap gas from a petrol-state, we not only contribute to global warming but also keep a bad regime in place, with negative global repercussions.

Beyond responsible trade policy that filters in economic, political and humanitarian considerations, what role does international business play? Are multinationals a force of good, leading to technology transfers and fostering prosperity and peace? It would be a nice story, and very convenient for the countries where these global players have their headquarters. Sadly, the fairytale does not match reality. Recent evidence suggests that multinationals –if anything – have a detrimental impact, especially when working in land-intensive sectors (think of the palm oil-heavy spread that you put on your bread in the morning) or in the mining sector. Thankfully, our tool kit contains various policy solutions. As the cherry on the cake, they do not even require all countries to get on board. The economic might of rich democracies is so strong that even on their own they can make a difference (although, of course, it would be even better to get everybody enlisted). In particular, as shown in Chapter 11, transparency and traceability initiatives, and a closer monitoring of corporate social responsibility have a significant impact in reducing the scope for armed fighting.

Last but not least, there is a case to be made for rich democracies (and of course all other countries) to step up their generosity in admissions of refugees. As discussed in Chapter 3, war exposure not only leads to immediate pain and suffering but also results in lasting trauma and lost years of education, thus triggering vicious cycles of future instability. We need to offer rapid admission to larger numbers of war refugees, and provide immediate school access as well as language courses. Each child should have the right to grow up in safety and accumulate positive experiences and knowledge.

While of course political leaders play key roles for the implementation of the set of peace-promoting policies sketched here, it is important not to forget our individual responsibility. One person can make a considerable difference. Think, for example, of the large-scale impact of Nelson Mandela, Mother Teresa or Mahatma Gandhi. As Henry Dunant, founder of the Red Cross, put it, "only those crazy enough to think that they can change the world will succeed in doing so."[3] Many of our leaders lack one of the components of smart idealism, and we cannot just stay passive and lazily have faith in their actions. Since we are all concerned and affected by conflict, we should therefore all be part of the solution. There is ample evidence that pressure from public opinion matters, both for the implementation of policies and the scope for preventing atrocities. There is a job to be done, so let us all work together to make a positive change.

Notes

I   SMART IDEALISM AND THE PEACE FORMULA:
INTRODUCTION

1. See the CIA World Factbook (www.cia.gov/the-world-factbook/field/ real-gdp-per-capita/country-comparison/).
2. See the Uppsala Conflict Data Program (https://ucdp.uu.se/ encyclopedia).
3. See Freedom House, Freedom in the World 2023 Report (https:// freedomhouse.org/).
4. See Dominic Rohner. "COVID-19 and conflict: Major risks and policy responses." *Peace Economics, Peace Science and Public Policy* 26, no. 3 (2020) (https://doi.org/10.1515/peps-2020-0043).
5. See www.rts.ch/info/suisse/1084123-visas-libyens-la-suisse-sous-pression-de-bruxelles.html.
6. See Eugen Dimant, Tim Krieger and Daniel Meierrieks. "Paying them to hate US: The effect of US military aid on anti-American terrorism, 1968–2018." Working Paper (2022) (https://dx.doi.org/10.2139/ ssrn.3639277).
7. See Oeindrila Dube and Suresh Naidu. "Bases, bullets, and ballots: The effect of US military aid on political conflict in Colombia." *The Journal of Politics* 77, no. 1 (2015): 249–267.
8. See Nathan Nunn and Nancy Qian. "US food aid and civil conflict." *American Economic Review* 104, no. 6 (2014): 1630–1666.
9. See Dominic Rohner and Alessandro Saia. "Education and conflict: Evidence from a policy experiment in Indonesia." CEPR Discussion Paper 13509 (2019).
10. See Eli Berman, Jacob N. Shapiro and Joseph H. Felter. "Can hearts and minds be bought? The economics of counterinsurgency in Iraq." *Journal of Political Economy* 119, no. 4 (2011): 766–819.
11. See www.olofpalme.org/wp-content/dokument/860221b_folkriksdag .pdf.

12. The video of the corresponding speech is available here: www.youtube
    .com/watch?v=2KESjF-W79Y.
13. See https://quod.lib.umich.edu/l/lincoln/lincoln6/1:757?rgn=div1;view=
    fulltext.

2 LOSS OF LIVES, LIVELIHOODS AND LOVE:
WARS ARE *NOT* GOOD BUSINESS

1. See Shawn Davies, Therése Pettersson and Magnus Öberg. "Organized
   violence 1989–2021 and drone warfare." *Journal of Peace Research*
   59, no. 4 (2022): 593–610.
2. See www.reuters.com/article/us-congo-democratic-death-
   idUSL2280201220080122/.
3. See Centers for Disease Control and Prevention (CDC) on "History
   of 1918 Flu Pandemic" (www.britannica.com/event/World-War-I)
   and Encyclopedia Britannica on "Casualties of World War I" (www
   .britannica.com/event/World-War-I).
4. See Hazem Adam Ghobarah, Paul Huth and Bruce Russett. "Civil
   wars kill and maim people – long after the shooting stops." *American
   Political Science Review* 97, no. 2 (2003): 189–202.
5. See Charles H. Anderton and Jurgen Brauer. "Mass atrocities and
   their prevention." *Journal of Economic Literature* 59, no. 4 (2021):
   1240–1292.
6. See James D. Fearon and David D. Laitin. "Ethnicity, insurgency, and
   civil war." *American Political Science Review* 97, no. 1 (2003): 75–90.
7. See Hannes Mueller and Julia Tobias. "The cost of violence: Estimating
   the economic impact of conflict." International Growth Centre (2016).
8. See Joseph E. Stiglitz and Linda J. Bilmes. *The Three Trillion Dollar
   War: The True Cost of the Iraq Conflict*. WW Norton & Company,
   2008.
9. See Alberto Abadie and Javier Gardeazabal. "The economic costs of
   conflict: A case study of the Basque Country." *American Economic
   Review* 93, no. 1 (2003): 113–132.
10. See Encyclopedia Britannica on "ETA" (www.britannica.com/topic/
    ETA).
11. See Luis Garicano, Dominic Rohner and Beatrice Weder di Mauro (eds.).
    *Global Economic Consequences of the War in Ukraine: Sanctions,
    Supply Chains and Sustainability*. CEPR Press, 2022.

12. See Timothy Besley, Thiemo Fetzer and Hannes Mueller. "The welfare cost of lawlessness: Evidence from Somali piracy." *Journal of the European Economic Association* 13, no. 2 (2015): 203–239.

13. See Massimo Guidolin and Eliana La Ferrara. "Diamonds are forever, wars are not: Is conflict bad for private firms?" *American Economic Review* 97, no. 5 (2007): 1978–1993.

14. See the Political Economy Research Institute (PERI) country profile on "Angola (1975–2002)."

15. See Stefano Della Vigna and Elian La Ferrara. "Detecting Illegal Arms Trade," *American Economic Journal*: Economic Policy 2 (2010): 26–57.

3 VICIOUS CYCLES OF CONFLICT: WHY WARS TODAY THREATEN OUR FUTURE

1. See Jose Galdo. "The long-run labor-market consequences of civil war: Evidence from the Shining Path in Peru." *Economic Development and Cultural Change* 61, no. 4 (2013): 789–823.

2. See W. Martin James III. *A Political History of the Civil War in Angola: 1974–1990*. Transaction Publishers, 2011.

3. See Sirimal Abeyratne. "Economic roots of political conflict: The case of Sri Lanka." *World Economy* 27, no. 8 (2004): 1295–1314; Nisha Arunatilake, Sisira Jayasuriya and Saman Kelegama. "The economic cost of the war in Sri Lanka." *World Development* 29, no. 9 (2001): 1483–1500.

4. See www.reuters.com/article/idUSKBN2BF1DD/.

5. See Stephanie Oum, Jennifer Kates and Adam Wexler. "Economic Impact of COVID-19 on PEPFAR Countries." KFF Global Health Policy (2022).

6. See Erhan Artuc, Guillermo Falcone, Guido Port and Bob Rijkers. "War-induced food price inflation imperils the poor." In Luis Garicano, Dominic Rohner and Beatrice Weder (eds.), *Global Economic Consequences of the War in Ukraine: Sanctions, Supply Chains and Sustainability*. CEPR Press, 2022.

7. See Robert Putnam. *Bowling Alone: America's Declining Social Capital*. Simon and Schuster, 2001.

8. See Dominic Rohner, Mathias Thoenig and Fabrizio Zilibotti. "War signals: A theory of trade, trust, and conflict." *Review of Economic Studies* 80, no. 3 (2013): 1114–1147.

9. See www.theguardian.com/news/2003/aug/18/guardianobituaries.

10. See Dominic Rohner, Mathias Thoenig and Fabrizio Zilibotti. "Seeds of distrust: Conflict in Uganda." *Journal of Economic Growth* 18 (2013): 217–252.

11. See Dominic Rohner, Mathias Thoenig and Fabrizio Zilibotti. "War signals: A theory of trade, trust and conflict." Review of Economic Studies 80, no. 3 (2013): 1114–1147.

12. See Luigi Guiso, Paola Sapienza and Luigi Zingales. "Cultural biases in economic exchange?" *The Quarterly Journal of Economics* 124, no. 3 (2009): 1095–1131.

13. See Vasiliki Fouka and Hans-Joachim Voth. "Collective remembrance and private choice: German–Greek conflict and behavior in times of crisis." *American Political Science Review* 117, no. 3 (2023): 851–870.

14. See Gianmarco Leon. "Civil conflict and human capital accumulation: The long-term effects of political violence in Perú." *Journal of Human Resources* 47, no. 4 (2012): 991–1022.

15. See Olga Shemyakina. "The effect of armed conflict on accumulation of schooling: Results from Tajikistan." *Journal of Development Economics* 95, no. 2 (2011): 186–200.

16. See Saurabh Singhal. "Early life shocks and mental health: The long-term effect of war in Vietnam." *Journal of Development Economics* 141 (2019): 102244.

17. See Eric B. Elbogen, Sally C. Johnson, H. Ryan Wagner, Connor Sullivan, Casey T. Taft and Jean C. Beckham. "Violent behaviour and post-traumatic stress disorder in US Iraq and Afghanistan veterans." *The British Journal of Psychiatry* 204, no. 5 (2014): 368–375.

18. See Eric B. Elbogen, Sally C. Johnson, H. Ryan Wagner, Connor Sullivan, Casey T. Taft and Jean C. Beckham. "Violent behaviour and post-traumatic stress disorder in US Iraq and Afghanistan veterans." *The British Journal of Psychiatry* 204, no. 5 (2014): 368–375.

19. See Mathieu Couttenier, Veronica Petrencu, Dominic Rohner and Mathias Thoenig. "The violent legacy of conflict: evidence on asylum seekers, crime, and public policy in Switzerland." *American Economic Review* 109, no. 12 (2019): 4378–4425.

20. See Dominic Rohner and Mathias Thoenig. "The elusive peace dividend of development policy: From war traps to macro complementarities." *Annual Review of Economics* 13 (2021): 111–131.

4   POVERTY, POPULATIONS AND PETROL: WHY DO PEOPLE FIGHT?

1. See James D. Fearon. "Rationalist explanations for war." *International Organization* 49, no. 3 (1995): 379–414.

2. See Matthew O. Jackson and Massimo Morelli. "Political bias and war." *American Economic Review* 97, no. 4 (2007): 1353–1373.

3. See Zeev Maoz and Bruce Russett. "Normative and structural causes of democratic peace, 1946–1986." *American Political Science Review* 87, no. 3 (1993): 624–638.

4. See Eoin McGuirk, Nathaniel Hilger and Nicholas Miller. "No kin in the game: Moral hazard and war in the US congress." *Journal of Political Economy* 131, no. 9 (2023): 2370–2401.

5. See Dominic Rohner. "Mediation, military and money: The promises and pitfalls of outside interventions to end armed conflicts." *Journal of Economic Literature* 62, no. 1 (2024): 155–195.

6. See Edward Miguel, Shanker Satyanath and Ernest Sergenti. "Economic shocks and civil conflict: An instrumental variables approach." *Journal of Political Economy* 112, no. 4 (2004): 725–753.

7. See Joan Esteban and Debraj Ray. "On the measurement of polarization." *Econometrica* 62, no. 4 (1994): 819–851; Joan Esteban and Debraj Ray. "Conflict and distribution." *Journal of Economic Theory* 87, no. 2 (1999): 379–415.

8. See José G. Montalvo and Marta Reynal-Querol. "Ethnic polarization, potential conflict, and civil wars." *American Economic Review* 95, no. 3 (2005): 796–816; Joan Esteban, Laura Mayoral and Debraj Ray. "Ethnicity and conflict: An empirical study." *American Economic Review* 102, no. 4 (2012): 1310–1342.

9. When it comes to the determinants of ethnic divisions in various countries, a key factor is the arbitrary border drawing imposed by colonial powers (see Stelios Michalopoulos and Elias Papaioannou. "The long-run effects of the scramble for Africa." *American Economic Review* 106, no. 7 (2016): 1802–1848).

10. See the numbers of the Federal Statistical Office (www.bfs.admin .ch/bfs/en/home/statistics/population/languages-religions/languages .html).

11. See Thorsten, Rogall. "Mobilizing the masses for genocide." *American Economic Review* 111, no. 1 (2021): 41–72.

12. See Hannes Mueller, Dominic Rohner and David Schönholzer. "Ethnic violence across space." *The Economic Journal* 132, no. 642 (2022): 709–740.

13. See www.theguardian.com/uk-news/2022/jun/14/ declassified-files-reveal-british-interest-in-falkland-islands-oil.

14. See www.washingtonpost.com/wp-srv/liveonline/03/special/iraq/ sp_iraq_fires032103.htm.

15. See Francesco Caselli, Massimo Morelli and Dominic Rohner. "The geography of interstate resource wars." *The Quarterly Journal of Economics* 130, no. 1 (2015): 267–315.

16. See Massimo Morelli and Dominic Rohner. "Resource concentration and civil wars." *Journal of Development Economics* 117 (2015): 32–47.

17. See Nicolas Berman, Mathieu Couttenier, Dominic Rohner and Mathias Thoenig. "This mine is mine! How minerals fuel conflicts in Africa." *American Economic Review* 107, no. 6 (2017): 1564–1610.

18. See Oeindrila Dube and Juan F. Vargas. "Commodity price shocks and civil conflict: Evidence from Colombia." *The Review of Economic Studies* 80, no. 4 (2013): 1384–1421.

19. See www.hrw.org/reports/1993/iraqanfal/ANFALINT.htm.

20. See Joan Esteban, Massimo Morelli and Dominic Rohner. "Strategic mass killings." *Journal of Political Economy* 123, no. 5 (2015): 1087–1132.

5   THE KILLER IN THE BOARDROOM: HOW FIGHTING IS FUNDED

1. See https://reliefweb.int/report/angola/angola-illegal-diamond-sales-funding-unita-war-effort.

2. See Massimo Guidolin and Eliana La Ferrara. "Diamonds are forever, wars are not: Is conflict bad for private firms?" *American Economic Review* 97, no. 5 (2007): 1978–1993.

3. See James D. Fearon. "Why do some civil wars last so much longer than others?" *Journal of Peace Research* 41, no. 3 (2004): 275–301.

4. See Michael D. König, Dominic Rohner, Mathias Thoenig and Fabrizio Zilibotti. "Networks in conflict: Theory and evidence from the great war of Africa." *Econometrica* 85, no. 4 (2017): 1093–1132.

5. The exact death toll of the Rwandan genocide is still debated in the academic literature. The recent work of André Guichaoua gives an account of the different fatality estimates. See for example André Guichaoua.

"Counting the Rwandan victims of war and genocide: Concluding reflections." *Journal of Genocide Research* 22, no. 1 (2020): 125–141.

6. See www.reuters.com/article/us-congo-democratic-death-idUSL2280201220080122/.

7. See Nicolas Berman, Mathieu Couttenier, Dominic Rohner, and Mathias Thoenig. "This mine is mine! How minerals fuel conflicts in Africa." *American Economic Review* 107, no. 6 (2017): 1564–1610.

8. See Raul Sanchez de la Sierra. "On the Origins of the State: Stationary Bandits and Taxation in Eastern Congo." *Journal of Political Economy* 128, no. 1 (2020): 32–74.

9. See Oliver Vanden Eynde. "Targets of violence: Evidence from India's naxalite conflict." *The Economic Journal* 128, no. 609 (2018): 887–916.

6   POWER TO THE PEOPLE: INCLUSIVE DEMOCRACY AND POWER-SHARING

1. See www.thejournal.ie/martin-mcguinness-nelson-mandela-2504246-Dec2015/.

2. See Encyclopedia Britannica, "Bloody Sunday" (www.britannica.com/event/Bloody-Sunday-Northern-Ireland-1972).

3. See Hannes Mueller and Dominic Rohner. "Can power-sharing foster peace? Evidence from Northern Ireland." *Economic Policy* 33, no. 95 (2018): 447–484.

4. See Encyclopedia Britannica, "Omagh Bombing" (www.britannica.com/event/Omagh-bombing).

5. This illustrates well the multidimensionality of inclusion, where equal democratic representation needs to be guaranteed for everyone, independently of ethnicity, gender, religion, sexual orientation or socioeconomic background, among others.

6. See Lars-Erik Cederman, Andreas Wimmer and Brian Min. "Why do ethnic groups rebel? New data and analysis." *World Politics* 62, no. 1 (2010): 87–119.

7. See Andrea Marcucci, Dominic Rohner and Alessandro Saia. "Ballot or bullet: The impact of the UK's Representation of the People Act on peace and prosperity." *The Economic Journal* 133, no. 652 (2023): 1510–1536.

8. See Daron Acemoglu, Suresh Naidu, Pascual Restrepo and James A. Robinson. "Democracy does cause growth." *Journal of Political*

Economy 127, no. 1 (2019): 47–100. See also their work on how colonial history affected institution building: Daron Acemoglu, Simon Johnson, and James A. Robinson. "The colonial origins of comparative development: An empirical investigation." *American Economic Review* 91, no. 5 (2001): 1369–1401.

9. Ronald Wintrobe. *The Political Economy of Dictatorship*. Cambridge University Press, 2000.

10. See Jeremy Laurent-Lucchetti, Dominic Rohner and Mathias Thoenig. "Ethnic conflict and the informational dividend of democracy." *Journal of the European Economic Association* 22, no. 1 (2024): 73–116.

11. See https://data.undp.org/countries-and-territories/CZE.

12. See Michael Mann. *The Dark Side of Democracy: Explaining Ethnic Cleansing*. Cambridge University Press, 2005.

13. See Joan Esteban, Massimo Morelli and Dominic Rohner. "Strategic mass killings." *Journal of Political Economy* 123, no. 5 (2015): 1087–1132.

14. See Rudolph J. Rummel. "Power, genocide and mass murder." *Journal of Peace Research* 31, no. 1 (1994): 1–10, on page 1.

15. See Paul Collier and Dominic Rohner. "Democracy, development, and conflict." *Journal of the European Economic Association* 6, no. 2–3 (2008): 531–540.

16. See https://georgewbush-whitehouse.archives.gov/news/releases/2003/05/20030501-15.html.

17. See www.theguardian.com/world/2005/jun/29/iraq.usa.

18. See https://data.undp.org/countries-and-territories/IRQ.

19. See www.eiu.com/n/campaigns/democracy-index-2022/.

7   STATE CAPACITY FOR STABILITY

1. See Sarah M. Glaser, Paige M. Roberts and Kaija J. Hurlburt. "Foreign illegal, unreported, and unregulated fishing in Somali waters perpetuates conflict." *Frontiers in Marine Science* 6 (2019): 704.

2. See Oriana Bandiera. "Land reform, the market for protection, and the origins of the Sicilian mafia: theory and evidence." *Journal of Law, Economics, and Organization* 19, no. 1 (2003): 218–244.

3. See Paolo Buonanno, Ruben Durante, Giovanni Prarolo and Paolo Vanin. "Poor institutions, rich mines: Resource curse in the origins of the Sicilian mafia." *The Economic Journal* 125, no. 586 (2015):

F175-F202; Arcangelo Dimico, Alessia Isopi and Ola Olsson. "Origins of the Sicilian Mafia: The market for lemons." *The Journal of Economic History* 77, no. 4 (2017): 1083–1115.

4. See Daron Acemoglu, Giuseppe De Feo and Giacomo Davide De Luca. "Weak states: Causes and consequences of the Sicilian Mafia." *The Review of Economic Studies* 87, no. 2 (2020): 537–581.

5. See Patrick Premand and Dominic Rohner. "Cash and Conflict: Large-Scale Experimental Evidence from Niger." *American Economic Review: Insights* 6, no. 1 (2024): 137–153.

6. See Eli Berman, Jacob N. Shapiro and Joseph H. Felter. "Can hearts and minds be bought? The economics of counterinsurgency in Iraq." *Journal of Political Economy* 119, no. 4 (2011): 766–819; Eli Berman, Joseph H. Felter, Jacob N. Shapiro and Erin Troland. "Modest, secure, and informed: Successful development in conflict zones." *American Economic Review* 103, no. 3 (2013): 512–517.

7. See Oeindrila Dube and Suresh Naidu. "Bases, bullets, and ballots: The effect of US military aid on political conflict in Colombia." *The Journal of Politics* 77, no. 1 (2015): 249–267.

8. See Eugen Dimant, Tim Krieger and Daniel Meierrieks. "Paying them to hate US: The effect of US military aid on anti-American terrorism." Working Paper (2022) (http://dx.doi.org/10.2139/ssrn.3639277).

9. See Navin A. Bapat. "Transnational terrorism, US military aid, and the incentive to misrepresent." *Journal of Peace Research* 48, no. 3 (2011): 303–318.

10. See Lisa Hultman, Jacob Kathman and Megan Shannon. "United Nations peacekeeping and civilian protection in civil war." *American Journal of Political Science* 57, no. 4 (2013): 875–891; Lisa Hultman, Jacob Kathman and Megan Shannon. "Beyond keeping peace: United Nations effectiveness in the midst of fighting." *American Political Science Review* 108, no. 4 (2014): 737–753; Andrea Ruggeri, Han Dorussen and Theodora-Ismene Gizelis. "Winning the peace locally: UN peacekeeping and local conflict." *International Organization* 71, no. 1 (2017): 163–185; Hanne Fjelde, Lisa Hultman and Desirée Nilsson. "Protection through presence: UN peacekeeping and the costs of targeting civilians." *International Organization* 73, no. 1 (2019): 103–131.

11. See Timothy Besley and Torsten Persson. *Pillars of Prosperity: The Political Economics of Development Clusters*. Princeton University Press, 2011.

12. See Halvor Mehlum, Karl Moene and Ragnar Torvik. "Institutions and the resource curse." *The Economic Journal* 116, no. 508 (2006): 1–20.

13. See Charles Tilly. *Coercion, Capital, and European States, A.D. 990–1992*. Blackwell, 1992.

14. See Kai Gehring. "Can external threats foster a European Union identity? Evidence from Russia's invasion of Ukraine." *The Economic Journal* 132, no. 644 (2022): 1489–1516.

15. See Alberto Alesina and Eliana La Ferrara. "Participation in heterogeneous communities." *The Quarterly Journal of Economics* 115, no. 3 (2000): 847–904.

16. See Dominic Rohner and Ekaterina Zhuravskaya. "Nation Building: What Could Possibly Go Wrong?" In Dominic Rohner and Ekaterina Zhuravskay (eds), *Nation Building: Big Lessons from Successes and Failures*. CEPR Press, 2023.

17. See Bruno Caprettini and Hans-Joachim Voth. "New Deal, New Patriots: How 1930s Government Spending Boosted Patriotism During World War II." *The Quarterly Journal of Economics* 138, no. 1 (2023): 465–513.

8   PLENTY MAKES PEACE: EDUCATION, HEALTH AND LABOR MARKET POLICIES

1. See Bénédicte de la Brière, Deon Filmer, Dena Ringold, Dominic Rohner and Anastasiya Denisova. *From Mines and Wells to Well-built Minds: Turning Sub-Saharan Africa's Natural Resource Wealth into Human Capital*. World Bank Publications, 2017.

2. See Ronald F. Inglehart and Pippa Norris. "Trump, Brexit, and the rise of populism: Economic have-nots and cultural backlash." Harvard Kennedy School Faculty Research Working Paper 16-026 (2016).

3. See Dominic Rohner and Ekaterina Zhuravskaya, eds. *Nation Building: Big Lessons from Successes and Failures*. CEPR Press, 2023.

4. See Clayton L. Thyne. "ABC's, 123's, and the golden rule: The pacifying effect of education on civil war, 1980–1999." *International Studies Quarterly* 50, no. 4 (2006): 733–754.

5. See Esther Duflo. "Schooling and labor market consequences of school construction in Indonesia: Evidence from an unusual policy experiment." *American Economic Review* 91, no. 4 (2001): 795–813; Dominic Rohner and Alessandro Saia. "Education and conflict: Evidence from a policy experiment in Indonesia." CEPR Discussion Paper DP13509 (2019).

6. See Madhuri Agarwal, Vikram Bahure, Katja Bergonzoli and Souparna Maji. "Education and domestic violence: Evidence from a school construction program in India." SITES Working Paper No. 17 (2023).

7. See Willa Friedman, Michael Kremer, Edward Miguel and Rebecca Thornton. "Education as liberation?" *Economica* 83, no. 329 (2016): 1–30.

8. See Matteo Cervellati, Uwe Sunde and Simona Valmori. "Pathogens, weather shocks and civil conflicts." *The Economic Journal* 127, no. 607 (2017): 2581–2616.

9. See Andrea Berlanda, Matteo Cervellati, Elena Esposito, Dominic Rohner and Uwe Sunde. "Medication against conflict." CEPR Discussion Paper DP17125 (2022).

10. See Christopher Blattman and Jeannie Annan. "Can employment reduce lawlessness and rebellion? A field experiment with high-risk men in a fragile state." *American Political Science Review* 110, no. 1 (2016): 1–17.

11. See Thiemo Fetzer. "Can workfare programs moderate conflict? Evidence from India." *Journal of the European Economic Association* 18, no. 6 (2020): 3337–3375.

12. See Mathieu Couttenier, Veronica Petrencu, Dominic Rohner and Mathias Thoenig. "The violent legacy of conflict: evidence on asylum seekers, crime, and public policy in Switzerland." *American Economic Review* 109, no. 12 (2019): 4378–4425.

13. See Benjamin Crost, Joseph H. Felter and Patrick B. Johnston. "Conditional cash transfers, civil conflict and insurgent influence: Experimental evidence from the Philippines." *Journal of Development Economics* 118 (2016): 171–182.

9   FORGIVING NOT FIGHTING: FOSTERING TRUST AND RECONCILIATION

1. See Encyclopedia Britannica, "Rwanda genocide of 1994" (www.britannica.com/print/article/1762747).

2. See https://peacekeeping.un.org/en/mission/past/unamirS.htm.

3. See David Yanagizawa-Drott. "Propaganda and conflict: Evidence from the Rwandan genocide." *The Quarterly Journal of Economics* 129, no. 4 (2014): 1947–1994.

4. See Dominic Rohner, Mathias Thoenig and Fabrizio Zilibotti. "War signals: A theory of trade, trust, and conflict." *Review of Economic Studies* 80, no. 3 (2013): 1114–1147.

5. See Charles de Montesquieu: *The Spirit of the Laws*. Cambridge University Press, 1989.

6. See Saumitra Jha. "Trade, institutions, and ethnic tolerance: Evidence from South Asia." *American Political Science Review* 107, no. 4 (2013): 806–832.

7. See Julio Cáceres-Delpiano, Antoni-Italo De Moragas, Gabriel Facchini and Ignacio González. "Intergroup contact and nation building: Evidence from military service in Spain." *Journal of Public Economics* 201 (2021): 104477.

8. See Oyebola Okunogbe. "Does exposure to other ethnic regions promote national integration?: Evidence from Nigeria." *American Economic Journal: Applied Economics* 16, no. 1 (2024): 157–192.

9. See Salma Mousa. "Building social cohesion between Christians and Muslims through soccer in post-ISIS Iraq." *Science* 369, no. 6505 (2020): 866–870.

10. See Emilio Depetris-Chauvin, Ruben Durante and Filipe Campante. "Building nations through shared experiences: Evidence from African football." *American Economic Review* 110, no. 5 (2020): 1572–1602.

11. See Jacobus Cilliers, Oeindrila Dube and Bilal Siddiqi. "Reconciling after civil conflict increases social capital but decreases individual well-being." *Science* 352, no. 6287 (2016): 787–794.

12. See Arthur Blouin and Sharun W. Mukand. "Erasing ethnicity? Propaganda, nation building, and identity in Rwanda." *Journal of Political Economy* 127, no. 3 (2019): 1008–1062.

13. See https://rsf.org/en/index.

14. See Elena Esposito, Tiziano Rotesi, Alessandro Saia and Mathias Thoenig. "Reconciliation narratives: The birth of a nation after the us civil war." *American Economic Review* 113, no. 6 (2023): 1461–1504.

15. See Elizabeth Levy Paluck and Donald P. Green. "Deference, dissent, and dispute resolution: An experimental intervention using mass media to change norms and behavior in Rwanda." *American Political Science Review* 103, no. 4 (2009): 622–644.

10 A ROLE FOR ALL OF US? *SMART IDEALISM,* GLOBAL PUBLIC OPINION AND INTERNATIONAL SUPPORT FOR PEACE

1. See www.theguardian.com/world/2004/mar/26/indonesia.philippines.
2. See Joan Esteban, Massimo Morelli and Dominic Rohner. "Strategic mass killings." *Journal of Political Economy* 123, no. 5 (2015): 1087–1132.
3. See Encyclopedia Britannica on "Khmer Rouge" (www.britannica.com/print/article/316738).
4. See Leonard Wantchekon, Marko Klašnja and Natalija Novta. "Education and human capital externalities: evidence from colonial Benin." *The Quarterly Journal of Economics* 130, no. 2 (2015): 703–757.
5. See https://worldhappiness.report/ed/2023/.
6. See Timothy Besley and Robin Burgess. "The political economy of government responsiveness: Theory and evidence from India." *The Quarterly Journal of Economics* 117, no. 4 (2002): 1415–1451.
7. See David Strömberg. "Radio's impact on public spending." *The Quarterly Journal of Economics* 119, no. 1 (2004): 189–221.
8. See Thomas Eisensee and David Strömberg. "News droughts, news floods, and US disaster relief." *The Quarterly Journal of Economics* 122, no. 2 (2007): 693–728.
9. A recent edition is Bertolt Brecht, *Die Dreigroschenoper.* Suhrkamp, 2021.
10. See Ruben Durante and Ekaterina Zhuravskaya (2018). "Attack when the world is not watching? US news and the Israeli-Palestinian conflict." *Journal of Political Economy,* 126(3), 1085–1133.
11. See Siwan Anderson, Patrick Francois, Dominic Rohner and Rogerio Santarrosa. "Hidden hostility: donor attention and political violence." United Nations University World Institute for Development Economics Research, 2022.

11 GLOBAL COORDINATION TO CURB CONFLICT

1. See www.worldbank.org/en/country/centralafricanrepublic/overview.
2. See www.washingtonpost.com/world/2023/09/18/wagner-central-african-republic-touadera/.
3. Anjan Sundaram. *Breakup: A Marriage in Wartime.* Catapult, 2023.

4. See Christine Binzel, Dietmar Fehr and Andreas Link. "Can International Initiatives Promote Peace? Diamond Certification and Armed Conflicts in Africa." Working Paper (2023) (https://dx.doi.org/10.2139/ssrn.4567734).

5. See Nicolas Berman, Mathieu Couttenier, Dominic Rohner and Mathias Thoenig. "This mine is mine! How minerals fuel conflicts in Africa." *American Economic Review* 107, no. 6 (2017): 1564–1610.

6. See Tommaso Sonno. "Globalization and conflicts: The good, the bad and the ugly of corporations in Africa." CEP Discussion Paper No. 1670 (2020).

7. See Frederik Noack, Dominic Rohner and Tommaso Sonno, "Multinationals vs Mother Nature? The Impact of Multinational Firms on the Environment," preprint (2023).

8. See Mathieu Couttenier, Veronica Petrencu, Dominic Rohner and Mathias Thoenig. "The violent legacy of conflict: Evidence on asylum seekers, crime, and public policy in Switzerland." *American Economic Review* 109, no. 12 (2019): 4378–4425.

9. See Quentin Gallea. "Weapons and war: The effect of arms transfers on internal conflict." *Journal of Development Economics* 160 (2023): 103001.

10. See www.international.gc.ca/country-pays/us-eu/relations.aspx?lang=eng.

11. See Solomon William Polachek. "Conflict and trade." *Journal of Conflict Resolution* 24, no. 1 (1980): 55–78.

12. See Martin, Philippe, Thierry Mayer, and Mathias Thoenig. "Make trade not war?" The Review of Economic Studies 75, no. 3 (2008): 865–900.

13. See Mathias Thoenig. "Trade policy in the shadow of war: A quantitative toolkit for geoeconomics." In Massimo Morelli, Debraj Ray, Tomas Sjostrom and Oeindrila Dube (eds.), *Handbook of the Economics of Conflict*, 1st edition. Elsevier, 2024.

14. See Quentin Gallea and Dominic Rohner. "Globalization mitigates the risk of conflict caused by strategic territory." *Proceedings of the National Academy of Sciences* 118, no. 39 (2021): e2105624118.

15. See Immanuel Kant. *Perpetual Peace: A Philosophical Sketch.* Cambridge University Press, 1970.

16. See Zeev Maoz and Bruce Russett. "Normative and structural causes of democratic peace, 1946–1986." *American Political Science Review* 87, no. 3 (1993): 624–638.

17. Freedom House. "Freedom in the world 2023: Marking 50 years in the struggle for democracy." Report (2023).

18. See Christian Gollier and Dominic Rohner (eds.). *Peace not Pollution: How Going Green Can Tackle Climate Change and Toxic Politics.* CEPR Press (2023).

19. See Marshall Burke, Solomon M. Hsiang and Edward Miguel. "Climate and conflict." *Annual Review of Economics* 7, no. 1 (2015): 577–617.

20. See Ulrich J. Eberle, Dominic Rohner and Mathias Thoenig. "Heat and Hate: Climate security and farmer-herder conflicts in Africa." Working Paper (2020); Eoin F. McGuirk and Nathan Nunn. "Transhumant pastoralism, climate change, and conflict in Africa." *Review of Economic Studies* (2024) (https://doi.org/10.1093/restud/rdae027).

21. See Kai Gehring and Paul Schaudt. "Insuring peace: Index-based livestock insurance, droughts, and conflict." CESifo Working Paper No. 10423 (2023).

12   CONCLUSION

1. See Hannes Mueller and Julia Tobias. "The cost of violence: Estimating the economic impact of conflict." International Growth Centre (2016).

2. See Dominic Rohner, Michael Lehning, Julia Steinberger, Nicolas Tetreault and Evelina Trutnevyte. "Decentralized green energy transition promotes peace." *Frontiers in Environmental Science* 11 (2023): 1118987.

3. See www.bps-suisse.ch/pdf/media_henry_dunant_coraggio_perseveranza_forza_delle_idee_1_en.pdf.

Bibliography

CHAPTER 1

Berman, Eli, Jacob N. Shapiro, and Joseph H. Felter. "Can hearts and minds be bought? The economics of counterinsurgency in Iraq." *Journal of Political Economy* 119, no. 4 (2011): 766–819.

Dimant, Eugen, Tim Krieger, and Daniel Meierrieks. "Paying them to hate US: The effect of US military aid on anti-American terrorism, 1968–2018." Working Paper (2022). https://dx.doi.org/10.2139/ssrn.3639277

Dube, Oeindrila, and Suresh Naidu. "Bases, bullets, and ballots: The effect of US military aid on political conflict in Colombia." *The Journal of Politics* 77, no. 1 (2015): 249–267.

Nunn, Nathan, and Nancy Qian. "US food aid and civil conflict." *American Economic Review* 104, no. 6 (2014): 1630–1666.

Rohner, Dominic. "COVID-19 and conflict: Major risks and policy responses." *Peace Economics, Peace Science and Public Policy* 26, no. 3 (2020): 20200043.

Rohner, Dominic, and Alessandro Saia. "Education and conflict: Evidence from a policy experiment in Indonesia." CEPR Discussion Paper DP13509 (2019).

CHAPTER 2

Abadie, Alberto, and Javier Gardeazabal. "The economic costs of conflict: A case study of the Basque Country." *American Economic Review* 93, no. 1 (2003): 113–132.

Anderton, Charles H., and Jurgen Brauer. "Mass atrocities and their prevention." *Journal of Economic Literature* 59, no. 4 (2021): 1240–1292.

Besley, Timothy, Thiemo Fetzer, and Hannes Mueller. "The welfare cost of lawlessness: Evidence from Somali piracy." *Journal of the European Economic Association* 13, no. 2 (2015): 203–239.

Davies, Shawn, Therése Pettersson, and Magnus Öberg. "Organized violence 1989–2021 and drone warfare." *Journal of Peace Research* 59, no. 4 (2022): 593–610.

Della Vigna, Stefano, and Eliana La Ferrara. "Detecting illegal arms trade." *American Economic Journal: Economic Policy* 2 (2010): 26–57.

Fearon, James D., and David D. Laitin. "Ethnicity, insurgency, and civil war." *American Political Science Review* 97, no. 1 (2003): 75–90.

Garicano, Luis, Dominic Rohner, and Beatrice Weder di Mauro (eds.). *Global Economic Consequences of the War in Ukraine: Sanctions, Supply Chains and Sustainability.* CEPR Press, 2022.

Ghobarah, Hazem Adam, Paul Huth, and Bruce Russett. "Civil wars kill and maim people– long after the shooting stops." *American Political Science Review* 97, no. 2 (2003): 189–202.

Guidolin, Massimo, and Eliana La Ferrara. "Diamonds are forever, wars are not: Is conflict bad for private firms?" *American Economic Review* 97, no. 5 (2007): 1978–1993.

Mueller, Hannes, and Julia Tobias. "The cost of violence: Estimating the economic impact of conflict." International Growth Centre (2016). www.theigc .org/sites/default/files/2016/12/IGCJ5023_Economic_Cost_of_Conflict_ Brief_2211_v7_WEB.pdf

Stiglitz, Joseph E., and Linda J. Bilmes. *The Three Trillion Dollar War: The True Cost of the Iraq Conflict.* W. W. Norton & Company, 2008.

CHAPTER 3

Abeyratne, Sirimal. "Economic roots of political conflict: The case of Sri Lanka." *World Economy* 27, no. 8 (2004): 1295–1314.

Artuc, Erhan, Guillermo Falcone, Guido Port, and Bob Rijkers. "War-induced food price inflation imperils the poor." In Luis Garicano, Dominic Rohner, and Beatrice Weder (eds.), *Global Economic Consequences of the War in Ukraine Sanctions, Supply Chains and Sustainability.* CEPR Press, 2022.

Arunatilake, Nisha, Sisira Jayasuriya, and Saman Kelegama. "The economic cost of the war in Sri Lanka." *World Development* 29, no. 9 (2001): 1483–1500.

Couttenier, Mathieu, Veronica Petrencu, Dominic Rohner, and Mathias Thoenig. "The violent legacy of conflict: Evidence on asylum seekers, crime, and public policy in Switzerland." *American Economic Review* 109, no. 12 (2019): 4378–4425.

Elbogen, Eric B., Sally C. Johnson, H. Ryan Wagner, Connor Sullivan, Casey T. Taft, and Jean C. Beckham. "Violent behaviour and post-traumatic stress disorder in US Iraq and Afghanistan veterans." *The British Journal of Psychiatry* 204, no. 5 (2014): 368–375.

Fouka, Vasiliki, and Hans-Joachim Voth. "Collective remembrance and private choice: German–Greek conflict and behavior in times of crisis." *American Political Science Review* 117, no. 3 (2023): 851–870.

Galdo, Jose. "The long-run labor-market consequences of civil war: Evidence from the Shining Path in Peru." *Economic Development and Cultural Change* 61, no. 4 (2013): 789–823.

Guiso, Luigi, Paola Sapienza, and Luigi Zingales. "Cultural biases in economic exchange?" *The Quarterly Journal of Economics* 124, no. 3 (2009): 1095–1131.

James III, W. Martin. *A Political History of the Civil War in Angola: 1974–1990.* Transaction Publishers, 2011.

Leon, Gianmarco. "Civil conflict and human capital accumulation: The long-term effects of political violence in Perú." *Journal of Human Resources* 47, no. 4 (2012): 991–1022.

Oum, Stephanie, Jennifer Kates, and Adam Wexler. "Economic Impact of COVID-19 on PEPFAR Countries." KFF Global Health Policy (2022).

Putnam, Robert. *Bowling Alone: America's Declining Social Capital.* Simon & Schuster, 2001.

Rohner, Dominic, and Mathias Thoenig. "The elusive peace dividend of development policy: From war traps to macro complementarities." *Annual Review of Economics* 13 (2021): 111–131.

Rohner, Dominic, Mathias Thoenig, and Fabrizio Zilibotti. "Seeds of distrust: Conflict in Uganda." *Journal of Economic Growth* 18 (2013): 217–252.

Rohner, Dominic, Mathias Thoenig, and Fabrizio Zilibotti. "War signals: A theory of trade, trust, and conflict." *Review of Economic Studies* 80, no. 3 (2013): 1114–1147.

Shemyakina, Olga. "The effect of armed conflict on accumulation of schooling: Results from Tajikistan." *Journal of Development Economics* 95, no. 2 (2011): 186–200.

Singhal, Saurabh. "Early life shocks and mental health: The long-term effect of war in Vietnam." *Journal of Development Economics* 141 (2019): 102244.

CHAPTER 4

Berman, Nicolas, Mathieu Couttenier, Dominic Rohner, and Mathias Thoenig. "This mine is mine! How minerals fuel conflicts in Africa." *American Economic Review* 107, no. 6 (2017): 1564–1610.

Caselli, Francesco, Massimo Morelli, and Dominic Rohner. "The geography of interstate resource wars." *The Quarterly Journal of Economics* 130, no. 1 (2015): 267–315.

Dube, Oeindrila, and Juan F. Vargas. "Commodity price shocks and civil conflict: Evidence from Colombia." *The Review of Economic Studies* 80, no. 4 (2013): 1384–1421.

Esteban, Joan, and Debraj Ray. "On the measurement of polarization." *Econometrica* 62, no. 4 (1994): 819–851.

Esteban, Joan, and Debraj Ray. "Conflict and distribution." *Journal of Economic Theory* 87, no. 2 (1999): 379–415.

Esteban, Joan, Laura Mayoral, and Debraj Ray. "Ethnicity and conflict: An empirical study." *American Economic Review* 102, no. 4 (2012): 1310–1342.

Esteban, Joan, Massimo Morelli, and Dominic Rohner. "Strategic mass killings." *Journal of Political Economy* 123, no. 5 (2015): 1087–1132.

Fearon, James D. "Rationalist explanations for war." *International Organization* 49, no. 3 (1995): 379–414.

Jackson, Matthew O., and Massimo Morelli. "Political bias and war." *American Economic Review* 97, no. 4 (2007): 1353–1373.

Maoz, Zeev, and Bruce Russett. "Normative and structural causes of democratic peace, 1946–1986." *American Political Science Review* 87, no. 3 (1993): 624–638.

McGuirk, Eoin F., Nathaniel Hilger, and Nicholas Miller. "No kin in the game: Moral hazard and war in the US congress." *Journal of Political Economy* 131, no. 9: 2370–2401.

Michalopoulos, Stelios, and Elias Papaioannou. "The long-run effects of the scramble for Africa." *American Economic Review* 106, no. 7 (2016): 1802–1848.

Miguel, Edward, Shanker Satyanath, and Ernest Sergenti. "Economic shocks and civil conflict: An instrumental variables approach." *Journal of Political Economy* 112, no. 4 (2004): 725–753.

Montalvo, José G., and Marta Reynal-Querol. "Ethnic polarization, potential conflict, and civil wars." *American Economic Review* 95, no. 3 (2005): 796–816.

Morelli, Massimo, and Dominic Rohner. "Resource concentration and civil wars." *Journal of Development Economics* 117 (2015): 32–47.

Mueller, Hannes, Dominic Rohner, and David Schönholzer. "Ethnic violence across space." *The Economic Journal* 132, no. 642 (2022): 709–740.

Rogall, Thorsten. "Mobilizing the masses for genocide." *American Economic Review* 111, no. 1 (2021): 41–72.

Rohner, Dominic. "Mediation, military and money: The promises and pitfalls of outside interventions to end armed conflicts." *Journal of Economic Literature* 62, no. 1 (2024): 155–195.

CHAPTER 5

Berman, Nicolas, Mathieu Couttenier, Dominic Rohner, and Mathias Thoenig. "This mine is mine! How minerals fuel conflicts in Africa." *American Economic Review* 107, no. 6 (2017): 1564–1610.

Fearon, James D. "Why do some civil wars last so much longer than others?" *Journal of Peace Research* 41, no. 3 (2004): 275–301.

Guichaoua, André. "Counting the Rwandan victims of war and genocide: Concluding reflections." *Journal of Genocide Research* 22, no. 1 (2020): 125–141.

Guidolin, Massimo, and Eliana La Ferrara. "Diamonds are forever, wars are not: Is conflict bad for private firms?" *American Economic Review* 97, no. 5 (2007): 1978–1993.

König, Michael D., Dominic Rohner, Mathias Thoenig, and Fabrizio Zilibotti. "Networks in conflict: Theory and evidence from the great war of Africa." *Econometrica* 85, no. 4 (2017): 1093–1132.

Sanchez de la Sierra, Raul. "On the Origins of the State: Stationary Bandits and Taxation in Eastern Congo." *Journal of Political Economy* 128, no. 1 (2020): 32–74.

Vanden Eynde, Oliver. "Targets of violence: Evidence from India's naxalite conflict." *The Economic Journal* 128, no. 609 (2018): 887–916.

CHAPTER 6

Acemoglu, Daron, Simon Johnson, and James A. Robinson. "The colonial origins of comparative development: An empirical investigation." *American Economic Review* 91, no. 5 (2001): 1369–1401.

Acemoglu, Daron, Suresh Naidu, Pascual Restrepo, and James A. Robinson. "Democracy does cause growth." *Journal of Political Economy* 127, no. 1 (2019): 47–100.

Cederman, Lars-Erik, Andreas Wimmer, and Brian Min. "Why do ethnic groups rebel? New data and analysis." *World Politics* 62, no. 1 (2010): 87–119.

Collier, Paul, and Dominic Rohner. "Democracy, development, and conflict." *Journal of the European Economic Association* 6, no. 2–3 (2008): 531–540.

Esteban, Joan, Massimo Morelli, and Dominic Rohner. "Strategic mass killings." *Journal of Political Economy* 123, no. 5 (2015): 1087–1132.

Laurent-Lucchetti, Jérémy, Dominic Rohner, and Mathias Thoenig. "Ethnic conflict and the informational dividend of democracy." *Journal of the European Economic Association* 22, no. 1 (2024): 73–116.

Mann, Michael. *The Dark Side of Democracy: Explaining Ethnic Cleansing*. Cambridge University Press, 2005.

Marcucci, Andrea, Dominic Rohner, and Alessandro Saia. "Ballot or bullet: The impact of the UK's representation of the people act on peace and prosperity." *The Economic Journal* 133, no. 652 (2023): 1510–1536.

Mueller, Hannes, and Dominic Rohner. "Can power-sharing foster peace? Evidence from Northern Ireland." *Economic Policy* 33, no. 95 (2018): 447–484.

Rummel, Rudolph J. "Power, genocide and mass murder." *Journal of Peace Research* 31, no. 1 (1994): 1–10.

Wintrobe, Ronald. *The Political Economy of Dictatorship*. Cambridge University Press, 2000.

CHAPTER 7

Acemoglu, Daron, Giuseppe De Feo, and Giacomo Davide De Luca. "Weak states: Causes and consequences of the Sicilian Mafia." *The Review of Economic Studies* 87, no. 2 (2020): 537–581.

Alesina, Alberto, and Eliana La Ferrara. "Participation in heterogeneous communities." *The Quarterly Journal of Economics* 115, no. 3 (2000): 847–904.

Bandiera, Oriana. "Land reform, the market for protection, and the origins of the Sicilian mafia: Theory and evidence." *Journal of Law, Economics, and Organization* 19, no. 1 (2003): 218–244.

Bapat, Navin A. "Transnational terrorism, US military aid, and the incentive to misrepresent." *Journal of Peace Research* 48, no. 3 (2011): 303–318.

Berman, Eli, Jacob N. Shapiro, and Joseph H. Felter. "Can hearts and minds be bought? The economics of counterinsurgency in Iraq." *Journal of Political Economy* 119, no. 4 (2011): 766–819.

Berman, Eli, Joseph H. Felter, Jacob N. Shapiro, and Erin Troland. "Modest, secure, and informed: Successful development in conflict zones." *American Economic Review* 103, no. 3 (2013): 512–517.

Besley, Timothy, and Torsten Persson. *Pillars of Prosperity: The Political Economics of Development Clusters*. Princeton University Press, 2011.

Buonanno, Paolo, Ruben Durante, Giovanni Prarolo, and Paolo Vanin. "Poor institutions, rich mines: Resource curse in the origins of the Sicilian mafia." *The Economic Journal* 125, no. 586 (2015): F175–F202.

Caprettini, Bruno, and Hans-Joachim Voth. "New deal, new patriots: How 1930s government spending boosted patriotism during World War II." *The Quarterly Journal of Economics* 138, no. 1 (2023): 465–513.

Dimant, Eugen, Tim Krieger, and Daniel Meierrieks. "Paying them to hate US: The effect of US military aid on anti-American terrorism." Working Paper (2020).

Dimico, Arcangelo, Alessia Isopi, and Ola Olsson. "Origins of the sicilian mafia: The market for lemons." *The Journal of Economic History* 77, no. 4 (2017): 1083–1115.

Dube, Oeindrila, and Suresh Naidu. "Bases, bullets, and ballots: The effect of US military aid on political conflict in Colombia." *The Journal of Politics* 77, no. 1 (2015): 249–267.

Fjelde, Hanne, Lisa Hultman, and Desirée Nilsson. "Protection through presence: UN peacekeeping and the costs of targeting civilians." *International Organization* 73, no. 1 (2019): 103–131.

Gehring, Kai. "Can external threats foster a European Union identity? Evidence from Russia's invasion of Ukraine." *The Economic Journal* 132, no. 644 (2022): 1489–1516.

Glaser, Sarah M., Paige M. Roberts, and Kaija J. Hurlburt. "Foreign illegal, unreported, and unregulated fishing in Somali waters perpetuates conflict." *Frontiers in Marine Science* 6 (2019): 704.

Hultman, Lisa, Jacob Kathman, and Megan Shannon. "United Nations peacekeeping and civilian protection in civil war." *American Journal of Political Science* 57, no. 4 (2013): 875–891.

Hultman, Lisa, Jacob Kathman, and Megan Shannon. "Beyond keeping peace: United Nations effectiveness in the midst of fighting." *American Political Science Review* 108, no. 4 (2014): 737–753.

Mehlum, Halvor, Karl Moene, and Ragnar Torvik. "Institutions and the resource curse." *The Economic Journal* 116, no. 508 (2006): 1–20.

Premand, Patrick, and Dominic Rohner. "Cash and conflict: Large-scale experimental evidence from Niger." *American Economic Review: Insights* 6, no. 1 (2024): 137–153.

Rohner, Dominic, and Ekaterina Zhuravskaya. "Nation building: What could possibly go wrong?" in Dominic Rohner, and Ekaterina Zhuravskay (eds.), *Nation Building: Big Lessons from Successes and Failures*. CEPR Press, 2023.

Ruggeri, Andrea, Han Dorussen, and Theodora-Ismene Gizelis. "Winning the peace locally: UN peacekeeping and local conflict." *International Organization* 71, no. 1 (2017): 163–185.

Tilly, Charles. *Coercion, Capital, and European States, A.D. 990–1992*. Blackwell, 1992.

CHAPTER 8

Agarwal, Madhuri, Vikram Bahure, Katja Bergonzoli, and Souparna Maji. "Education and Domestic Violence: Evidence from a School Construction Program in India." SITES Working Paper No. 17 (2023).

Berlanda, Andrea, Matteo Cervellati, Elena Esposito, Dominic Rohner, and Uwe Sunde. "Medication against Conflict." CEPR Discussion Paper DP17125 (2022).

Blattman, Christopher, and Jeannie Annan. "Can employment reduce lawlessness and rebellion? A field experiment with high-risk men in a fragile state." *American Political Science Review* 110, no. 1 (2016): 1–17.

Cervellati, Matteo, Uwe Sunde, and Simona Valmori. "Pathogens, weather shocks and civil conflicts." *The Economic Journal* 127, no. 607 (2017): 2581–2616.

Couttenier, Mathieu, Veronica Petrencu, Dominic Rohner, and Mathias Thoenig. "The violent legacy of conflict: Evidence on asylum seekers, crime, and public policy in Switzerland." *American Economic Review* 109, no. 12 (2019): 4378–4425.

Crost, Benjamin, Joseph H. Felter, and Patrick B. Johnston. "Conditional cash transfers, civil conflict and insurgent influence: Experimental evidence from the Philippines." *Journal of Development Economics* 118 (2016): 171–182.

De la Brière, Bénédicte, Deon Filmer, Dena Ringold, Dominic Rohner, and Anastasiya Denisova. *From Mines and Wells to Well-built Minds: Turning Sub-Saharan Africa's Natural Resource Wealth Into Human Capital.* World Bank Publications, 2017.

Duflo, Esther. "Schooling and labor market consequences of school construction in Indonesia: Evidence from an unusual policy experiment." *American Economic Review* 91, no. 4 (2001): 795–813.

Fetzer, Thiemo. "Can workfare programs moderate conflict? Evidence from India." *Journal of the European Economic Association* 18, no. 6 (2020): 3337–3375.

Friedman, Willa, Michael Kremer, Edward Miguel, and Rebecca Thornton. "Education as liberation?" *Economica* 83, no. 329 (2016): 1–30.

Inglehart, Ronald F., and Pippa Norris. "Trump, Brexit, and the rise of populism: Economic have-nots and cultural backlash." Harvard Kennedy School Faculty Research Working Paper 16-026 (2016).

Rohner, Dominic, and Alessandro Saia. "Education and conflict: Evidence from a policy experiment in Indonesia." Working Paper (2019).

Rohner, Dominic, and Ekaterina Zhuravskaya, (eds.). *Nation Building: Big Lessons from Successes and Failures.* CEPR Press, 2023.

Thyne, Clayton L. "ABC's, 123's, and the golden rule: The pacifying effect of education on civil war, 1980–1999." *International Studies Quarterly* 50, no. 4 (2006): 733–754.

CHAPTER 9

Blouin, Arthur, and Sharun W. Mukand. "Erasing ethnicity? Propaganda, nation building, and identity in Rwanda." *Journal of Political Economy* 127, no. 3 (2019): 1008–1062.

Cáceres-Delpiano, Julio, Antoni-Italo De Moragas, Gabriel Facchini, and Ignacio González. "Intergroup contact and nation building: Evidence from military service in Spain." *Journal of Public Economics* 201 (2021): 104477.

Cilliers, Jacobus, Oeindrila Dube, and Bilal Siddiqi. "Reconciling after civil conflict increases social capital but decreases individual well-being." *Science* 352, no. 6287 (2016): 787–794.

De Montesquieu, Charles. *Montesquieu: The Spirit of the Laws.* Cambridge University Press, 1989.

Depetris-Chauvin, Emilio, Ruben Durante, and Filipe Campante. "Building nations through shared experiences: Evidence from African football." *American Economic Review* 110, no. 5 (2020): 1572–1602.

Esposito, Elena, Tiziano Rotesi, Alessandro Saia, and Mathias Thoenig. "Reconciliation narratives: The birth of a nation after the us civil war." *American Economic Review* 113, no. 6 (2023): 1461–1504.

Jha, Saumitra. "Trade, institutions, and ethnic tolerance: Evidence from South Asia." *American Political Science Review* 107, no. 4 (2013): 806–832.

Mousa, Salma. "Building social cohesion between Christians and Muslims through soccer in post-ISIS Iraq." *Science* 369, no. 6505 (2020): 866–870.

Okunogbe, Oyebola. "Does exposure to other ethnic regions promote national integration? Evidence from Nigeria." *American Economic Journal: Applied Economics* 16, no. 1 (2024): 157–192.

Paluck, Elizabeth Levy, and Donald P. Green. "Deference, dissent, and dispute resolution: An experimental intervention using mass media to change norms and behavior in Rwanda." *American Political Science Review* 103, no. 4 (2009): 622–644.

Rohner, Dominic, Mathias Thoenig, and Fabrizio Zilibotti. "War signals: A theory of trade, trust, and conflict." *Review of Economic Studies* 80, no. 3 (2013): 1114–1147.

Yanagizawa-Drott, David. "Propaganda and conflict: Evidence from the Rwandan genocide." *The Quarterly Journal of Economics* 129, no. 4 (2014): 1947–1994.

CHAPTER 10

Anderson, Siwan, Patrick Francois, Dominic Rohner, and Rogerio Santarrosa. *Hidden Hostility: Donor Attention and Political Violence.* United Nations University World Institute for Development Economics Research, 2022.

Besley, Timothy, and Robin Burgess. "The political economy of government responsiveness: Theory and evidence from India." *The Quarterly Journal of Economics* 117, no. 4 (2002): 1415–1451.

Durante, Ruben, and Ekaterina Zhuravskaya. Attack when the world is not watching? US news and the Israeli-Palestinian conflict. *Journal of Political Economy*, 126, no. 3 (2018): 1085–1133.

Eisensee, Thomas, and David Strömberg. "News droughts, news floods, and US disaster relief." *The Quarterly Journal of Economics* 122, no. 2 (2007): 693–728.

Esteban, Joan, Massimo Morelli, and Dominic Rohner. "Strategic mass killings." *Journal of Political Economy* 123, no. 5 (2015): 1087–1132.

Strömberg, David. "Radio's impact on public spending." *The Quarterly Journal of Economics* 119, no. 1 (2004): 189–221.

Wantchekon, Leonard, Marko Klašnja, and Natalija Novta. "Education and human capital externalities: Evidence from colonial Benin." *The Quarterly Journal of Economics* 130, no. 2 (2015): 703–757.

CHAPTER 11

Berman, Nicolas, Mathieu Couttenier, Dominic Rohner, and Mathias Thoenig. "This mine is mine! How minerals fuel conflicts in Africa." *American Economic Review* 107, no. 6 (2017): 1564–1610.

Binzel, Christine, Dietmar Fehr, and Andreas Link. "Can International Initiatives Promote Peace? Diamond Certification and Armed Conflicts in Africa." Working Paper (2023). https://dx.doi.org/10.2139/ssrn.4567734.

Burke, Marshall, Solomon M. Hsiang, and Edward Miguel. "Climate and conflict." *Annual Review of Economics* 7, no. 1 (2015): 577–617.

Couttenier, Mathieu, Veronica Petrencu, Dominic Rohner, and Mathias Thoenig. "The violent legacy of conflict: Evidence on asylum seekers, crime, and public policy in Switzerland." *American Economic Review* 109, no. 12 (2019): 4378–4425.

Eberle, Ulrich J., Dominic Rohner, and Mathias Thoenig. "Heat and Hate: Climate security and farmer-herder conflicts in Africa." Working Paper (2020).

Gallea, Quentin. "Weapons and war: The effect of arms transfers on internal conflict." *Journal of Development Economics* 160 (2023): 103001.

Gallea, Quentin, and Dominic Rohner. "Globalization mitigates the risk of conflict caused by strategic territory." *Proceedings of the National Academy of Sciences* 118, no. 39 (2021): e2105624118.

Gehring, Kai, and Paul Schaudt. "Insuring Peace: Index-Based Livestock Insurance, Droughts, and Conflict." CESifo Working Paper No. 10423 (2023).

Gollier, Christian, and Dominic Rohner (eds.). *Peace not Pollution: How Going Green Can Tackle Climate Change and Toxic Politics*. CEPR Press, 2023.

Kant, Immanuel. *Perpetual Peace: A Philosophical Sketch*. Cambridge University Press, 1970.

Maoz, Zeev, and Bruce Russett. "Normative and structural causes of democratic peace, 1946–1986." *American Political Science Review* 87, no. 3 (1993): 624–638.

Martin, Philippe, Thierry Mayer, and Mathias Thoenig. "Make trade not war?" *The Review of Economic Studies* 75, no. 3 (2008): 865–900.

McGuirk, Eoin F., and Nathan Nunn. "Transhumant pastoralism, climate change, and conflict in Africa." *Review of Economic Studies* (2024). https://doi.org/10.1093/restud/rdae027

Noack, Frederik, Dominic Rohner, and Tommaso Sonno, "Multinationals vs Mother Nature? The Impact of Multinational Firms on the Environment." preprint (2023).

Polachek, Solomon William. "Conflict and trade." *Journal of Conflict Resolution* 24, no. 1 (1980): 55–78.

Sonno, Tommaso. "Globalization and conflicts: The good, the bad and the ugly of corporations in Africa." CEP Discussion Paper No. 1670 (2020).

Sundaram, Anjan. *Breakup: A Marriage in Wartime*. Catapult, 2023.

Thoenig, Mathias. "Trade policy in the shadow of war: A quantitative toolkit for geoeconomics." In Massimo Morelli, Debraj Ray, Tomas Sjostrom and Oeindrila Dube (eds.), *Handbook of the Economics of Conflict*, 1st edition. Elsevier, 2024.

CHAPTER 12

Mueller, Hannes, and Julia Tobias. "The cost of violence: Estimating the economic impact of conflict." International Growth Centre (2016).

Rohner, Dominic, Michael Lehning, Julia Steinberger, Nicolas Tetreault, and Evelina Trutnevyte. "Decentralized green energy transition promotes peace." *Frontiers in Environmental Science* 11 (2023): 1118987.

Index